THE ANGRY MIDDLE-AGED MAN

Also by Pat Watters

Down to Now: Reflections on the Southern Civil Rights Movement
The South and the Nation
Climbing Jacob's Ladder: The Arrival of Negroes in Southern Politics
(with Reese Cleghorn)

Edited by Pat Watters

Investigating the FBI *(with Stephen Gillers)*

THE ANGRY MIDDLE-AGED MAN

Pat Watters

Grossman Publishers

A Division of The Viking Press
New York   1976

First published in 1976 by Grossman Publishers
625 Madison Avenue, New York, N.Y. 10022

Published simultaneously in Canada by
The Macmillan Company of Canada Limited

Printed in the United States of America

Library of Congress Cataloging in Publication Data
Watters, Pat.
    The angry middle-aged man.
    1. Watters, Pat. 2. Journalists—United States— Biography. 3. United
States—Social conditions—1960–   I. Title.
PN4874.W295A3   070.4′092′4 [B]   76-27763
ISBN 0-670-12684-5

ACKNOWLEDGEMENT:
The New York Times: from Edward B. Furey's "The Fear, the Numbing Fear," April
1, 1975 (Op-Ed). ® 1975 by The New York Times Company. Reprinted by
permission.

To my mother and father

THE ANGRY MIDDLE-AGED MAN

1

Glenda and I were sitting in the middle room, having a drink before lunch, taking a breather from Saturday chores watching the NCAA quarter-finals on the tv, saying how relaxing it was to see the patternings of the players, the swift, skilled action, the beauty of the upthrust arms shooting—when the phone rang. I jumped to get it, and heard the old-lady voice, excitement, almost glee in it, a voice of doom, one I knew I had been expecting for years: "Pat. You better come. Your mother's fallen. We're at the Big Star supermarket at Ansley Mall. . . ."

It had happened. She had lived alone now—how many years?—in the old family house on Virginia Avenue that I grew up in, a gloomy and graceless place at best, decrepit now and ill kept. Steep, rickety back steps down which she had to cart the garbage. Steep, cement front steps, two tiers of them, from front porch to sidewalk. She, with glaucoma and cataracts, taking her poodle, Joy, on its leash up and down them, how many times a day? Driving her 1960 Studebaker to the grocery store, the bank, church, at what peril to everybody en route, let alone herself? Her eye doctor had said she needed an operation for the cataracts. So she got a new one who said she didn't. The glaucoma is controlled by drops she puts in three times a day on the conviction that if she misses once she will immediately go blind, a belief unfounded in medical fact. A neighbor called her every morning to be sure nothing had happened to her during the night, and several times the neighbor had summoned me early in the morning in foreshadowings of what was happening now, and I had rushed over there to walk through room after gloomy room, fearing to find her fallen, stricken, what? only to discover that she had forgotten to tell the neighbor she was going early to Myrt's, the beautician on the corner who has done her hair as long as I can remember, or to the grocery store.

Now it had actually happened at the grocery store. And I, after gulping my martini, empty-stomached, was driving the familiar route to it, not wanting to think it through, hoping it wasn't serious—but knowing it had to be.

There had been other forebodings that weekend. I had gone to lunch on Friday with Francis Kent, excellent newspaperman, good friend of my own age with whom I had much in common. I had sat across from Fran at the 1776 Restaurant and he, just like the old lady on the telephone, began uttering words that I didn't want to hear— could barely stand to hear. He had developed an ulcer, and during the course of examinations they had X-rayed his chest and found something there. He was to go into the hospital on Monday to have it cut out to determine if it was cancer. He told it calmly and he said, "I'm not afraid. I just don't feel like anything is wrong."

I had lain on that metal table the previous spring, with the big metal insect-head-shaped thing pointed at my chest, and I knew the feeling Fran was talking about. The doctor had said after the routine physical that they had found something that looked like a scar and wanted to know more about it. Lying there, wanting a cigarette, I knew, first, that I wasn't afraid to die but didn't want it to happen in the obscenity of cancer treatment, and second, that five years of marriage to Glenda was more from life than most people ever get—so I could face death. But like Fran, I didn't *feel* anything was wrong with me, and held to that through the long weekend of waiting for the verdict. When I called on Monday morning, dry-mouthed, to ask the results of the X-rays, the impersonal young woman's voice said the doctor had not gone over them yet. Great God, why not? Don't they know what goes on inside the mind, the being, of someone for whom the second of telling means either continued life, the good with the bad, or an obscene death? She called back a half-hour later to say that the doctor had examined the X-rays and "your lungs are in perfect condition." The tension, the fear, the dread, not fully acknowledged until that moment, went out of me, replaced by a feeling not of wild exhilaration, but quiet relief at being able to get back to the routine of work, of life.

Fran had also talked at our lunch of the story he was doing on unemployment in Atlanta, where the rate was among the highest in the nation. He told of the long lines at the unemployment office, of talking with middle-class men down there, standing in line, applying for the pittance of unemployment compensation. "Think what it must be like," Fran said, "to be middle-aged, used up, thrown out—nothing to fall back on."

There had been a meeting at my office on Thursday. We had known for a couple of months that the Council—the Southern Regional Council, nonprofit, foundation-supported, do-good organization—was in trouble because the foundations were in trouble on account of the stock market. But an audit just completed had revealed that the Council was in far worse trouble than anyone had suspected, least of all the accountant in charge of the incredibly complicated books. Emergency action was to be taken by the executive committee over the weekend to cut the operating budget in half. Some programs would continue; some would be abolished; some would be dormant until funding could be found. Some of the fifty or so employees would continue in their jobs; some would be transferred to other jobs; some would be given the choice of leave without pay, until the fate of their program could be determined, or of quitting.

We had had to suspend publication of *Southern Voices*, the Council's fine new magazine of which I was editor, back in November, after only four issues. It had been underfinanced from the start; costs had gone up; income had not been as high as anticipated; foundation support was lagging. Our days had been engrossed in reworking the financial plan on a realistic basis, seeking revenue through a renewal campaign frankly calling for a show of support, trying to find foundation support. It was early March and we still did not have the means to resume publication. I assumed at the meeting that the magazine was one of those projects that would lie dormant until it was determined if funding could be found. And I assumed that I would be one of those employees transferred, if only temporarily, to some other job. After all, I had worked there twelve years and my work had been valuable.

Even so, the tension, the hint of dread and fear, was there—to be pushed back, in a startled waking in the dark of that Friday night, by the logic of my assessment of the situation. And there, too, in the lonesome dark of sudden wakening, were worry and fear about Fran. Let him be all right.

And now to be faced was not the fear but the reality of disaster. I walked into the confusion and clamor and crowd of the Saturday afternoon supermarket. Mother was seated on an office chair beside the manager's high booth, her friend standing beside her. Shoppers moved their carts all around her, oblivious of her. She was pale; her hands trembled. How thin she was.

What had happened? A boy, a clerk in the store, had been walking ahead of her and had suddenly turned to go back the other way and bumped into her, knocking her down. Her friend had helped her up and—"I couldn't stand up. My foot just seemed like jelly." Oh God. Could she stand now? No. No. Was she in pain? No. Not a bit.

I said, "Well, we better get you looked at." The chair had wheels on it. I told her friend to stay with her while I got the car to the curb where you load your groceries. Her friend said she had not yet checked her groceries out, and bustled off to get her cart and stand in one of the long lines. I stood beside Mother as she smoked a cigarette with trembling fingers, blinking her big eyes.

I looked at the busy shoppers in the familiar aisles. We use this store, too. We both get the bends, a feeling of unreality, doing grocery shopping, and nearly everyone I have ever mentioned this to feels the same. It is in part the tremendous concentration required to select among the illogically assorted goods, in part the lighting, and in part, I suspect, unconscious resentment that the thing, like so many other businesses, is organized so that the customer has to do most of the work, down to the unloading of the badly designed carts and the hauling of the bags to the car. Selecting the foods that will sustain you and pleasure you for a week ought to be, as Glenda says, a joyous occasion. But it has been reduced, like so much else, to low-grade unpleasantness, one more unrewarding mechanical act to be gotten through each week. The workers in such a place know no joy either, and they make little money out of the ever increasing flow of cash. Nor, one reads, do the farmers profit much. I prefer this store because its aisles are a little wider than most, its goods slightly more logically arranged, and because the other grocery in this shopping center was used by my former wife.

The manager came up and began in about how he had made out an accident report, and that the boy said he had not run into Mother. Her friend, finally through the line, clutching a partially filled sack, said oh yes he did, she had seen it all. Oh Lord. I gave the manager my card, said I would get in touch with him, and went to get the car.

What in the hell were they doing in there at the busiest time of the busiest day of the week when they could go any time to buy that piddling sack of groceries?

I wheeled her out to the car and lifted her into it. How light she was. She has always been small, barely five feet tall. But I hadn't realized how thin, downright emaciated, she had become—her arms showing the bone outlines under loose, pale flesh. Lifting the feather-weight of her into the front seat of the Mercedes, I felt bad about not having seen her much lately, neglecting her. I told the friend that I would take her out to West Paces Ferry Hospital, where I knew the emergency clinic was almost humane. (I went out there almost a year ago to the day with a damned broken rib incurred in a fall down icy porch steps after a party.) Mother said no—wait, we must go by the house first and get her hospitalization papers.

She assured me she wasn't hurting. So off we went to the old house. Her papers, she said, were in the bottom of the clothes hamper in the bathroom, along with other valuables for safekeeping. (Later, I was to learn that her other place to hide important papers was under the living room rug.) Her friend had followed in her car, and picked up Joy to take to stay with her own two poodles. And damned if they didn't insist on my following her home so she could ride with us out to the hospital. It was a long way to her house. I felt trapped in absurdity. When at last we were on the way to the hospital, Mother said for at least the tenth time how she hated for this to have happened. "I've always been so careful. I've always tried not to be a bother to anyone." The conversation between her and her friend was built on this theme. "I just wish it hadn't happened." "Well, it did. Maybe it won't be so bad." Oh yes it will, I knew.

The first newspaper job I ever had was covering the emergency clinic at Atlanta's city hospital, Grady, on Saturday nights while I was in college. There I eagerly recorded the mayhem of wrecks and shoot-ings and other routine disasters and occasional unusual ones, making the front page once with a story about a man who had a chestnut explode in his mouth, knocking out several teeth. So I knew what I was about in the emergency clinic, filling out forms, telling the woman doctor what had happened, moving with Mother as they wheeled her on the examining table to the X-ray room, and waiting for what seemed forever for the verdict. How much of our lives we spend waiting for a crucial verdict. At last the woman doctor was saying that it was just as she had feared. Mother's hip was broken. Commonplace catastrophe for the aged. Shefellandbrokeherhip.

I told the nurse the name of the doctor who had put an Ace

bandage on my rib for twenty-five dollars that time a year before, and they summoned him—Dr. Loughlin, a quiet-voiced, amiable young man, pulled in from who knows what Saturday afternoon pleasure. He was beautiful with Mother, explaining that he would have to operate the next morning, would have to put a pin in her hip, that she would be in the hospital about two weeks, but would begin right away to learn to walk again. Then she would have to be in a nursing home for a while to continue the processes of healing and learning to walk again. She need have no worry about the bills because Medicare fully covered a broken hip. Mother said she wasn't covered by Medicare because she was a retired federal employee and was covered under a separate program. He said he thought it was the same. A fresh anxiety: Was it really the same?

Dr. Loughlin said to her gently, "Now I know how people your age feel about nursing homes—that they're places where they put people away when nobody wants them. That may have been true ten or fifteen years ago. But it isn't any more. There are very nice places and they are set up to help you get well as quickly as possible, so you can go back home and live a normal life."

Mother's friend broke in: "You have to watch out about those nursing homes. I read the other day about them beating up some poor old lady in one of them." Dr. Loughlin and I both stared in amazement. "That may have been slightly exaggerated in the press," he said. "I believe that sometimes happens in the press, doesn't it?" To me. I smiled. No profession is perfect.

He took me aside in the waiting room. The store would probably pay the expenses from its insurance, he said. Just tell them you don't want to gouge them, don't want to put her through the ugliness of a court suit. Then to the most serious part: "It's not a bad fracture. She seems in good physical condition, but we'll check her more tonight. She is light and that makes the operation easier and recovery quicker. But she is old. If it were a borderline matter, a hernia, I wouldn't advise taking the risks involved. But the choice here is between being bedridden the rest of her life and operating. Her chances, at her age, are about eighty-five percent."

So I said, "Certainly. Operate." Then I asked if she would be able to see people that night. He looked at me as though I hadn't fully grasped the situation. And I hadn't. "You have to realize," he said, "there is the chance that would be the last time for you to see her."

So I went home for a brief respite from this world of 85 percent chances, of a maybe last time to see her, home to a martini on the front porch, leaning back in the wicker rocker, breathing in the peace of the trees, the quiet of our little street, watching a rain come up. Then back the considerable distance to the hospital. Mother's parting request when I had left her in the pleasant double room was that I bring her the stuff she uses to glue her false teeth in. They had taken them out during her examination; she couldn't eat without having them glued back in. I barely thought of it in time to stop in a little neighborhood store to snatch a box of the stuff up, and head on through the rain.

She was groggy on sedatives when I got there. I hovered over her, lighting her cigarette, arranging things so she could reach them better on the bedside table, and proudly presented the tooth stickum.

"Oh, that's not the kind I use. I don't like that kind at all."

It was the possibly-last-time visit, and we really didn't have anything to say to each other beyond the amenities of my asking if she was comfortable and her expressing concern that I looked tired.

"Maybe," I ventured, "this is all for the best. You've needed to do something about your situation for a long time, and now you'll be able to."

Yes, she said, maybe it was all for the best, the good Lord took care of us. "But oh, I hope my little dog is all right. I know she misses me."

I stayed through another cigarette, wished her well for the morning, kissed her cheek, left. The phone was ringing as I came into our house, and Glenda coped with the call. It was Mother's friend and the burden of her message was that it was my duty to be there in the morning when they wheeled Mother off to the operating room instead of getting there, as I had planned, just before they wheeled her back to her room. Yes, my duty. I realized that all through this thing I had been trying to be the dutiful son that I really had not been for years— avoiding her, as I had, avoiding resolute action on getting her moved to a safer, more manageable place. *Dutiful son*. An abstraction. It was the beginning of many realizations. Her friend had said to me that Mother had often told her what a good son I was, and I am sure she told many old ladies that I was a perfect son. But somewhere back there I had quit trying to be a perfect any of those things your family demands that you be and tells everyone you are. Because when you get the false-teeth stickum and proudly present it, it's the wrong kind.

But I made myself be there the next morning for that dutiful mo-ment of the wheeling off. Mother was grateful that I had come and seemed unafraid. Her friend had already called to inform her that Joy had kept her awake all night hollering. "My poor little dog. . . ."

I went again the long way back home, drank coffee and read the Sunday *Journal-Constitution*, more than ordinarily aware of what a terrible newspaper it is. Then back to the hospital, and I became conscious for the first time of the sadism behind the arrangement that made anxious people pay fifty cents a throw to park their cars to visit suffering people paying the exorbitant prices the hospital charges for room and care. Somebody had placed the ticket machine at the top of a steep rise, so that to get the parking ticket you had to brake hard and then perform, if you have manual gears, the feat of starting on a steep hill—such a goddamned petty burden to add to heavy ones people already had.

I went in and sat in the little waiting area where I was to meet Dr. Loughlin after the operation. A family was there, mother and father and two youngsters, faces strained, an older boy having just been admitted with some injury sustained in yesterday's soccer game. They sat on the ugly, uncomfortable plastic furniture. Why not make it pleasant for people in here? Who designs and manufactures such furniture? Who picks it out for the waiting area of the orthopedic section of a hospital?

Another kid had been in the emergency clinic the day before with a soccer injury to his head. They had added soccer to the everyday violence and overorganization of kids' play—what ought to be fun ends in the emergency room.

Dr. Loughlin finally arrived, looking weary, saying that the operation was completely successful, that Mother was doing as well as could be expected. Again—the time of verdict, the breathing out of unacknowledged anxiety, which had surfaced, disguised, in my impatience with everyday idiocies I usually ignored or suffered silently. And, I realized, waiting for them to bring Mother back to her room, I was also anxious about what was going to happen to my job. We were all to learn our fate the next day.

Mother was woozy, of course, but in her incoherence obviously glad to be alive. I felt more strongly toward her that moment than I had during any of the rest of it—the natural, good, strong will in us to keep on living.

On that next morning of reckoning, a list of the appointments each of us had with George Esser, the executive director of the Council, was posted at the office. Mine was one of the earliest. I was apprehensive sitting across from owl-eyed George. It was one more time of verdict. George's middle-aged face was pale and drawn. A Virginia Military Institute graduate, the good Army officer looking first to the care and comfort of his troops, the pioneer poverty program architect, the consumate manipulator of foundations—old George. Waiting for him to get beyond small talk, I realized that I had never really liked or fully trusted him. Nor have I liked or fully trusted any of the other men I have worked for in the thirty years of working I have done, even though each, like George, had been a decent and likable human being, entirely trustworthy. But each had the power to take away the job that my existence depended on and plunge me into that abyss of terror where there is no monthly check coming in to pay all the bills, buy the food, keep things going. You can't fully like and trust anyone with that much power over you. Driving to work to the first job I had on a newspaper, feeling humbly undeserving that I had got up to a hundred dollars a week, I would pass every day a dreadful slum of poor whites, full of squalor, pasty-faced kids in mud yards, and more than once I would say to myself, you are only one paycheck from that.

And now I sat hearing words I did not want to hear, words I had dreaded all the years since driving through the slum. George was saying that until funding could be found for the magazine, all of us on its staff would have to take the unpaid leave of absence. There was some kind of arrangement with unemployment compensation that allowed us to draw one full week's pay a month in addition to the ninety dollars a week they regularly dole out. I said that was impossible for me. I had obligations to meet. Then I could resign, effective April 15—a month away. There would be severance pay and the like, enough for another month's support.

At the meeting the previous week, George had said some people would be transferred to other jobs on the basis of ability, with racial and sexual balance and seniority also considered. I had twelve years' seniority—among the longest in the organization. I looked across at George and said to him that I knew the job of directing an intact program, the investigative journalism project, was open, and that I wanted to put in for it. This had been my defense against terror through the weekend—the assumption that the job would be offered to me. Now George told me why it would not. Members of the executive committee felt that, if possible, a black person should have it. The ultimate irony. We had struggled through the 1960s in this work for equal rights. I had given up a good future in the newspaper business because the paper I worked for would not allow reporters to do a professional job of covering the civil-rights struggle, the biggest story then going on, and had gone to work for the Council because it was covering the story right. My motivation had been professional, but certainly a large part of it had also been devotion to the cause of equal rights, principled opposition out of my Southern experience to discrimination against a person because of the color of his skin. And this was what it had come to: I couldn't have the job because of the color of my skin.

I told George that I wanted to put in for it nevertheless. "Do you have any reservations about my qualifications to do that job?" I asked him. A strange little smile played on his face. He shook his head no. The job was half administrative, half writing. I told George that I would consider taking it as a half-time proposition, administration only, and use the other half of my time to do writing on my own. (When it had become apparent a month before that the magazine might not make it, I had begun to play with the dream of free-lance writing.) George said he would have to talk with various people, and would let me know something by the end of the week. I raised one other thing with George. We had already discussed the possibility of finding people to take over the magazine with private money, set it up as a commercial venture separate from the Council. Had the time come to try to do that? He said certainly, explore it.

I left that office with thoughts of free-lancing, thoughts of getting the magazine out from under the Council, exhilarating me, but all the while angry at coming to this end after giving the organization twelve of the most productive years of my life. In the pit of my stomach, I was scared. It was gone, the assurance of the check that would pay the bills, pay the alimony and child support, keep things going. Facing me was the possibility of losing the house, losing everything, the specter of the slum.

I called Glenda and told her what had happened. "Wonderful," she cried. "You're free. You're free at last of the Council. You can do what you want to do." A wild surge of exhilaration, and love for her.

There was a note to call Mother at the hospital. That had all been out of my mind. It came back fully with the demanding voice on the phone: "Get me my radio. Get me my clock. And oh, Pat, don't forget to get me the right kind of adhesive for my teeth. There's a full package of it in the living room." In the living room. Of course.

I had lost myself in the conversation but, as I put down the phone, the terror returned—no job, no money. I pushed the terror back. That's a month away. Concentrate on the free-lance thing. When I had talked to people about that a month before, it had been different. I had had a choice. Back around Christmastime, in another surge of wanting to get free, I had answered an ad in *Editor and Publisher* for an adviser to student publications at Southern Methodist University in Dallas. I got a letter back saying that they had narrowed the hundreds of applications down to three or four and would I come out for an interview? By then the dream of writing full time was upon me and I replied by saying that I had decided to withdraw my application. But in that situation, too, I had had a choice. Now I thought of the check that would have come every month in Dallas.

The memory was comforting. My qualifications were good. When you are told you no longer have a job, you are conditioned to think your performance must have had something to do with it.

On my desk was a message from the office accountant. I had filled out the forms, endless forms, for a claim on my medical insurance for two hundred and forty dollars in medical bills my son had run up in Boston. The message said the insurance company had sent yet another form, attached, which must be filled out by college officials certifying that my son was a full-time student, and by his mother and me certifying that he was dependent. Goddamn them. I mailed the form off to him.

I made a list of people I needed to call and started in on it. I had learned just recently that an old friend, John Somerville, was back in Atlanta, representing a newspaper syndicate. I wanted to talk with him about the possibility of my syndicating a column. I could find neither him nor his syndicate listed in the phone book, so I made a person-to-person call to him at the syndicate's headquarters in Cleveland, assuming they would give me his Atlanta number. Instead, the man there said John was traveling in Canada but would be calling in and did I want to leave word? Rattled, I said yes. And then realized I had laid myself open to paying for a long-distance call from Canada.

I called editors and writers I knew to try to line up free-lance work. During one of the first of these calls, I heard myself describing my situation, the words coming too fast, my voice strained. "Heavy," said my friend on the other end of the line. "Heavy." And the emptiness in my stomach, the terror, was the strongest yet.

I left the office in midafternoon and drove to Virginia Avenue and got the radio and clock and tooth adhesive. I was startled to see how much better Mother looked—less wan, even less thin. They had fed her glucose before and after the operation and they had been bringing her good meals. She was getting enough to eat, for God's sake, for the first time in how long? She had been starving herself over there on Virginia Avenue.

I realized something else, a new terror to add to all the others. Each time I walked into the room the previous two days, she seemed asleep, did not turn to greet me until I spoke. But this time her eyes were open. She was not asleep. She didn't see me. Now she was complaining about the darkness of the room. It was still raining, overcast, but there was good light from the window, and a long lighting fixture beamed down from the headboard of her bed. Had they neglected to put the glaucoma drops in her eyes while she was groggy from sedation? Or was it the cataracts that the other doctor had said must be operated on a year before? Where could she live, crippled and blind?

As I was getting ready to go, she said, "Oh, let me have that adhesive. I sure am glad to get the kind I like." I handed it to her, and she shook the can. "Why, this one's nearly empty. I had a full one right there in the bedroom."

"Living room," I said. "That's where I got this. You said living room."

That night I wrote letters to other editors stating I was available for assignments. Glenda was at her real-estate class. She had decided a month before to become an agent, and both of us were excited that she would be able to use her love and knack for house hunting and her enjoyment of dealing with people in this gainful way. She had for years been putting people and houses that would be good for each other in touch. Now she could do it for a living. When she got home, we talked of the change that was to come in our lives: my writing and her selling real estate would mean that we would both be working from the house, and would see more of each other. It would mean, too, that both of us, for the first time in our working lives, would be free of office hours, bureaucracy. This realization was the beginning of a feeling that good could result from all this upset. We held each other in the bed, and for the first time since Saturday, peace came with sleep.

I woke up in the early morning—two-thirty—and after a moment of lying in the darkness, all of the anxiety spilled into my mind again. Glenda is the one who usually does her worrying in the predawn hours. My time is after the alarm goes off, the first befuddled waking moments before I go into motion for the day. There is always something to worry about.

Now, getting up, lighting a cigarette, I went into the living room to sit in the darkness and deal with each level of anxiety. The job. Two months to get the writing going. Surely some kind of pay would come from the Council on the investigative thing. Then: Mother's insurance. Surely she had federal coverage. If not, she had some money, some income. And the grocery store was liable. (Her eyes. Call her eye doctor tomorrow.)

I looked about the darkened living room, the familiar shapes of furniture, the fireplace. Strong pang of despair at the thought of having to sell the place. It and the dogs and Glenda and my children were the only things I needed. Now the house seemed threatened. I had worked all those years and didn't, as they say, have a thing to show for it. No stocks, no bank account. Just the car and the house. Then I started through the anxieties all over again—the job, Mother's predicament—but in the midst of it, I stopped and said to myself, So this is what it gets you. All the years of work, of doing what they said you should do, all the strain and striving, and now. . . .

Sitting here in the darkened living room at two-thirty in the morning, unable to sleep, smoking, looking at the familiar shapes of the furniture, the fireplace, forcing the will to deal with each level of anxiety, to face down with facts, bad enough in themselves, each stab of unreasoning terror.

Sitting here, forty-eight years old and jobless, Mother in the hospital with a broken hip and maybe facing blindness.

Sitting here after thirty years of working hard and nothing to show for it, blessed only with the love of a good woman.

Sitting here thinking about giving twelve years of loyalty to an organization only to find that those in charge of it had not the first sense of loyalty toward me, and it an organization supposed to be devoted to human relations.

Sitting here thinking how through thirty years this country has taken so much of the joy and creative pleasure from the basics of my existence—idiocies and atrocities I was suddenly so aware of.

Sitting here, forty-eight and jobless, thinking back over thirty years of harassed existence, of being abstracted and programmed and almost robbed of any identity at all.

Sitting here, with that empty ache of defeat and disappointment in my gut, knowing that I had done my best, done everything I was supposed to do, and for what? The worst of it was knowing that if I had not lost my job, if Mother had not broken her hip, if all that trouble had not so suddenly come upon me, what I had before wasn't worth a damn anyhow.

Sitting here, dreading to go back to bed, to sleep, because to wake would be to plunge into the anxiety all over again, the opposite from waking out of a nightmare into pleasant reality. Sitting here in reality become a nightmare.

I had been numb, really, since the meeting with George, the surprise catastrophe of being laid off on top of the hellish weekend with Mother too much for my feelings to cope with. Now feeling rushed back into me, filled me, almost too much to control. Not self-pity. Some fear, yes. But mainly anger.

I was angry. Angry as hell.

2

It was to go on and on, the anger smoldering, the awareness growing of all the reasons it was stoked so strong in me, the anxiety about making a living. Meanwhile I spent precious time on errands and dealings with bureaucracies over Mother's predicament. On one rainy morning, with nothing ahead for the whole day but unpleasant duties at work and on behalf of Mother, I heard myself whimpering. But on another, getting out of bed, I caught sight in the mirror of a good, strong morning erection, felt ready for anything.

I turned off worry and escaped the drear, defeated atmosphere of the office by immersing myself in whatever work was to be found there. The first heady order of business was trying to find private money to take over the magazine. We had a list of likely prospects and at its top was a wealthy older woman of Atlanta. I had known her years ago as one of those furtive white supporters of the early Negro movement and other good causes. I couldn't find her listed and spent a good part of a morning tracking her down, finally reaching her at the welfare office of a small town nearby where she does volunteer work. "Oh, good heavens." Her strong old Southern voice crackled on the phone. "I can't do anything like that. I've still got the dairy farm you know, and taxes are eating me up, eating me up."

The others on the list had similar reactions. All the while, good people were pouring money into an effort to save the city's Fox Theater, one of those monuments to the bad taste of movies in the 1920s, a pseudo-Oriental, strange sort of architectural monstrosity, and I couldn't help feeling it was a shame they weren't putting their money into something truer to their culture and decent background.

Every day I had to read letters from readers and writers alike, expressing real concern for the magazine, disappointment at losing its serious treatment of the South's problems and its awareness of the region's many virtues. I would sit there reading them one after the other, heartsick, that rage I hadn't known was in me rising again. We had struck a chord with the very best in the South at a time when its worst evil, its racism, had largely been shed. And there was so much good—manners, sensitivity, feeling for the specific and individual, love of language, love of the sight and climate and feel of place. These were all there in the letters. And the Council's purpose was to better the lot of the South's many unfortunate people. What better Goddamned way, I would sit there fuming to myself, than to encourage the good instincts of the kind of Southerners who were reading the magazine, people with intelligence and, more important, the ability to get things done, to point out to them the opportunities for change and improvement?

But no, I realized, it wasn't going to happen. George Esser and a fund raiser he had taken on in the midst of his sea of troubles had put applications in to a half-dozen foundations, and a final decision on whether to fold the magazine would not be made until May 1. But after I satisfied myself that we couldn't find private money, I gave up on it. Foundations don't deal in so simple and basic a thing as instilling pride and the determination to solve problems in people capable of making a real change in society. They deal in making miserable people a tiny bit less so.

So I had the saddening task of drafting form letters to send to our writers once the magazine was pronounced officially dead. We had a big inventory of manuscripts, some paid for, some the writers were letting us hold until the fate of the magazine became known. In both categories, there was much beautiful material. It was depressing and infuriating to see what amounted to a new Southern literary movement die a-borning. Most of these fine manuscripts would not see print in the national magazines. And I realized, with more fury, that nobody in the organization other than our staff was aware of what was being lost.

My first morning of phoning rich people was the day of Fran Kent's operation. His secretary had promised to call as soon as she knew the outcome. Every time I picked up the phone for an incoming call, there was that expectation. And inevitably in moments like that, a dread feeling of unreasoning anxiety would fill me. No job. No paycheck. No more credit cards. No hospitalization. The call about Fran came in the afternoon: "He's all right. It was a benign tumor." Once again, the release of tension built up for a life-or-death utterance. Thank God he was all right. But the operation itself, having his chest cut open, was a terrible thing for him. He would be in the hospital at least another week, and would be unable to work for at least another six weeks. Great God, suppose that happened to me?

A few nights later, our neighbor, Billie Blalock, called and asked if we'd come over and try to cheer up her husband Frank. He had not been feeling good. They are in their sixties. Frank had retired not long before, and the slowing of his energy, the increase of his emphysematous coughing, we had put down to the strain of adjusting to not working after a lifetime of work. Frank had lived in the family home, two doors down from ours, since he was a boy. He took care of his mother until she died in her nineties, and only after that did he and Billie, who had been in love for years, get married. That was six years ago. Frank, small, red-headed, bandy-legged, was one of the gentlest, sweetest-spirited men I had ever known. We would stop by there in the evening, often bringing the dogs to play in the backyard with their dog, Kanza, a coyotish creature. They always had their bottle of Old Barton bourbon on the kitchen table, and being with them for a couple of drinks, being in contact with that gentle, happy love between them, always freshened our spirits, made life seem sweeter. "Aw, come on, darling," Frank would say to Glenda. "Y'all can have one more. Don't go yet." Not so this night. He didn't seem despondent—just distracted. Everything seemed to be going to the bad.

One bright spot. John Somerville, the syndicate man, had had the good sense not to call me from Canada but from his apartment in Atlanta when he got home for the weekend. He was enthusiastic about the column idea; we agreed to get together on Friday night to talk about it, and to renew acquaintance. You know, he told me, Barbara and I got a divorce, and I have a new wife. Me, too, I said. His new wife, Laverne, turned out to be a stalwart, no-nonsense, yet entirely fun-loving person, and we had a good evening with them.

Toward the end of it, John got going on all the things that bothered him about the country, and I thought how often this became the burden of talk with men our age. He spoke of Watergate and crime, and said how different it was in Canada, what a changed feeling he had every time he traveled up there. He had taken over the Canadian territory for the syndicate, in addition to working the South. Finally, after asking Laverne if it was all right, he confided that they were going to move to Canada and take out citizenship papers there.

"I'm just fed up with this country," John said. "It's so nice to be in a place, around people that are civilized." It was late. I promised myself that I would talk more with him some other time, compare the things we were angry about.

We agreed that night that I would write five or six prototype columns for him to take to the next sales meeting to see if the syndicate would take me on. This was something I could fit, the next morning, into the equation of good and bad that filled my mind on waking. Two months of income still to come, phone calls to two agents in New York and long follow-up letters, and now the syndicate possibility —all balanced against the terror of no job, no paycheck, in the offing. I had an appointment that morning at eleven with George Esser for an answer about the half-time investigative journalism job, and through the evening with the Somervilles I could feel the tension building in me over this one more crucial yes or no to come.

So we said on that morning to hell with it, they are having a cheapie auction at the good old Atlanta Gallery, and off we went to sit among the cheapie regulars and watch and occasionally enter the bidding on the incredible array of beat-up old furniture, tacky bric-a-brac, strange things like a submarine light.

I left Glenda there and drove to town to face the hour of decision with George. It was a pretty day, the endless rain finally over. Downtown was Saturday quiet. During the past four or five years developers had been tearing down old buildings, often usable and beautiful, and throwing up undistinguished slabs of office buildings and outlandishly designed hotels. Terrible, incessant noise came from those construction sites on weekdays. Dust and debris swirled into the already dirty air. Equipment blocked traffic lanes in the streets, forcing cars and trucks into a turmoil; horn-blowing added to the general clamor. People on the sidewalks looked harassed and angry where once they had nodded to one another and observed the rules of politeness.

Now, unpleasant encounters were commonplace, often with rampageous black teen-agers or hostile young black men in pimp apparel. Whites, particularly those who had moved to the suburbs and seldom got into town, had developed a paranoia about crime on the downtown streets. I had never been mugged or otherwise molested, and had never seen anything like that occur. But God knows I could attest to the bad manners and needless unpleasantness of many lower-class blacks, whose presence in such large numbers, whose freedom of movement, were, in part, the result of the civil-rights work I had given such a chunk of my life to. I was thinking about this as I walked to the office to find out whether I would give any more of it, feeling that this was my town still, my downtown. Why hadn't it ever occurred to me, or to anybody, to try to stop what the developers were doing to it? The sentimental (to me, misguided) effort to save the old Fox was the only such endeavor so far.

Old George looked, if anything, worse than at our last confrontation. He wanted to know if I would still settle for part time, and I said yes, that is what I would prefer to do. Then with much nervous smiling, he said that he had worked it out for me to do that, not administering the investigative journalism program, but rather writing for it. I would have an expense account, and be able to keep my hospitalization. Also, George said, my severance pay would be considerably larger than it had first been thought. Well, hot damn. What could be better? The program would subsidize me to write magazine stories and I would retain a little of that security I had been conditioned to value inordinately.

In the slow unraveling of things, none of the happy conditions we talked about that morning was fully met. And as it turned out, a white, after all, was hired to administer the program. But on that sunny, happy Saturday morning, I didn't know how things would turn out, and the fear and worry slid from me, and oh, jubilantly walking the Saturday quiet sidewalks of my downtown, all I could think about was getting back to Glenda and telling her the good news, and bidding on everything they put up at that funky auction.

Driving back out there, I stopped at a red light and heard a siren, close, and looked into the rear-view mirror and saw a cop car bearing down fast on the rear of my Mercedes, no sign that the driver would be able to veer by me. Terror. I could not see if anything was coming on the left of the intersection. The light was still red. I jammed down the accelerator and made a left turn, taking the risk, and the damned cop car shot on by, still in my lane. I was trembling.

Sometime during the previous week of dread and rain, I had been driving on a four-lane, one-way street, bent on some one of my countless errands for Mother, going over in my mind the equations of anxiety, when I looked up to see the light changing well in time to stop for it. But somehow I didn't, just went right through it, red before I entered the intersection. It had been a suicidal second, and I felt the fear of it afterward. But now I was mad—at the insane and meaningless menace of the cop car, at the way we have given over the streets to them, without knowing whether such dangerous speed is ever necessary—and mad, too, I realized, that their sirens sound like those in movies we used to see about Nazi Germany. I had been through a time of torment and now some of the worry and fear had been allayed, but all of it could have been wiped out, the good and the bad, everything, by that son-of-a-bitch cop, because I was in the path of the unchecked murderousness America has loosed everywhere in the name of keeping military and civil peace.

I remembered visiting Booty Scott, Glenda's cousin, who is mayor of the little south Louisiana town of New Roads. Nothing would do but for Booty to take me down to the police station to see all the equipment and meet the force, two men, a white and a giant of a black, both decked out in a multiplicity of belts and badges and weaponry, frightening to look at. Booty, a decent man deeply devoted to his little town, was far more intrigued by his police force than by the rest of his official duties. And so it has been with all our Presidents as long as I have lived. Damn 'em, I thought. Goddamn 'em.

But then there was the shining moment of telling Glenda the good news, feeling her hug me and say you're not jobless any more. I had the satisfaction, too, of telling a friend of ours who was at the auction, a special kind of satisfaction because one of the psychological torments of being jobless is the impression (maybe accurate, maybe imagination) that people are pitying you, and there had been much talk by this friend and various of *her* friends about doing something about Pat not having a job. Probably "poor old Pat."

When we got home that afternoon, we learned that Billie had called an ambulance and had Frank taken to the hospital. He had quit eating and was too weak to get out of bed.

Mother, meanwhile, was to be dismissed from the hospital during the coming week. I had finally gotten hold of her eye doctor on the phone, and he, pleasant-voiced, young-sounding, said that at her last examination the cataracts showed growth, and that if this kept up, she would have to be operated on. I had already talked to Dr. Loughlin about that possibility, and he said she was in good enough physical condition to have the operation done while she was still in the hospital. She would probably better regain her walking in the nursing home, he added drily, if she could see where she was going. I raised this with the eye doctor and he said she would have to come to his office to be examined again. I pointed out that this seemed out of the question since she couldn't walk. Couldn't he examine her in the hospital? No, not the proper light or instruments. Damn 'em, damn 'em, damn 'em. The process of transferring her from hospital to nursing home had already been set in motion, so presumably she would leave the hospital, go to the nursing home, soon after go back to the hospital, and then back again to the nursing home. There seemed no end to it.

I got to the hospital at nine-thirty the Tuesday morning she was to be transferred. The ambulance was supposed to come at ten. I went down and filled out the many forms connected with checking her out, and when I got back to her room, she said not to worry about the bill because she had six thousand dollars in her checking account for just such emergencies. I said that all I had done was sign the papers; her medical insurance would take care of the bill. Six thousand dollars, drawing no interest, in her checking account!

The ambulance attendants did not get there until after eleven—a long-haired youth and a girl who didn't look to be over sixteen. They had not arrived when I got to the nursing home. I sought out the pleasant, vague-voiced lady with whom we had arranged the admission on Friday, and told her I guessed Mother would be arriving any minute.

"What? Why I don't have her down to be admitted. I don't think we have a room."

Tight-lipped: "But ma'am, we arranged it all on Friday. Don't you remember?"

Oh, everything had been so busy. She would try to find a room. A long wait, no sign of Mother, and then everything happening at once: A room was found. Mother arrived. It had taken so long because they had driven her to the wrong nursing home. I had reached the point where all I wanted to do was laugh.

I went up with them to ensconce Mother in her room. The other occupant was a frail, very old looking woman, unconscious, with a tube in her nose. Great God. In the nursing home literature, and in our interview, I had been assured that much would be done to see roommates were "compatible." This is only temporary, the woman assured me in her vague voice. We'll move Mrs. Watters as soon as there is another vacancy. As it turned out, the roommate, a stroke victim, had a black woman attendant who stayed all day every day, and the black woman and Mother became fast friends, the black woman waiting on her and taking on over her. And since the roommate was not sentient, Mother could play her radio as loud and as late as she wanted to. So she never did get transferred.

At last, driving away from the nursing home that morning, a new, exotic anxiety seized me. In the hubbub of getting Mother checked in, I had been filling out one more form when the ambulance driver came up, wanting to be paid. I had had Mother sign a blank check for this and took it out of my pocket to fill it out. The long-haired young man politely asked if I would like him to fill it out. Sure, thanks, I said, and went back to filling out my form. Now I realized I hadn't looked to see what amount he had written on the check. Suppose during all that journeying from wrong to right nursing home, Mother had confided in them about that six thousand dollars in her checking account, and he had wiped her out?

An anxiety like that would bubble up and assume horrendous proportions, then gradually dissolve. I had lost the ability to differentiate between big worries and little, plausible and implausible, just as my anger lashed out with equal energy against large outrages and small, major injustices and minor irritants. I had taken to giving the finger to my fellow citizens in moments of stress and antagonism, usually in traffic, when some asshole behind me blew his horn the second the light changed. So many bad things had happened at once that I found myself expecting more. The barriers of confidence, of a feeling of reasonable well-being and safety, that I had built to get through day-to-day frustrations and dangers had partially crumbled. Even before the cop car tried to kill me, I had found myself dreading to drive, fearing a wreck.

Nothing seemed certain any more. I found myself indulging a tendency to hypochondria I had shed in my youth, worrying about my heart, my blood pressure. Was all of this worry and anger really appropriate to what had happened? Or was I cracking up? I found myself wanting to talk with others who had been through similar experiences, compare notes with somebody like Jim Wood.

But then the feeling of confidence and safety began to return. When I got home from the nursing home, Glenda was on the front porch waving a letter. It was from the real-estate board. She had passed the state exam. We found out later that out of two thousand who took it, only two hundred passed. It was a much tougher test than usual; someone felt too many people were getting into the business. Glenda's was the second highest grade—even though, we found out, they hadn't used the right book in her classes.

In the process of confidence rebuilding, the telephone began to take on a magic life of its own. The earliest sound of its magic was an assignment from one of those magazine editors I had written. While I was writing the story, it sounded again—a call from one of the two agents I had written, Joan Raines, saying she liked my work, would try this story here, that one at another place. I responded to the competence and confidence and nonloser quality of her crisp voice. Great, I said. Wonderful. Go to it. I had an agent! I was a writer! Right there, a story in the typewriter. And Glenda was a real-estate person. A whole new life would start for us both.

Meanwhile, though, the first of those two months of steady income was dwindling away. I forced myself as often as I could to go to the office, go through the motions of punctuality and attendance I had been going through in one way or another since I started first grade forty-one years before. The office was a dismal place. Four of us on the staff had been promised our old jobs back should the miracle of funding occur by May 1. In a gratuitous piece of cruelty none of us could understand, Jim Wood had not even been offered that. He had planned to take the leave of absence, but didn't even have that slim hope to hang onto, so had begun the tedious process of filling out all the forms necessary to seek federal government employment. Before he and his good wife Kathy were ostracized for their public stand against segregation in Mobile, Alabama, in the 1960s, Jim had been a successful grain merchant. Now he had gotten his reward from the Council for his stand on principle, and he couldn't go back to the grain business. So he applied for a federal job as an equal opportunities officer for the U.S. Department of Agriculture, offering the rather rare qualifications of experience in race relations and agriculture-related work. He didn't get the job. Equal opportunity officers, by unwritten rule, have to be black. Whites, even ones as principled as Jim, need not apply.

Maddening. But through that dreary time, I had the consolation and excitement of starting anew. And there was a feeling of old friends gathering around. Writers called to tell me about assignment possibilities. Newspaper friends expressed their regrets about the magazine, told me about job possibilities. A friend who is a book salesman put me in touch with an editor at his firm. A writer who has on occasion had to take free-lance work from ad agencies told me how to go about this. In the midst of it, I realized that the friends gathering around were all people of my profession. Not one in the do-good business came forward. And that led to one further sad realization. People in the movement had no appreciation for the professional qualities I had given to it, might still have to offer. To them, I was just one more interchangeable part of a big effort. It was a painful realization.

I had worked for both a newspaper and a cause institution, and in neither, I realized, did it matter to the people in charge how well or how badly I performed. On the paper, all they were interested in was making money. The cause organization was more complicated. Ostensibly, and for the most part sincerely, it wanted to achieve certain ends. But money had to be raised to do that and, too often, it became an end in itself. Not the goals, but keeping the organization going, became the important thing, pleasing the foundations or whoever is doing the financing. Soon I was to have, for the first time in my career, the joy of knowing that how well or how badly I performed did matter. The harder I worked, the better off I would be. The extra effort was worth it. I would be working for myself.

We were both coming to such realizations. Glenda was working for herself already. Every extra effort had meaning. The feeling of freedom, of opportunity, was rising in us. We talked late into one night about the many meanings of freedom, and we agreed that after the little taste of it we had then, we would never give it up, even if it meant selling the house to survive. "I could lock the door behind me and never look back," Glenda said.

3

Immediately, though, it was not our house we were faced with selling. It was Mother's. She had agreed, while in the hospital, that she wasn't able to keep the place up any more. We had found a good home for Joy, the poodle, and Mother had sadly accepted that as best for the creature. So she had no reason not to move into the retirement home where several of her friends were. Glenda would list the house for sale.

But before that could be done, there was the matter of disposing of its contents, the furnishings and clutter of the three generations who had lived there. We would go into its gloomy interior in the evening and spend hours sorting things out, cleaning things up. In a low-ceilinged room in the basement, I found trunks full of old letters, some dating back to the 1920s. Occasionally I would read one of them, by a ghost speaking from a time I never knew, mostly telling the minutia of lives that are no more. One was a terrible letter, painful for me to read, though I was unable to stop, from one family member to another, accusing him of stealing. I have never been able to feel the revulsion so many people do about American materialism. I like good living, machines that do things for me (as long as the damn things work), gadgets, entertainments. What had become awful to me was that ugly thing in the letter out of the past; the threat people feel about the pitiful things they have put together out of a lifetime of work, the way they hold to them fearfully, dreading that they will be taken away, that somebody will steal them or that they will have to be sold. How much of my initial panic about being jobless was grounded in that unreasoning fear instilled in us about the things we own? America giveth so much, and ever threatens to take away.

I realized, too, going about the depressing task of sorting that familiar little horde of things a family might fight over, that while I had had a reasonably happy childhood, very little of the happiness had occurred within the walls of this gloomy old house. I had always sought outside it for my happiness. And when I got a house of my own, I was out of it more often than not, earning the money that enabled me to have it, operating still, I am sure, on the old knowledge that happiness is more likely to be found without a house than within it.

My attitude toward houses, toward home, I realized, had been a major cause of the breakup of my first marriage, and one of the few things that had ever come between Glenda and me. She and I were contemplating now a life in which for both of us work would be based in the house. Already, I had been working some at home and had begun to feel the peace and rhythm of a functioning house through all the day and all the week. Before, home had been little more than a motel for me to use at night, the burdens of maintaining it and repairing it an annoying distraction from that work I did away from it. I would come in tired from the office, and Glenda would show me something she had done to make the house nicer during the day, furniture rearranged, something painted, a new plant, and I would say yeah, that's great, let's go mix a drink and sit on the porch. Now I was getting to know each of the many plants she had lovingly potted for our home. Now I would do some little something, clean the tops of the kitchen cabinets, rearrange some of the plants while she was gone, and proudly show her when she came in, and she would genuinely respond, be happy and proud with me. I realized what hurt I had caused all those years by not being interested in one of the most important parts of existence. That, I thought, surely is behind women's outrage, what feeds the energy of their movement: their knowledge of the fundamental meaning of home and a crazy culture that blocks their men from that knowledge and thereby destroys for both the whole meaning of it. We had picked up on Fred Powledge's term, "house-husband," and used it jokingly, but both of us were beginning to realize how profound a concept it is.

We finally got the old house on Virginia Avenue in shape to sell off its contents, and hired a young man experienced at such things to conduct an estate sale. On the first morning of the three days of it, there must have been seventy-five people waiting. They were mostly old women and they surged into the house, grabbing things, hardly looking at them. There was a feverish greed to the whole scene. I watched an old man down on his hands and knees frantically picking through a bunch of old rags we had tossed on the floor of an empty closet, thinking to throw them away later.

I got out of the house as soon as I could. It was a disgusting sight, and pitiful too. All those old people, all those old things. And an entity that will always live in my mind was disappearing, too, the furniture and furnishings of that early home I never had really known as a home. Mother was to show herself incapable of accepting that it was no more. Months after the sale, she would say, "Now, if you'll look in the dresser in Mama's room, I think there's some more of my costume jewelry." It was sad.

When we got home on one of the nights of the sale, Anna next door came to the back fence to tell us that they had finally found out what was wrong with Frank. He had lung cancer and it was spreading into his brain.

Life had to go on for us. Glenda was to spend an inordinate amount of time selling the old house. It was a short course for her in some of the less pleasant aspects of her work. Mother's brother, Uncle John, owned a third interest in the house, and it was not easy to get them to agree on such details as the asking price. Both had for many years harbored the great hope that the property would "go commercial." The city had a few years back condemned and begun to tear down a swath of houses through that fine old neighborhood, and northward into a better one, to build an expressway. A citizen's group blessedly got the damnable thing stopped. Now vacant lots and ruins of empty houses stood as a monument to heedless and destructive planning, and people like Mother and Uncle John clung to the vain hope that the project would be resurrected and their property be worth a fortune. Glenda was to discover that many other old people in the old neighborhoods of the city clung to the same hopeless dream and held on to their squalid, rundown old houses in the hope it would come true. It was of a part, I felt, with the estate sale—that terrible insecurity about things that haunted people all their lives.

When finally the house was sold, it was to a Cuban family, and I hoped it would come alive for them as the real home it had never been for me. But I was bothered by the strong feelings of distaste— disgust, actually—that I was feeling toward so many people. So many new understandings were still tumbling into my mind. I thought about our feeling for animals. A while back when our Old English sheep-dogs, Annie and Oscar, had a litter of puppies, one of them required an eye operation before he could be sold. When they brought him to us from the operating room and put him down on wobbly little legs, he uttered three little grunts, deep from within him, his only protest at all that had been done to him, and I felt a great surge of love for him, his calm and his dignity and his decency. I realized that I had felt more toward him in his eye operation than I did toward my own mother facing hers, and immediately felt guilty.

When we were first married, Glenda and I had thought we would have children, fat babies, "big fats" about the house. When that did not happen, we did not seek a medical explanation and remedy. It had been an unspoken thing between us, but what it amounted to was that we really did not want to have babies. This was not the fashionable thing of not wanting to add to overpopulation or not wanting to bring children into a doom-threatened world. What was it? Always before, I had believed in people, their potential. Now I said to myself, you are loose in a land of loveless, unlovable people, made that way by a country you can't bring yourself to feel is fit to raise children in.

What are the terrible things that America does to people? What was it doing right now to my own humanity in this crisis of being laid off? Again, I had the strong urge to go out among people in similar predicaments, talk with other men my age, compare my anger with theirs, mesh our angers together. Part of the impulse was to get back some of my old belief in people. So much of the positive I had found to weigh against the negative in my equations had involved the simple good of people. The old friends gathering around. The sense of getting started again as a writer, of returning to a land I had departed from years ago, renewing ties with people I had left behind. I had been for so many years immersed in the world of the movement and its people, oblivious to, and worse, contemptuous of, everybody else, people in ordinary work, involved in everyday business that many like me had learned to despise.

I realized I had stayed in the movement far too long. When they passed the 1965 Voting Rights Act, after the 1964 Civil Rights Act, the story I had been so fascinated with, the great overthrow of apartheid law and governments in the South, was ended. That's when I should have gotten out. And how good it felt now to be out. I drove up to Chattanooga to do a travel article. For so many years, trips I had made to do stories had been fraught with tension and outright peril. At first, it was animosity from whites who didn't like anybody writing about the Negro situation in their town. Then, more and more, it was hostility from black people. But now I was telling the Chattanooga Tourist Bureau people I had come to write about their tourist attractions, and they shouted huzzah and welcome and tried to pay for my motel room and couldn't be helpful enough.

Chance encounters with good people, certainly lovable, were part of what sustained me during the worst of my fright and anger. In that selfsame grocery store of Mother's disaster, shopping one Saturday, I was greeted by Mr. Cole, father of one of the closest friends I had in high school and college. Before his retirement, Mr. Cole sold machinery to cotton mills and was part of the tradition in that business of noblesse oblige, dating back to the South's romantic and unrealistic approaches to commerce after the Civil War. He is a big, heavy-set man, and his large face is wrinkled with lines of humor and kindness. Mr. Cole is a bibliophile, a true intellectual, deeply involved in what he reads.

On this day he said he was thinking about writing a book on economics. "I never did finish high school," he said. "But I've seen a lot and I think I could write about it." "You've read a lot," I said. He smiled. He read to me from a notebook things he had jotted down about Robinson Crusoe, and told me, "I read somewhere the other day that somebody said people have a right to jobs. They don't. A job is not a right. It's a deal. Robinson Crusoe is the only one who ever did work without having to make a deal with somebody. You find somebody needs work done and you come to terms with him." It was a point I could appreciate. I said to Mr. Cole that what working people needed to learn in this country is how to make a better deal. He nodded, looking down at me with his humorous old eyes the way he used to at his son Harold and me when we were kids and one or the other of us said something that confirmed him in his hope we might be bright.

He was a refreshing contrast to all those clutching and holding-on old people we had encountered. The period of selling the house and its contents had been the most depressing and, with its consumption of time, frustrating of all. Now that was done, and there was but one more move to make with Mother—to the retirement home. Her progress in regaining the ability to walk had been remarkable; she was getting about with a cane quite easily. We had made many trips to the nursing home and were always impressed with the genuine concern the people there showed for their elderly or incapacitated wards. One patient was a young man whom we would see in his wheelchair, a look of startled blankness on his face. He had been in a motorcycle wreck and sustained brain damage so severe he would never be more than the virtual vegetable he was now. Mother had made friends with him and with old ladies up and down the hall of her floor. She had been so long isolated from people in the old house; it was good to see her reaching out.

On one of the visits to her, I heard my name called and turned to see a man I had not seen since we were in high school together. It was Harold Chapman. I didn't remember his name but knew his face immediately.

We shook hands and Harold started in, without small talk, standing there in the nursing home hall, his long face serious and strained looking, about what was happening to him. It was his mother-in-law in the room next to Mother's. She had had a stroke. And: "You know I'm a contractor. And I've got just one little job over at Tech to complete. After that, nothing. No prospect of anything. Now it is just not right. It's not only me. My workers. Skilled craftsmen who have worked hard all their lives. They can't buy groceries. They're losing their houses. And they want to work. That's all they want. Why can't the government do something? What kind of country is that where a man who is honest and skilled and wants to work, has to work to support his family, can't find work to do? I don't know. I swear I don't know. But something's got to be done." Later, I was to hear this complaint over and over again. But now his words stirred in me the strongest will yet to talk with such men, compare notes. Could we get together later and talk some more—and get some of his crew to join in? Sure, he said. He would like that.

I went downtown to see about the retirement home, look at the different kinds of rooms available. When I got there, the woman in charge was on the phone and motioned me to sit down in her little office. She was telling one of the residents, some poor soul, that the doctor had said she was not able to take care of herself there any more; she would have to find some other place. When she put down the phone, she put her forehead down on her knuckles for a moment, pain and grief in her face. Here again, a good person. And there for the future, another worry.

We took the rocker and the marble-topped desk and the personal effects we had kept out of the estate sale into the room I selected, and then moved Mother into it. She was to report that the meals were better than in the nursing home. But there was no tub in her bathroom; she was afraid of the shower. She set her considerable will to adjusting to this whole new environment and way of life, and was genuinely pleased not to have to make so many demands on our time now. As was I, for I had the compelling, urgent need to work, to do the magazine stories and book work I had lined up against the day when I would have nothing more to do at the office.

That day, April 15, had come during the gloomy time of the selling of the house. I went down to the office that one last time, picked up my last check, and went to sit in on one last meeting of Council staff people. I have ever hated meetings, sitting in airless rooms for hours while people talk their way to obvious conclusions, spread their egos, consumately waste time by the multiple man-hour. This one was called to discuss what to do about the two issues of the magazine we still owed our first-year subscribers.

I urged a cheaply produced tabloid containing the stories we had already bought. But the consensus was for sending those loyal subscribers of ours copies of standard Council reports, of interest to specialists but deadly dull stuff. I raised the question of what would be done about the twenty-five hundred people who had gone the extra mile and resubscribed to the magazine in the hope that it would be started up again. I was assured their money would be returned to them and that a strong letter of gratitude and regret would be sent to all subscribers. Incredibly, not one of these things was done during the next six months—no reports were sent out, no refunds, not even the letter to subscribers. Thus do such organizations defeat themselves. I sat in on that last, frustrating meeting thinking, Thank God I'll never be trapped in one of these again.

April 15. In all the years I had paid taxes, there had been only a few, three or four, when I did not owe more than they had withheld from my pay. Why, I would think, if they are going to take my money and use it before it is even due, can't they at least take it accurately? We had given our accountant all the data the week before, and he had said it looked as if everything was in order. Then he had called three nights later to say, with real anguish in his voice, that we owed twelve hundred dollars more than had been withheld. The final Goddamned outrage. Somehow that same accounting department that had miscalculated the Council's financial situation so disastrously had assumed I had ten dependants in figuring my withholding.

One more reason to be glad to be away from there. But there were brighter reasons. Already, by the circumstance of what had happened to me, life was better in its very basics. I had gotten up every weekday morning for nearly thirty years and put that noose of a tie around my neck and donned that uniform of a suit and marched off to the sterility and banality and waste of time that is office routine. Now, suddenly, I didn't have to. I could set my own hours. And ah! to work uninterrupted, no meetings suddenly called, no intrusion of unwanted visitors. To get up and eat lunch not at the appointed time, but whenever I felt hungry, to fix lunch in the kitchen that I now have a part in running, since I am no longer totally dependent on a woman's knowledge and mastery of its mysteries. And then eat the lunch out in the quiet beauty of the front porch. How different it is to be able to eat lunch like that instead of crowding into a noisy, jangling restaurant and getting half drunk on martinis and gulping down tasteless stuff, paying exorbitant prices for it and having to tip the waitress who, more likely than not, has served the table with dreadful indifference.

These were other good things I could put into the equation against anxiety, good things I had not even known I was missing. I would still wake up startled at the insecurity of my situation, but now the good things about it were beginning to outweigh the bad. I still had emotional onsets of worry on the first and fifteenth of every month, those important paydays during all the years in the past. On those days I would pace to the mailbox more often, more anxiously, seeking some harbinger of success, some assurance that money would still be coming in. The first two times, I called my good agent and asked anxiously about this project, that one, and then finally realized what I was doing, and explained it to her.

Soon after that week of April 15, that first week of real freedom for me, the phone rang. It was Anna. "Pat, did Billie call you?" No. "Frank died tonight at eight-fifteen." Another tragic utterance. There was no tension built up around this one that might be released, only grief, and we had been feeling that all the time he had been in the hospital. We didn't go out to see him, knew he would not want us to. We had speculated that Frank knew what was wrong with him before he had had to go to the hospital and had hoped to be able to die at home, the home he had lived in all his life and loved so. He had all manner of things growing in the yard, fussed over them. When we first got to know him, he had been engaged in a hopeless effort to heighten the back yard fence with chicken wire to prevent Kanza from jumping over it. Fort Blalock, we called it, and Kanza had her final victory when, the last gap closed, she ran halfway up a tree trunk to clear the strand of chicken wire Frank had just put up.

But he wasn't allowed to die in the place he loved; he had to go through that final indignity waiting for us all—sterile death in the hospital. Further indecency: for some reason, when he retired, his hospitalization was not kept up. (Do I have mine still? shot through my mind when I heard about this.) He was a month away from sixty-five and Medicare when he died. Billie had to take care of the expenses he incurred dying indecently.

The funeral was at an old cemetery amid quiet woodland and ponds. Frank had planned it—the preacher's words were blessedly brief, someone sang "Leaning on the Everlasting Arms." Frank had expressed for the last time his love and consideration for us, his friends. There were many of us there.

Frank had died and Fran Kent had lived, and there was no way to know why. Free of the office and the rituals of punctuality and attendance, for the first time in my life I had the time and the solitude to reflect, to think deeply. After Frank's funeral, I not only felt grief, but also thought about death, its certainty, my own mortality. (On one of those awful mornings of rain and drear duty, I had wakened early and felt something in my chest. I smoke too much, have been badly addicted since I was fourteen. That morning I could feel Death inside me. I got up, lit a cigarette, made some coffee, got the paper, fought him off.)

Now I realized that the archetypal experience of schooling had unconsciously influenced my attitude toward life, and death. You go through grade school, with all the trials and triumphs, and then you graduate to junior high, making it through there, and on to high school and college, each time starting a new cycle. By the time I finished college and started working to make a living, I was conditioned to feel that these continuous endings and new beginnings would go on forever. This was a feeling I had only now probed, not a conscious belief, but that feeling had been a big part of the mechanism by which I had assimilated and endured such public outrages as the repeated assassination of the best leaders of my lifetime, and all those everyday outrages and obscenities afflicting my life. We live, the truism goes, as though we would live forever. I had lived as though I was going to keep on graduating to another school forever, and surely the next one would be better than the one I was in now.

Well, I said to myself, thinking about Frank, there ain't going to be no next one. Something has got to be done about this one.

Frank's death and funeral triggered the acknowledgment of my own mortality, which was to be the climax of all the sudden realizations I had come to. I felt now the very strong need to get outside of myself. I kept coming back to that urge to talk with other men my age. How did others respond to the terrors of joblessness? I had been lucky, on that score. At least I had some chance because of the kind of work I do. What of those with no chance?

Someone sent me a clipping of what Edward B. Furey, a recently fired middle-aged executive, had written on the Op-Ed page of *The New York Times*: "But to be fifty-two years old and jobless is to be frightened—frightened to the marrow of your bones. Your days start with it, and end with it. It's all pervasive. It's numbing. . . ."

How I could respond to those words. And: "It's to realize the simple stunning fact that you are without meaningful representation in this society. . . . Finally, it's to lie sleepless in bed waiting for the dawn of a new day and realize that something is terribly wrong in America."

Yes, yes. Exactly! I determined to find men like the writer of those words, articulate and angry. Angry about their joblessness, angry about their country. I would set out on a quest of such men, compare notes with them, seek in them the particulars of how America renders its people loveless, maybe even find my way back to some of the belief I used to have in people. But most of all, I would seek anger in others like that which still burned in my own brain.

4

My quest of angry middle-aged men was to prove at the outset far more difficult than I had expected; for a time, I was frustrated at every turn. I set out to find unemployed men first. They would be the most angry of all, I believed, and I needed to hear how they were handling what had come so close to throwing me.

The first man I thought of was Harold Chapman, the contractor I had encountered in the nursing home. I hadn't gotten his phone number at the time, and when I dialed the only Chapman construction firm in the book, a recording came on saying the phone had been disconnected. I called the likely Chapman residences, but none was his. I tried another old high school friend who is in the construction business, and he checked trade directories in his office but couldn't find anything. I had the feeling a lost soul had been swallowed up out there. Later the other construction man called with a phone number and home address he thought were right. I called the number and this time the recording said it had been changed to unlisted. Damn. Finally I drove out to the address and found a house that should, by the progression of street numbers, be the right one. It had no number on it, and there was an air of desertion, even desolation, to the place, though an old car was parked in the side yard and a dog barked inside the house when I rang the bell. No one answered, and I left a note asking the resident to call me if he was Harold Chapman. I never did hear from him.

Then I went to the Atlanta unemployment compensation office, located downtown on Marietta Street, in an ancient building the developers should have got. I talked with a young woman on the staff about what I wanted to do and she took me into a little office with a glass wall that looked down on a huge, gloomy room where men and women of all ages stood in ten long lines waiting to sign for their compensation, to give their defeated testimony that they had not yet found a job. I shuddered to see it. On busy days, the young woman said, the lines merge into one at the door and it stretches back a block to the corner and another block around the corner.

She gestured at those people in the lines and said I should just go down there and see if any of them would talk to me. I shrank back. It would be like going into a pit. Wouldn't they resent it, my approaching them that abruptly? I asked the question hoping she would intercede for me. She smiled, with not a lot of sympathy. "Some of them probably will resent it," she said.

I bent my shoulders and went down the steps and started searching up and down the lines for middle-aged men. There was a fat fellow in overalls, but he went off behind the counter somewhere, I guess to be interviewed. Only one other man looked likely, and I feared he was too young. He had on a good business suit, a neat, compact, decent-looking guy. I gritted my teeth and approached him, told him what I was about, getting in early that I had been laid off myself not long ago. He said, "Okay, I'll meet you over by those chairs when I get through signing up."

We sat side by side on folding chairs. I got the age thing straight first. He smiled and said he guessed he qualified; he was forty-five. I told him he looked much younger. He smiled again and said that was an asset looking for work, wasn't it? Jesus. He told me he had been executive vice-president of a food brokerage firm, making forty-five thousand dollars a year plus bonuses. Last year he had grossed sixty-two thousand. He was married and had four sons, eight to twenty. He had been out of work for four months. It wasn't the economy that had cost him his job, but politics in the firm.

When I told him I would like to get our talk on a tape recorder, he started backing off. I don't need to use your name, I assured him. And I can disguise your identity. This book I'm doing, it might just do some good. He smiled. "It can't do any harm."

Could we set up an appointment? He said he wanted to think about it. He would have to be anonymous. I asked if I could call him next week because I wanted to hear his whole story. He got out his wallet, took a card out, then put it back in. "I was about to give you my card.

Then I wouldn't be anonymous. Let me have your phone number. I'll call you." He had no reason, of course, to trust me. But my God, to be that cautious, that afraid. I never did hear from him, another lost soul I still think about occasionally.

An old newspaper friend who does public information work for the state labor department had promised to line up some men for me to talk with. Weeks had gone by and each time I'd call him about it, he would have some excuse for not having found anybody. I decided to try the DeKalb County unemployment office. DeKalb is a bedroom community and a lot of middle-management men live there.

The office is in a former Arlan's department store, huge, with hideous lighting. In its glare, again those long dreary lines of jobless men and women. I made my business known and was turned over to Mrs. Jeanette Cofer, a pretty, pleasant-faced black woman, and from her, sitting in her little office, I was to find out why my friend hadn't found any men for me. The problem is, she said, that people out of work, especially the older ones, the middle-aged ones, are reluctant to talk about their situation. She said tv crews had done a lot of filming of the unemployment lines, and people resented it. They felt an injustice was being done. I could tell Mrs. Cofer felt the same way.

I heard myself delivering an impassioned speech. "Look, I'm on their side. I got laid off myself not long ago. I'm trying to do something to help out in this situation. This book could do some good. Couldn't you tell some of the men what I'm doing, that I'm one of them, and see if they would agree to talk with me?"

She gave me a long, appraising look, then smiled and said, "All right. But it may take a week or so. I'll get some files out and talk with the men when they come in to sign up." Bless her heart, she did that, and called me with names and phone numbers, sounding genuinely pleased and excited about it, proud of herself.

I asked Mrs. Cofer that day in her little office about the middle-aged men she had dealt with during her five years in such work. She said most were "rebellious." She said she didn't mean rebellious like a kid, but that "they feel like the world is down on their backs." They had gotten used to a life-style and now they had to change it. That made them irate and upset, hostile. Hostile toward workers in the unemployment office sometimes. They would raise Cain if their checks were late. They were not used to standing in lines, resented having to fill out forms. And they resented very much the companies that had discharged them or laid them off. I could sure as hell empathize with all of that. I looked out at the lines and thanked God I wasn't standing in one of them.

"They do look for work," Mrs. Cofer said, sympathy and concern in her voice. "They don't want to settle for ninety dollars a week, the maximum we can pay. Most of them don't stay unemployed long. If one of them is out of work for as long as twelve weeks, he gets really depressed. If he feels like he's exhausted all possibilities for getting work, he's just very depressed."

Twelve weeks. I tried to imagine myself there. Then by chance, that very day, I found out about a man who had been out of work for two years. Two Goddamned years. I had gone by Manuel's Tavern for lunch and Manuel waddled over to sit in the booth a few minutes with me. I have known him since my newspaper days, and over the years he has called me when he was irate about some specific outrage, or just depressed about the bad state of things in general. We would bitch together and commiserate with each other. On this day, he was angry and depressed about evidence he had found that one of his political rivals had been tapping his telephone. Manuel is a member of the DeKalb County government body, a recent development out of his long involvement in liberal-reform movements.

I told him about my book and how frustrated I was at not being able to locate out-of-work guys who would talk with me. Manuel's big, creased, frowning Lebanese face brightened. "I know a guy who has been out of work for two years. He's had it rough. A nice guy. He'll talk to you."

I called Jim Buchan that night and he said sure, if I was a friend of Manuel's, he'd see me. "Come on by the office tomorrow," he said. He had a job now. Not a permanent one, just temporary. "I'm hoping I can make it into a permanent one."

I was excited, setting out to talk with him the next day. At last, after all that time of living with my own emotions about being jobless, of looking inward and feeling the anger building, I was going to hear someone else tell his experience of the same terrible thing. It had been a long time since my own experience. It was midsummer now and I had been building my anticipation since April.

I guess I expected thunder and lightning bolts from Jim Buchan, out of work for two whole years. Instead, as with all the jobless men I met, I found a balanced, quiet kind of anger, all the more impressive when it did break out in the midst of telling the details of what had happened. I was to find myself deeply involved in each man's story, in all the familiar details, and was eventually to realize that those details could be woven into a broad pattern that depicted, damningly, what was wrong with this country, what had happened to it during the time of our particular middle-aged lives.

Jim's office was in the Atlanta Center Ltd., a high-rise office building in the last stages of completion. The incompletion, the emptiness of the place, made me uneasy. There were no signs marking the labyrinth of parking ramps, and I had the fear I would never be able to find my car again.

Jim's voice on the phone had been genial, almost jovial. I was surprised when at last I found his office to see a solemn, almost stern-faced man with an air of formal dignity. His face was roundish, deeply tanned, and he wore black-rimmed glasses. I had told him on the phone that I had been laid off back in April, and he had laughed and said, "You're just a rookie." But now he was all seriousness, and he sat across his desk from me and quickly, quietly, and precisely told me about himself.

He was born in Grand Island, Nebraska, in 1922, and has lived in Georgia since he was five, in towns around Atlanta, but did most of his growing up in Atlanta. His father was a teacher, "a dedicated schoolteacher." Jim spent three years in the Army, eighteen months of it in the Quartermaster Corps in Europe during World War II. He came back to Atlanta to finish high school and, after working three years for a manufacturing company, entered the Atlanta Division of the University of Georgia. His GI Bill ran out after three years, and by that time he had decided he wanted to sell real estate, so didn't finish. Jim said he meant to join the Reserves when he got out of the Army, but didn't. "I wish now I had."

He went to work for a large real-estate firm in Atlanta, and worked there for twenty-five years. "So I've had only two jobs in my life. I'm fifty-three years old. So that's much more than fifty percent of my working life spent on one job." He started out in the bookkeeping department, then went into property management, and then into sales, which with that company was mostly leasing of office space and commercial property.

What had happened to his job? "Well, in a way it's a mystery to me." It was a local company. Its founder died about fifteen years ago. "He was one of the finest people I have ever known," Jim said. "It seems that when he died, the leadership of the company died." The company was finally sold three and a half years ago to a Chicago firm. "At first," Jim said, "I felt a little insecure because I felt they were going to come in and maybe weed people out and bring in their own people. But when they sent the man down to take charge of things, I had good rapport with him. I figured I had been silly thinking about looking for another job. I had confidence in him as a leader. If it had happened right at the time they took over, it wouldn't have surprised me. But when it happened after a year's time, it did." He said he had several opportunities to work elsewhere during that year, but did not take them. "I thought I was just as secure as I would be had the company not been sold."

He told of two older men who had sold for the company more than forty years each who were retired before they wanted to be, and of another man who didn't get along with the new management and was fired. One other man with twenty-nine years' experience was treated as Jim was. Jim described that treatment. "I was called into Mr. Big's office and was told that they could no longer keep me on board. That's the way he put it. He gave me no reason. So I told him I was surprised, that I had confidence in him, and was looking forward to a good year."

The other man who was thus "phased out" told Jim that they had informed him he had not projected enough business for the coming year, that if he couldn't make thirty-five thousand dollars he ought not to be there. Jim said that to earn thirty-five thousand dollars you had to do seventy thousand dollars' worth of business on a fifty-fifty split with the company. He had projected twenty-five thousand dollars himself, which was the highest amount he had made in any of his twelve years of selling. "The only way to make money in real estate is to invest," Jim explained. "It takes money to make money."

When had the phasing-out occurred? "My fate fell on January 8, 1974," Jim said. Part of his problem was that shortly after that time the real-estate business began a decline from which it had not yet recovered. "I'll always blame myself for that. I didn't go out immediately and start looking for work. And by the time I did, I realized how bad the real-estate market was. I had to look for a property management job or something with a salary because I knew the market was too tough to jump in it cold turkey on a commission basis."

He didn't start looking at once because the firm gave him a six-month period to continue selling and draw commissions on previous sales and leases as a sort of severance pay. This is how they "phased me out." I asked Jim how that differed from being laid off or fired. "It differs in no way. That was just a nice way of putting it." After the six months, they would apply Jim's commissions to paying off money he had been advanced on the draw. I asked him if he would get any money from those commissions after the debt was retired, and he said no, there might not even be enough to pay off the debt.

Well, I thought, business is business, cold and hard, and they have the right to tell an employee he's got to make thirty-five thousand dollars or get out. But Goddamn. To kick a man out after twenty-five years. I asked Jim how he felt about the firm's disloyalty.

"I definitely have a strong feeling of—not disloyalty on the part of the former owners. But, as I say, twenty-five years is a long time." He was disappointed in one respect. Four executives of the old company were given five-year contracts when the new company took over. The old owners had insisted on that. "You would have thought that the four other people and me, because of longevity, should have been given some sort of contract."

Jim said that the thing he was angriest about was the commissions they were collecting to pay off his draw. They were withholding income tax from them and that had caused him trouble when he signed up for unemployment, and besides, it seemed to him like a tax on a loan. And not letting him work long enough to repay the draw seemed unfair, too. They could have just written the draw off. One officer said they should have, but it was too late by the time he thought of it.

Rude little shocks kept bumping my naïveté. I couldn't follow the whole story about the commissions and asked Jim if he had thought of taking the thing to the Legal Aid Society. He said he had tried it. The place was pandemonium, nobody but blacks there. "They were prejudiced against me. I had on a coat and tie."

So many disappointments, small and large. I could feel myself where Jim had been two years ago: suddenly, overnight, cast out in a world where nobody wanted me. What would I do? *What do you do, Jim? What the hell do you do?*

"After twenty-five years of working, you don't know how to look for a job. You don't realize how times are. Before the six months were over, I had begun looking. I had gone to several brokers and asked them if they would put me on a drawing account or if they had any salaried jobs either in sales or property management. And, of course, I found that everybody was trying to cut back because of the slowdown in the real-estate market. Then I tried to get into another field.

They would put me down in a flattering manner. They'd say, 'We feel you're overqualified—overqualified to go out and sell something other than real estate—' or something like that. It's a compliment, but it's also a put-down. I would say, 'Look, I need to make a living. Give me a tryout.' "

At last he found a residential real-estate firm that wanted to start a commercial department. He got his license transferred and: "The first day I went to work I became ill. I had a cerebral hemorrhage or stroke or whatever you want to call it."

Good God. The troubles, with so many of these men I was to find, as with me, come in bunches. And that's understandable. We are at an age when parents become ill, die; children get in trouble, struggle with their growing up; our own health has to be watched. These natural kinds of troubles piled onto the unnatural one of joblessness make life almost unbearable. Jim's stroke was probably brought on by the strain of his joblessness.

"I had a pretty tough time," Jim said. "Of course, I came through it fine. In fact, the doctor was surprised I didn't wind up with a speech impediment or some kind of paralysis or something. But I'm in better health now than before it happened." Thank God. That's all you would need on a new job as a salesman—a speech impediment, paralysis. Jim was in Georgia Baptist Hospital three and a half days, and it cost him eleven hundred dollars. Then he went to the VA hospital for two and a half weeks and it didn't cost him a penny. He went back there as an outpatient for blood-pressure checks for six months. His blood pressure stayed perfectly normal all the while. Now he gets it checked free through the Georgia Heart Association at a private hospital. "As I say, I've looked in every nook and cranny, not just for jobs but for where I can get a service done for nothing," Jim said.

When he got out of the hospital, he kept in touch with his new employer, who said, "Now, Jim, just take it easy. Come on back when you feel like it." The doctors told Jim to stay off his feet for a couple of weeks. "Then when the time came for me to go to work, my man said, 'Well, we just decided not to hire you.' I said, 'Why, you have hired me. You have my real-estate license.' Then he said, 'Well, we just feel that since you've had this severe illness you couldn't pass our physical. We could not insure you.' I said I would be willing to waive insurance. But anyway, that was just an excuse, you know. Since the real-estate market had soured, they decided why pay an extra man? So it was just bad timing all around."

Jim said his next move was to go to the Georgia Vocational Rehabilitation Department, a state agency. He thought they would help him get a job. What they did was give him a physical to see if he was disabled. He also spent four hours with a clinical psychologist and went to the Georgia Mental Health Institute to take a bunch of job evaluation tests. "I came through with flying colors on all of that. In fact, it was an interesting thing. One of the tests showed I should have been a musician." We laughed, and I thought how much better that might have been for him. "But still, sales came to the forefront on most of those tests." They finally told him he was not disabled so they couldn't help him find a job. Jim hadn't realized that was what they required. Still, he got a free physical and he enjoyed taking those tests. So it was time well spent.

By then he was drawing unemployment compensation. "Of course, I had more job interviews. Pat, you just can't believe the number of people I talked to about jobs. Résumés. I wish I had all the money I've spent at fifteen cents a copy to have them Xeroxed and ten cents for a postage stamp." He got responses to some of the résumés and had interviews, but still no job. There were offers for him to sell real estate on a straight commission. But that would mean giving up the unemployment pittance for likely less income. How cruel the traps they have set for us. "I needed something with a salary. After all, you have to eat and pay the rent. With the real-estate market deflated, it was very bad. Of course, it's picking up now." I told him I hoped so, because my wife was in that business. We laughed. A life insurance firm offered him a sales job with a one-year salary while training. But they insisted that he would have to give up his real-estate license. He just couldn't bring himself to do that.

He said he hoped to place his license with the firm he was working for temporarily. "I have no assurance that this is going to be a permanent job because I was hired on a two- to three-month basis, possibly six months, but if the work is there, it could become a permanent job. I hope so because this is still related to what I have done in the past. This is real estate here, even though I'm working for a developer, not a broker."

The import of all he had been telling me, what Manuel had said, hit me anew. This man, quiet and easy-voiced, solemn, dignified in his business suit, had been out of work for nearly two years, had been looking for work that long, and until now had not been able to find any. Nineteen months, Jim said, and he had lived through every day of every one of them. How, Jim?

He had only himself to support. He is divorced, his children grown.

He was given a small GI disability pension after the stroke. Once he gets a job, that will stop. And, of course, he was getting unemployment compensation. "I've just been a-living pretty close to the bone really. It's tough. But I needed to. I felt the job market would open up pretty soon. I sure was not the big spender I once was." Luckily, he said, he had not had to cut back on his living quarters. He had been in his apartment several years, and even though he was "a little behind" in his rent, they let him stay on because of his long tenancy. "I don't eat steak any more, anything like that. Anybody offers me a free meal, I take advantage of it," Jim said.

"It affected my personality very strongly," he went on. "I've always had a good sense of humor—think I still have basically. But some friends of mine have accused me of being overly sensitive. I'm sure that I have been. Like I say, when you have to kind of change your theme of living and depend on others when you never did before, it really affects your personality. I don't think it's a permanent thing, though. I've been just as happy as a lark since I got this job three or four weeks ago. Just something to do. You get up and know you're going out to do something instead of looking for a job. It has been very depressing. There's no doubt about that."

I told him my first reaction was panic: I was scared to death. Did he go through that? Are there levels of it, different degrees as time goes by? Jim said sure, he had been scared, and then worried about his health after the stroke. And the debts. "I owe people right now." His gas credit card. More than seven hundred dollars still to the hospital. About two hundred and fifty dollars to a clinic and a doctor. "That's what bothered me most. Being in debt and not being able to do anything about it—because what little income I had from the pension and unemployment would barely pay my rent and feed me. Eventually it catches up. The longer you're unemployed, the longer you have no income, the more you're going to go into debt. You've got to live. You've got to survive."

His anger came through in his quiet words. Others were to speak vehemently about the need for a government medical program, but Jim didn't go into that. He felt he'd been lucky in his medical experience. It was the defeats that were not his fault that made him mad. Like his age being held against him. His company had no pension program when he was phased out, but now they have one, and health insurance. "So I think that age definitely had something to do with it." He was the youngest of the five let go. And when he applied for a job at a bank, his friend there said, "Jim, we'd like to hire you. But we have mandatory retirement at sixty years of age. You could only put in nine years." Well that was honest, Jim said. "I don't consider that discrimination." But if the company he had worked for for twenty-five years had been honest enough to tell him that, he would have hollered discrimination to high heaven.

And what, I asked, about the assets you had to give to your company—your experience, judgment, the things you can learn only through long, hard years of work? "Well, I don't know. They were bringing in, you know, these kind of hot-shot salesmen and college graduates and such. I learned what I know about real estate from experience, that's true. Enough to bring me all the way from bookkeeping to where I was." At one time early in his career, he said, he was holding down·three jobs for the company, and filling in when a bookkeeper was out. Now he had his reward. It wasn't right, we were agreed on that. But what was to be done? He had sought out free services. What else, from his long experience of being jobless, did he think the government might do for middle-aged men in his predicament?

He wasn't sure, but he was certain that what it was doing was not enough. Unemployment wasn't enough to live on. Manuel had put him onto the federally supported Community Educational Training Aid program (CETA), administered by the city. All it amounted to, Jim said, was another employment agency, a few jobs for people doing that. Who needed another employment agency? He was already going to the unemployment office every week and getting lists of fruitless possibilities. The CETA people had given him a test for entry into training as a housing expediter, which sounded close to real estate. A Philadelphia lawyer with three degrees in accounting couldn't have passed it, Jim said. If this was a training program, he said, they should have trained him first and then given him the test. He thought the government funds there were being misappropriated. "By that I mean they're not being put to good use, they're not helping the person who is really desperate for a job. But I'm not saying I want a pension or anything like that. I want a *job*. I want to earn. Even if this thing I'm on now works out to be only temporary, it's something to go to in the morning. Get up and have somewhere to go and put forth some effort."

What else are you mad about? I asked. He spoke of "annoyances." The twenty-five years of loyal work—he mentioned that again. And smaller things. Having to convince people at the unemployment office that even though taxes were being withheld from commissions he wasn't actually getting, he was unemployed, and their bossily telling him he had to put his license with the Real Estate Board before he could draw compensation. "That annoyed me." He continued:

"The whole thing just annoys you when you know you're qualified and you go down and you almost beg a person to hire you. And they hire someone else. Somebody younger. Or property management— you know, resident manager—they want to hire girls. Here again, they don't come out in the open and tell you that. But it always turns out to be a girl. There have been situations where I know I could have done the work as skillfully if not more so than the person they hired. But they're going in for the young college graduates. And here again, the put-down: you're overqualified. Things like that have annoyed me. In fact, I'd say they made me furious. It seems the timing was so bad on everything. The unemployment situation and the real-estate market both hit the bottom at the same time."

And the illness, I said. But on that, Jim maintained, "I feel I was lucky. I came through that and the doctor says I'm in better shape now than I was before."

I shook hands with him in that fine, sparkling new office and prayed that he would be allowed to stay there. He promised that if he thought of anything else he wanted to say, he would "make some notations" and give me a call. He did call two nights later to say, "The whole thing, Pat, made me lose confidence in things. In myself. And now it makes me feel so good to have somewhere to go in the morning. I've got to do a good job for them so that it will be permanent."

I was on fire now to get on with the quest. I had expected thunder and lightning from Jim Buchan, but found his quiet words of measured anger and desperate struggle far more moving, and disturbing. What else in the stories that such men have to tell would feed my anger and increase my awareness? I tried to sort out my motivations. It was comforting to know that Jim had felt the same kind of anger and anxiety I had, and finding similar reactions in other men was to steady me increasingly. What else was I doing? Seeking reassurance by talking to men worse off than I was? I hope not. Looking for catharsis? Sure. Finding misery in company? There was that on both sides. Joblessness was a bond. It had done Jim good to talk with someone who had been there, if but briefly, who could understand and empathize. And it had done me good, Lord knows.

I just couldn't wait to see whether Mrs. Cofer would succeed in finding other men for me to talk with. I called my friend at the labor department again, and this time he suggested that I check out Americus in southwest Georgia. They had one of the highest unemployment rates in the nation. When I called the woman in charge of the Americus unemployment office, Mrs. Eula Hill, she was cooperative and very concerned about the hard times in the town. Grown men were standing in the unemployment lines crying, she said. In her friendly, slurring southwest Georgia voice, she gave me names of men to call. Each one I called long distance was cautious, noncommittal at first. Then I would say that I had been laid off myself back in April, and they would become cordial, saying sure, come on down, I'll talk to you.

I drove into Americus at midday, feeling joy just at being back on reporting duties again, going out to talk to folks. I love south Georgia anyhow, always feel good down there, probably because I lived there during my formative years, five to ten years old. It was hot that day as only south Georgia can be hot, and the big old sky was cloudless. I lifted my face to the sun. I had pulled up to the Windsor House in the middle of downtown, an incredible old hulk of a red-brick hotel with turrets and other flourishes. Traveling before, I would never take a chance staying in such a place, would seek the stale certainty of a standard motel. Now I marched up to the big old front door, and found it padlocked. I asked the lady in the gift shop next door what had happened, and she said, "Bankruptcy. Times are hard down here. They just couldn't keep it going any more."

I felt guilty about all that elation I had brought into town. After all, hard times was why I was here. Americus has always been an agricultural market town, once cotton, still tobacco, some soybeans, lumber. And in the South's postwar grasping at any kind of industry it could get, Americus had become, also, a center for the mobile home industry, at best a low-paying, exploitative kind of business. The collapse of the housing market in 1974 that Jim had talked about had brought down most of the mobile home plants in the town. The unemployment rate was 14.5 percent in May 1975, and was still about that when I got down there in early August.

I checked into a standard motel and then went to the unemployment office to talk with Mrs. Hill. Here again, those men and women standing in lines. Things were a little better now, Mrs. Hill said. The town's agricultural base had kept the bottom from dropping out. And men laid off had been able to grow their own food during the spring and summer months. Since I had called her from the motel, she said, a man whom I might want to talk with had come in, and he had agreed to wait around to see me. She looked about and said, "Well, my goodness, he's gone."

The office has No Smoking signs plastered all around, which seemed to me a cruel thing for smokers in those long, unhappy lines. When I came in, I had noticed a fellow hunkered down on the sidewalk by the door, having himself a good long-drawing smoke. I said "I bet that was him," and sure enough, we looked out and Mrs. Hill said, "Yes, here he is." She introduced me to Horace Smith.

I asked him if he wouldn't rather talk at his house, that I found people were more relaxed in the rooms they lived in. He said he would just as soon talk here at the office, and I realized he probably didn't want me to see the kind of place he lived in. Mrs. Hill found us a little office and said it would be all right for us to smoke in there. So we sat across from each other and talked, puffing away. Horace said at one point that he hoped he would live to see his youngest son graduate from high school, and thought he would if "these things" didn't get him. He said he wished he could quit. I said me, too.

Horace Smith, deeply tanned, with brown curly hair, a broad forehead, blue eyes behind his eyeglasses, wore on his heavy-set body a tan shirt and trousers identifying his former job on the assembly line at one of mobile home plants. He smiles easily, and laughs the ironic laugh of country people in southwest Georgia, even as he tells you something awful. "I'll be glad to talk to you," he said at the outset. "If you just don't git me put in the chain gang."

He was born in 1919 in Thomaston, Georgia, not far from Americus, and was raised on a farm in nearby Dooly County. His education: "I went to the Vineville School." He farmed with his father until World War II. Then he workd briefly at Warner Robbins Air Force Base in Macon, Georgia, and served in the Army. He got out to go back to the farm to help his father, who was in ill health. He stayed on the farm and worked around in machine shops, cotton gins, and the like until he got married in 1952. That was the last year he made a crop. He and his wife moved to Florida, and Horace worked at such places as paper mills and a lumber company, "knocking down houses and all that." After other laboring jobs in Florida and Georgia, he came to Americus in 1962 because he had heard about the mobile home plants, and he got work on the assembly line at one of them. It was the best job he had ever had, he said.

"I been used to hard work all my life," Horace said. "When I was the age of my youngest boy now, fourteen, fifteen years old, I was doing more than a man's job. You know those old-timey peanut pickers? I was tailing one of them for a dollar a day. And then hoeing hay at night till ten or eleven o'clock. I was working fourteen or fifteen hours a day. And back then, labor in the field wasn't but fifty cents a day. That was from sunup till sundown. It wasn't no eight hours or nothing. 'Course, my kids, when I tell 'em about it, they laugh at me. They wouldn't think of doing it. Shoot. I had to."

In Americus, he was laid off from the job at the first plant, and went to work at a sawmill. There he lost a part of one of his fingers. Then he went back to the mobile home plant, only to be laid off again. He worked at a spring manufacturing plant for four years, and then was once more taken on at the mobile home plant in July 1969. He was laid off again in September 1974, and this time the plant went out of business. Except for a short-term, low-paying job in Charleston, South Carolina, he had not been able to find work in twelve months. He had applications in all over, but nobody was hiring.

He lives with his wife, their youngest son, and their married daughter and her two-year-old son in a rented house. Of his daughter and oldest son, he said, "They ain't grown, but they claim to be." His wife has varicose veins and cannot work. His daughter helps out some, and he has been drawing unemployment compensation. His original twenty-six-week application had been extended, so he had two more checks coming. Would they extend it again? "They go have to, because I can't find nothing to do. They got to do something. That's all I know."

He had some hope of getting on with the city, reading water meters. But he had had a heart attack in 1970, and it made him short of breath. "I can walk. But I have to rest a right smart."

How had he spent his time during this year of unemployment? "I'm just a-looking. I'll be out walking and looking, trying to find me a job. I go to these places and ask, and if they don't have anything, maybe I go a-fishing in the afternoon, something like that. I get worried and go fishing and pass it off. But when it's all over with, it's the same thing again. So there you go. I don't go to bed till late at night. I sit there and think and think. Then when I go to bed, it's hard for me to go to sleep. I keep thinking, which I reckon it's wrong to do, but I can't help it. Because I know what responsibilities I got on me. I know what I got to do, and that's why I keep trying to go."

I knew that feeling. He spoke of his daughter and grandson as part of his responsibilities, but one of his blessings, too. "If they leave, I reckon I will go crazy. He just pitty-pats, pitty-pats across that floor and—" He laughed. "I tell you, if she ever gets out and takes him with her, I reckon I will go crazy."

Naïvely, I asked if the unemployment money was enough to get by on. He laughed. "It ain't barely enough to get by on. It ain't enough. But you have to do the best you can." His family was also getting food stamps, ninety-six dollars' worth for fifty-seven dollars. "And everything's gone so dern high and still going higher. It's just a mess."

He said he had some doctor bills from his wife's condition that he couldn't pay. But the main worry was paying the rent. He was two weeks behind. But the old woman he rents from had been understanding so far, had been mighty nice. But if she ever got teed off, she could put them out in the street. "And that's bad. I told my wife, back in them Hoover days, living on a farm, a man had the house. They didn't charge you no rent. Had the water. No water bill to pay. And you go to the woods and cut the wood for the fireplace. There's three or four things back in those days you didn't have to pay for that you have to pay for now."

What, I asked Horace, do you think is going to happen to this country with folks like you and folks like me who want to work and can't get jobs? And there are a whole lot of us, I said. He laughed that southwest Georgia laugh once more. "Somebody's going to have to keep 'em up, I reckon. If we get another Republican President, I know they will. I don't know whether you're a Republican or a Democrat, but that's the way it's turned out for me. This is the fourth time I've been through 'em. Looks to me like they set down on the money and you can't find no jobs or nothing." He told about the time he tried to get a job and the man asked him if he knew who was President. He answered Eisenhower. And the man said, "That's why I don't have no job for you." In Hoover days, he was doing more than a man's work at fourteen. Then Nixon, and now Ford, ran up the price of gas, Horace said, instead of rationing it. He didn't remember too much about Roosevelt, only that he had pulled the kinks out a little. "I wasn't no politicking man. But I could sho' tell the difference when a Republican or Democrat was President."

Would he want to see something like the WPA again? He laughed. "I hope not. You can't never tell though." It'd be better than this, I said. "Oh yes. You better believe it." On other matters, he stuck to the things he had believed when he was relatively better off. He had had hospitalization from the mobile home plant when he had the heart attack. He didn't have it now, of course, just a little life insurance "you have to die to collect." But he wouldn't want a federal medical program for everybody, didn't want anybody doing for him as long as he was able to work for such things. (He had told me about the health problems of two of his three brothers. One had been sickly all his life and died on the operating table when his lungs flooded with blood. The other got hurt somehow or another working down in Florida. "Something fell on his back and messed him up for life. He ain't good for nothing.")

When I asked him if he didn't feel that somebody had kind of let him down, he gave that southwest Georgia laugh and said, "Well, naw, I don't guess so. These things happen. I don't guess so that I know of." It seems though, I said, if a man works hard all his life and all he wants to do is work some more and can't get a job, it's a rough kind of a deal. "Well, yeah," he said. "I'm one of them kind—I like to work. As long as I can work, I want to do it. I get miserable setting still. That's the way my daddy was. He never could set still. He wanted to work all the time."

He believed the mistakes he had made in his life were partly the cause of his predicament. He wished that he had stayed in the Army. He could be retired now. Another time, a section foreman on the railroad had offered to hire him. "I couldn't see it. Now, after it's all over with, it was my mistake."

Had he ever in all his working years gotten a little bit ahead of bills and expenses? Yes. One time while working for the mobile home plant. They gave him a two-week vacation and he worked during those two weeks and was able to save his vacation pay. I knew that kind of willingness to work, keep working, and admired it in him. It bothered me that he was so inclined to take most of the blame for his desperate situation on himself. I started in again: "They're just going to have to do something to get jobs for people." And he responded this time: "They're going to have to, I reckon. If they don't, I don't know what people are going to do. I tell you, it'll be like these foreign countries and all that. Be where we'll be on starvation. And that's bad. I feel for little babies dying over there—ones like my daughter's got. Bring one into this world in the shape it's in now—it's bad.

"Now I tell you, the way I always looked at it, ain't nobody going to give me anything. I'd have to work for it—one way or the other.

But it's like a fellow told me here a while back. I'm too old for 'em to hire and too young for the old-age pension. So there you go. Just in a sweat. I get a check this week and I got one more coming. If they don't give more after that, I don't know what I'll do. I'll do something. If everybody else does it, I guess I can, too. I don't want to steal— nothing like that. But if it was to come down to it, I'd have to before I'd starve."

"That's a desperate way to have to feel," I said to him. He laughed. "I always wanted to work for mine. I never have been one to want to take or steal because I tell you if I stole something—get out here and people'd be a-looking at me and I'd be guilty—and they'd know I was guilty, just looking at me." He laughed. "But if I work for it and the man pays me off, I can spend it like I want, and I'll be free to do as I please with it. I want mine honest if I can make it."

I asked him about religion. "To tell you the truth"—his voice was low—"I should go to church, but I don't. These churches around here ain't the church I used to go to in no way. These churches here, if you ain't got a seventy-five-dollar or hundred-and-fifty dollar suit of clothes on, they won't even look at you good. You ain't going for them to see you, the way I look at it, but for the benefit of the Lord. It don't matter whether you're dressed like a rich man or whatever, we're all going to be treated alike when the time comes. So that don't bother me. But I want to look halfway decent. So I don't go. My wife goes. I'm going to start back one of these years—as soon as I can get me something decent to wear." He spoke fondly of the little country church he went to as a boy in Dooly County, and said his religion still meant a great deal to him.

I asked him about the schools—whether he thought his children would have a better chance than he had. He said he didn't like the school situation but there was nothing he could do about it. His youngest boy had been in a different school every year since he started. Was he getting a good education? "He's doing as good as the rest of 'em," Horace said. Then: "I don't like the situation with all these niggers and all. But what am I going to do about it? I got to go along with it. It's one person against a hundred and fifty or two hundred." He laughed his southwest Georgia laugh. "So what's the use to raise sand about it? It comes. You have to go along with it." I thought about how I used to believe that people like him, the South's dispossessed poor whites, might eventually join the movement, make it a populist cause. But all the movement had done for him was add to his sense of helplessness.

Then he talked at great length about his children, how people can't afford to raise big families any more, how kids don't help out around the house the way he did as a boy, how they don't obey as his father made him obey with a hickory stick, how they wouldn't work as he did as a teen-ager. "They ain't got the strength or energy that we had back then, or something. I don't know what. They're lazy or something. I don't know what it is."

He said he used to walk everywhere he went, and now kids thought they had to have cars. He bought his two eldest a car because they said they needed it to get back and forth from school. Turned out they were using it for anything but that—all kinds of devilment. His oldest boy tried to drive it down to Florida and burned up the motor, and Horace had to go and haul it back to town for him. Then his children got mad at him because he wouldn't give them money for a new motor. Soon after, he had to sell his own car because he had been laid off. "I got out of the car business," he said.

Then: "My two oldest ones, they got nearly about through the eleventh grade and they quit school. That hurt me worse than anything. Every time I think about it, it makes me sick. Times I worked when I was sick just to keep them in school, get 'em an education." How come they quit that far along? I asked. "I don't know. They got in with the wrong bunch of people." He had tried to get them to go back, and said he hoped it still wasn't too late. Meantime, his oldest boy had been laid off at the pulpwood mill and was working in a filling station.

"This other one I've got, I told him I wanted to see him graduate out of the high school if I could. I don't know whether I'll make it or not. He's got five more years to go. He's going to have to have it, all this here electronic stuff and all. Anybody ain't got their education, they're just out of luck. I see my mistake. It's too late now. If I had my time to go over again, if I had to stay in every grade in school three years, I'd go at it until I finished. You better believe it."

Things were different back when you quit school, I offered. "Yeah. Back then, when you went to get a job, it didn't matter whether you had an education or not. They just wanted you to work. But now that's the first thing they want to know: Did you finish high school? If you ain't finished high school, they don't even want to talk to you. They want somebody else. But that's true enough, too, because there's plenty of them has got it."

More of them than are needed, I commented. "So that makes it hard on somebody like me," Horace agreed. "And I got a little age on me, too." I said the way I figured it, experience and skill and judgment ought to count for something. "That's right. But they want a younger guy because they figure a fellow like me, in a few more years —if I live—I'd be ready to retire and wouldn't have but about eight or nine years work in. Take the younger guy, they git twenty-five or thirty years work out of him before they retire him." He laughed. "That's what they want." *Age. The echoes of bitter knowledge—Horace with his life's history, Jim with his. Echoes.*

As throughout our conversation, Horace's mind went back to the good life he had known as a boy on the farm. "We'd work. We'd go fishing. There was so much to do. Finish and go fishing, in a bateau out there. Just go fishing. Wasn't worried about who was President because I knowed we had plenty to eat. Some clothes, which wasn't the finest in the world, but covered our skin anyway. And happy, and had neighbors. We'd all gang up and go to the creek swimming, go and play baseball or something like that. And have a good time. That's another thing with young kids today. If they ain't got a-plenty of money and an automobile and get out here and run up and down the road with it, they ain't happy."

He thought some more about the farm. "You go back to them days now, it'd take fifty-thousand dollars for me to git started farming again like I farmed then. Naturally, with everything else changed, that was going to change, too. The old mule went out of style and tractors come in. Oh, I like to farm. I wish I was on one now. But I couldn't farm it like I did then. They'd all think I was a damn fool, see me plowing a mule." He laughed. "Think I was crazy. And fertilizer and stuff has gone so high, you couldn't buy it. But I believe—I believe if I had me a place like that, I could make a living off it. I couldn't make none to sell to nobody else. I could raise everything I need except a little sugar, this and that, flour. Fact is, I could eat cornbread if I could git the corn ground. That's what I was raised on. Cornbread and milk and vegetables out of the yard. And they was hard to beat and they still are. Now you go to town and buy this stuff that's in a can, and it ain't good." And they charge you six prices, I said. "That's right. And it ain't fit to eat."

He talked again of being able to cut firewood for fuel. "We'd cut up fifteen load of stovewood and fifteen load of firewood every year. That'd last the whole year around. Every time it'd rain, Daddy'd say, 'Well, boys, you better cut up some firewood.' We'd have a pile up there fifteen or twenty foot high. About thirty foot around. It'd last all year."

Yes. Yes. I could see it. Twenty foot high. Enough for all year long. And the fires. Warmth. Comfort. Security. And a man was certain of his place, not baffled and bewildered and frightened. And could feel that his children were being raised right and would continue this good life.

"Well," said Horace. "That's about all I know about. That's about the story of my life, I reckon."

Then: "Well, they always told me in something like this, times had to get worse before they got better. I don't know if they could git any worse, or any better either." He laughed his southwest Georgia laugh.

And: "They always told me if there's a will, there's a way. I think there'll be a way. Might not be like the one we'd want, but there'll be a way. Might not like it. Just have to go along with it."

Goddamn. Goddamn the cruelty of such a country, I thought. The insane waste of the life of such a man, of other men like him all across the continent, raised to farm and driven from the land. Once I had interviewed young people in jail for a magazine story on youthful crime, and after talking with them realized that what they were saying was they weren't going to do the kind of hard labor Horace had done all his life. They were no better prepared for anything else than he was. So they stole or sold dope or kited checks—anything to avoid the fate this Goddamned insane country had molded them for. And there was Horace in the unemployment office, worried and scared. After working hard since he was fourteen, all he wanted was the chance to keep on working hard, and the country couldn't even give him that.

"Well," he said. "That's about it. That's about all I know."

I talked with other jobless men in Americus, and then in Atlanta when I got back, and became just as involved in their stories, just as angry hearing them. Jim and Horace had set out the basic story they all had to tell: work done for half a lifetime suddenly stopped, the effect this had on them, the struggle to survive on not enough money, the strong desire to get back to work. But the details were different, and out of them patterns emerged. Jim told how business practice and ethics had deteriorated during his and my lifetime, and Horace how the quality of life had deteriorated since his youth on the farm. All the men I was to talk with were also to describe this deterioration, a terrible thing that had been going on all my life, though I had not been fully aware of it. "Naturally, with everything else changed, that was going to change, too."

Curiously, neither of these men had expressed the awareness I had come to of what a sorry thing my job had been all along. They just wanted theirs back. Maybe my awareness was just sour grapes. Or maybe it was different for me since I had writing to fall back on. How hard would I have fought for my old job or sought desperately for a new one just like it if I hadn't? Jim and Horace seemed to accept unquestioningly all the roles assigned them in personal and public life, and did not rail out, as I had expected them to, against the government and society.

How similar were the little life stories of all the men I interviewed. Before the quest, I had had an insight into how we had all been abstracted from our humanity. Now I was to become aware of just how that had happened.

We were, most of us, good little boys, good scouts, game players, determinedly heterosexual suitors, and dutifully monogamous husbands. We fought that largest of wars, GI Joes, and after that: a silent generation, not to be trusted because we were over thirty, the power structure; racists, if white (though we might protest not so), inferior, if black (though the opposite might be demonstrable), and chauvinist pigs, all. At the same time, good husbands, proud fathers, grimly enduring the rat race, men in gray flannel suits, organization men, and paying the bills, buying the split-levels, paying the taxes that each year made us dread the beautiful onset of spring, buying the insurance that made us worth more dead than alive, attending the PTA, boosting the Little League, footing the college bills, paying the alimony and child support—and ever the dutiful sons, seeing after sick and enfeebled parents, guilt-haunted when we had to put them in nursing homes.

The jobless men I met did not talk about these things, but I wondered how many of them were fed up with being abstractions—chauvinist, bill payer, dear old Dad. Every other element in society has risen up and thrown off some yoke of abstraction—blacks, women, youth. But not *the man*. All we have done was what was expected of us in all those abstract roles. Blacks and whites of us, we kept things going while the black movement won its victories. Women and youth could not have mounted their movements if we had not been going to work and paying the bills. When, I asked myself, would it be our turn to be heard, we who are supposed to belong to the most powerful group in the land?

Returning from Americus, I was on an old two-lane U.S. highway, getting back to the accursed expressway, when I stopped at a filling station. There, drinking a Coke, I looked about me at the gashed landscape common to such roads all across the country: garish signs, graceless little galvanized-steel or cement-block buildings, Brazier Burger, Dairy Queen, Kayo Gas Regular 53.9¢, Hasty House. Across the way, a fenced-in grassless storage area by a railroad track, huge gravel piles. Litter everywhere. My anger was still indiscriminate. This ugly sight made me almost as angry as the tales I had heard from Jim and Horace, or the thoughts I had had about how abstracted we all were.

I was Goddamning all of it, Goddamning this country just as vehemently as I had when I sat listening to Horace. I could see myself making a career out of my anger, hurling thunderbolts at idiocies and idiots across the land for years, the way Mencken did.

When I got back home, I talked with Francis Kent. The time had come to talk with men who *had* jobs, but were angry nevertheless. Because they were not consumed with the agonizing search for a job, I thought, they would speak out on these other matters, things like being abstracted. What better person to begin with than Fran Kent?

We have much in common—newspapering, a love of the natural-fiber clothing of our youth (which we seek out in exclusive shops yet), and a loyalty to the music of our youth, the civilized sound of jazz and swing. Yet we come from entirely different backgrounds.

Fran was born in Gary, Indiana, in 1925, and finished high school there. "I went into the Navy in 1942, spent four years there, and went back to school after I got out." (How often these men pass over that important, dangerous period of their lives, the hell of being in World War II, with such a sentence. Did you see action? I asked Fran. "Oh yes." Where? "Sicily, Salerno—you know, we had landings there." That was pretty fierce, wasn't it? Fran laughed. "I guess.")

He went through two years of college back in Gary, and then worked for papers in Hammond, Indiana, and San Diego before joining the *Los Angeles Times*, on which he has worked ever since. He was promoted to various editing jobs and then, at his request, went back to being a reporter, assigned in 1964 to Rio de Janeiro with responsibility for covering the entire continent of South America. He was transferred to Mexico City in 1969 and covered that country until 1973, when he came to Atlanta to cover the South. (When someone asked him once if he had requested Atlanta, he laughed. "I had the choice of Atlanta or *Australia*," he said, making the latter sound like an obscenity.) He was married to Lee in 1949, and they have one son, born in 1950.

Lee is a beautiful woman, Fran a handsome man. He and I talked in their apartment way out in Chamblee. It is spacious, tastefully decorated with furnishings from Latin America. But the apartment complex is depressingly ugly, oppressively modern, bright red carpet in the halls. Glenda says it is like walking into a stomach. Fran, his hair and moustache graying so that he resembles the movie Topper, leaned back, relaxed, and talked in his staccato delivery.

I asked him, to start out, what his impressions of America had been when he returned after ten years away from it. "The most obvious thing was that everything had become much more expensive. And people had become much more permissive about everything—from the way children are raised to the things people are allowed to get away with in government, climaxed, of course, by Watergate. And differences generally in standards and values, a more relaxed sort of attitude, even toward manners, people's behavior toward one another. Men didn't open doors for women any more, or get up and give them seats." And this, I said, in the South, more deterioration I hadn't even noted. "Yes," Fran said, "and the South is supposed to be the origin of gentlemanly behavior. I found that people, certainly in the business world, are no more gentlemanly here than they are anywhere else." He said, though, he didn't mean to knock the South: "Even though there are a lot of dishonest people here, I have found more people in the South who are, in fact, ladies and gentlemen, courteous people, than anywhere else in the world I've been."

I asked him to elaborate on the changes in politics, and he quoted former Senator Fulbright to the effect that men in government are no longer guided by ethical standards. "Anything that isn't specifically forbidden by the law is all right."

"So," I said, "I reckon you are like me in having given up on the government?"

His eyebrows raised, Fran asked what I meant. I told him how I had realized that I no longer believed in liberal-reform politics one night while watching a Ford press conference. Gazing at that face suggestive of so much stubborn stupidity, watching him posture, listening to him uttering other people's words, ideas, I had shouted at Ford, "Why the hell don't you just be yourself? Say, 'Look. I didn't ask for this. I'm just an ordinary guy doing the best I can.' " Then I asked myself if there had been a President in my lifetime who had revealed his real personality to the public, or told the truth. Maybe Roosevelt on the radio—before the war started, anyhow. None of the rest, not even Kennedy with pragmatism ever dictating what he said. And then I remembered how ever since high school, I had believed that if we could just get the right man elected President, and the right men in Congress, and the right laws passed, then America could be the good, just place for everybody that it promises to be. Now, I just didn't believe it would work. "Haven't you come to that?" I asked Fran.

"Oh, no," he said, almost vehemently. "I think, with a lot of other people, that our government is far from perfect. But it's about as good a thing as has been devised. Of course, when it's run by scoundrels, that's altogether different. And much of the government, from the federal to the local level, has been run by scoundrels in the last few years."

"You think Nixon was an aberration, not a norm?" I asked. "Oh, I hope so. Yes. I can't imagine this country would put up with it a second time." Then he added that it would be less likely again if Nixon had been properly punished for his crimes. "It's almost as though he were allowed to cop a plea. He got slapped on the wrist and told not to do it again."

All this was true enough, but certainly not what I had expected from old Fran. I began to feel I was in some kind of a duel. One experienced reporter parrying with another—as though Fran were putting me on my mettle to ask the kind of questions that would elicit the kind of answers I was seeking. (How often do we do that in our profession, if no more than unconsciously? And is there something wrong with that?) "But surely," I said to Fran, "you don't believe any more in that business of getting the right man elected, the right laws passed?"

"I think that's a myth really," he said. "I don't think anybody is one-hundred-percent right on every issue. I think if you have a man who is right on the major issue of his time, it's fortunate. Even if he's wrong about everything else. FDR made a lot of mistakes. But I think he was right about most of the important things of his time." Truman? I asked. "Oh, I think Harry Truman made some very good decisions."

And some very bad ones, I said to myself, thinking about the bomb being dropped, and the cold war. But what the hell. I was full of anger and Fran was sounding like a statesman, weighing his words. He had been through that hell in the hospital. "What about medical care in this country?" I asked him.

"You mean how costly it is?"

"Yeah. And what it was like, the whole process when you had to go into the hospital."

"It's something you want to put out of your mind and forget as quickly as possible," Fran said. "It's all kind of dehumanizing. You're treated like a piece of machinery—a used car or something. People sticking things into you. And expensive. God. Fortunately, I've got good insurance. I was in the hospital eleven days and the bill was something over three-thousand dollars." The doctor bills and others brought the total cost up over four-thousand. X-rays alone were several hundred dollars. With his insurance, he had to pay only a couple of hundred dollars. But without insurance, it would have been disastrous, he said. "Nobody has that much money in his checking account for that kind of rainy day."

I mentioned that here again we were caught in the middle. Old folks have Medicare. Poor folks have Medicaid. Young folks don't run the health risks we do. Rich folks can afford it. "Sure," said Fran. "The guy who isn't in one of those programs is just over a barrel. And it's his taxes supporting all the programs." He said some sort of government health program, like the British have, seems indicated. It hadn't been as disastrous in Britain as the AMA would have us believe, he told me.

Well, that was a little better. But not the sparks I had expected to be struck. I had thought we had so much in common to bitch about. Our work. Newspapering is a frantic kind of fun. But on the paper I worked for (and it was better than most), management was a constant restraining force, ever thwarting the simple but impossible goal we had of telling the comprehensive truth about what was going on. Then I got into the common predicament of being promoted to a job completely detached from the fun, the creativity of newspapering, just as Fran had. I stood two years of the strain and joylessness of being city editor, and then went back to writing—this time a daily column. That was when I found they wouldn't let me cover the biggest story going on, and moved over to the Council. There for a brief time in the 1960s I had the opportunity and privilege of reporting with no restraints, no arbitrary management pressures. But increasingly, from 1965 on, the people and the organizations involved in the struggle for racial justice were plunged into unclear, ambiguous ideology and programs. For a time, it took courage on the part of blacks and whites alike to continue to express belief in integration. The brief time of editing the magazine had been as close to doing fully professional work as I had come since the early 1960s, and even that had been frustrated by inane management pressures from George Esser and the executive committee. I told Fran some of this and asked if he had been subjected to such pressures, if he had been able to find full satisfaction in all his years of newspapering.

"Oh yes," he said. "There isn't anything else I would want to do. I don't regret a minute of it. I'd do it all over again." But could it have been better? Could the papers that he worked for have been run better? "Oh sure. Until I went to work for the *Times*, I had worked for two newspapers and I always went around apologizing for it. But I never had to do that in Los Angeles." I remember making those apologies myself.

Fran recalled how on those first two papers he was told, more than once, you can't report that kind of story. "I don't know how many times I've been told, 'We don't want any crusaders, anybody stirring up the advertisers.' Oh God, yes." He recalled that when he was telegraph editor of the San Diego *Union* during the McCarthy years, "the standard identification of Wayne Morse that we had to write into the wire service copy was, 'Wayne Morse of Oregon, who calls himself a Republican.' Then when Morse became a Democrat, the identification was changed to 'Wayne Morse, the turncoat senator from Oregon.' " We laughed. Fran went on: "When somebody attacked Joe McCarthy, we couldn't get it in the paper. The next day, when McCarthy would respond, we'd have to write in the background." He chuckled. "Why McCarthy is saying this." But at the *Times*, nobody had ever told him to violate professional standards.

I asked him about that time he had found himself promoted to a job he didn't really want. "Oh, that's a disease in the newspaper business," he said. "To reward a good reporter, they make him an assistant city editor or something. And he's doing something that he doesn't know anything about, really. That he doesn't really like. He got in this business in the first place because he likes reporting and writing."

I asked Fran how he would rate the San Diego paper. Was it standard or pretty bad? Pretty bad, he said. Only a small percentage are that bad. And two or three pretty good ones, I suggested, and the rest in between. Fran said to make it half a dozen good ones. I thought our resigned acceptance of this outrage was a hell of a commentary, that it said a lot about the profession we had given so much of our lives to and believed in, still, so strongly. *Belief.* Fran had far more of it than I had expected, than I had. And so much less anger.

But then he did speak, with a little more feeling, about "reporters getting their own views into what really ought to be even accounts. By even, I mean temperate accounts of what happened. They're supposed to be reporting who, what, where, when, why, how, to whom. They're not supposed to be opinionating—unless it's an interpretative story clearly labeled such with their name on it. A news story ought to be written calmly." And these are people working for the Establishment press? Not the underground papers? Oh yes, Fran assured me. I had gotten out of it before that started, and didn't read the papers as a newspaperman any more, noting such violations of standards. I had my own ambivalence about the new journalism. Writers like Norman Mailer and Gay Talese freed a lot of us to write more naturally and maybe even more truthfully. But they loosed on the country, too, all kinds of bad writing by people whose objectives have to do with anything but the truth. Lord knows, I agreed with Fran that loose and opinionated semifictional writing had no place in the news columns. In one more field, one I still consider partly my own, deterioration of standards and ethics.

Fran went on about how he had seen people working for reputable newspapers, "running around in dirty overalls, unshaven, unwashed. I don't know. If someone were representing me in a public situation, I'd want them to be well dressed. I'm certain that they're paid enough to wear decent clothes. And the women are worse than the men. These girls running around unwashed, unclean. And women who work in offices dressed as though they were going off on a beach party or something." He said maybe that made him some kind of fuddy-duddy. "But I don't think so. I think very rigid standards ought to be maintained."

Fuddy-duddy, indeed. We are aware of the prevailing disdain for so many of the things we believe in, so we throw in such little apologies for our own beliefs, even on so fundamental a thing as standards of decency in appearance.

Well, this was a little better. If not on the big issues, then on such little ones we were finding common ground. And oh so many such subjects were boiling in my head to throw out to him. Cars. "What's been your experience with automobiles, coming back to America after all those years?" I asked, adding that my own had never been happy. (Until I drove the Mercedes that Glenda owned before our marriage, I had never driven a car I felt fully safe in. The Mercedes is beautifully engineered, and I still love to drive it. But anxiety about breakdowns is as great for me in it as in any rattletrap Ford I ever owned. It's not the superb piece of machinery; it's the incompetents who do the maintenance. We were on the way to a meeting one day and the Mercedes just stopped running in Talladega, Alabama. It took a mechanic not familiar with diesel motors half a day to discover that the fuel filter was clogged with filth. We had paid a king's ransom for a checkup just two weeks before, and included in the bill was a charge for replacing the fuel filter. Not long afterward, we slung a rod at midnight on the highway, and had to be hauled by wrecker one hundred miles to Atlanta. The mechanic who put in the new short block [parts and labor, one thousand dollars] said the bolt on the oil pan on the old one had not been tightened properly. A newspaperman friend of mine later told me I had become a legend in my own time. A young reporter had told him with awe he had heard I was a hell of a fellow— had a young wife, drove a Mercedes, and, when we broke down on the road, rode back behind the wrecker in the back seat drinking and singing. I told my friend the story was true in all but one particular. I didn't sing. I cursed. When I was most furious about being laid off, I got to thinking about that episode and got furious about it all over again.)

But about cars, Fran said, "Oh, no trouble." No trouble with the one he had owned since he got back. "You can see they're kind of shoddily put together. But they seem to work pretty well." He told of talking with an auto worker who said people on the assembly line didn't care what they did, so long as the car passed inspection. If a screw head broke off where it could be seen, the screw was replaced. But if it was out of sight, they let it go. No sense of pride in the work or obligation to the buyer, Fran said. One more piece of deterioration. Appliances? "Oh yes," Fran said. "Bad experience with those. Television sets, radios, kitchen things. They're just not well made." Again, it goes back to assembly line. "Nobody identifies with what he makes. It's just an eight-hour-a-day job. Put a screw in the thing as it goes by."

It's the same, I said to him, with the workmen we've had fixing up our old house. Incompetent and unreliable and arrogant. And you are paying them a hell of a lot of money to work on the thing most important to you, your home. I told him what Glenda had said about how we don't have the challenge of barter in the ordinary things we buy—groceries, clothes, furniture—but are plunged, without any bargaining experience, into sharp-dealing, treacherous transactions loaded against us when we buy the two most important things—our automobiles and our houses. "What about all that?" I asked Fran. "In general," I put it, "have you found your place of habitation to be a source of great pleasure to you?"

No, Fran said, no, a sadness in his voice. "It's just a place to hang my hat now. When I owned a house, I'd take great delight working in the garden and on the house itself. But an apartment—it's just a place to live." He and Lee had talked off and on about buying a house in Atlanta but had not made a decision.

The thing was still all backward. I was the one making the angry statements. My first angry middle-aged man with a job, who I had imagined would be lashing out at all those things beyond joblessness, was proving himself hardly angry at all. I thought again about the pattern of deterioration that had emerged from my talks with Jim and Horace. "What about the quality of life here now, compared with when you left the country? Have the basic things gotten shoddy and rotten?"

"I don't know," Fran said. "I think there're a lot of things that go into the quality of life. I don't think it's all that bad. You don't *have* to eat processed cheese. You can buy decent cheese. You don't *have* to buy frozen food or powdered food. You can grow it in your backyard. Or go out to the farmer's market and buy it. I suppose no matter where you are, there are going to be all sorts of irritants—the traffic, neighbors."

"But—but," I interrupted, "if you get good cheese, you're going to pay ten prices. And who the hell wants to go out and dig in a vegetable patch after working all day in an office? Or go to the farmers' market? It takes a day."

Fran said that people pretty much get what they want, or are willing to put up with. "It's like television. Why isn't television better? I don't think there's a person in this country who thinks television is what it ought to be." He said they weren't kidding when they talked about programming for the lowest common denominator. "They point that thing at people with a mental age of about nine." And yet, I said, the damn thing is addictive. "Yeah. It's easy. You watch the news and then you have a drink—and then, rather than go in the other room and pick up a book, you keep watching it."

Another thing, Fran said, that he had been thinking about was "the changes that have happened in the whole world of sex." He said that to him, sex had always been a very private matter. "What a man does or a woman does with someone else is his or her own business. But everything is all out in the open today. Girls running around with their breasts bouncing up and down. Shorts that—just nothing is concealed. I think it was more interesting when there was some mystery about it. That's all gone." He spoke of the kids sleeping with one another, sort of encouraged to, sharing dormitories in college. I asked if he saw that as all bad. "I don't know whether it's all bad or not. It's certainly different. And I don't like it. I don't see anything wrong with people living together. That's their own business. And I don't see anything wrong with people being DC or AC or whatever it is. But I don't see any point in their running around flaunting it. I would say that if I were a homosexual, the last thing in the world I would do would be to join a group and wear a button proclaiming it."

What about other kinds of movements? The black one, the antiwar one? He said he couldn't be in the newspaper business and be out demonstrating. He tried to maintain objectivity." What about us, though?" I asked him. "Here we are supposed to be the most powerful kind of people in the country"—and Fran interrupted. "Powerless," he said. "We're power*less*." Supposed to be the most powerful, I insisted. "But we are powerless, in fact. What do these people expect? The Democratic party is controlled by minority elements. And I would have great difficulty voting with the Republicans, who are a minority to begin with." This was as succinct a statement as I was to hear of what was perceived by so many of the men who had the perspicacity that I didn't to see what is wrong with much of politics today. The playing off of minority groups against one another and the ignoring of the general welfare.

Fran went on: "What are we going to do if we get into another war? In 1941, people ran off and joined the Army out of a real sense of patriotism, I think for the very last time." Everybody realizes that the government did not level with the people about Vietnam, he said. "When I say government, I don't mean any one party. I think Jack Kennedy, Lyndon Johnson were every bit as guilty as Richard Nixon. They did the same thing. Just lied to the American people about what they were doing out there. What's going to lead anybody to believe he isn't being lied to again? When maybe he isn't."

There now, at last, real echoes of my own thoughts, a real spark of anger. I jumped in to ask him about loss of faith, not in the system of government, but in the way it now operates. "There shouldn't be lots of faith in the people who are running it now," Fran said. "I don't know. I think we're going to have to have a long, long spell of people in office being frank and open, and being able to demonstrate it, before confidence in the government will be restored. And I'm not sure that Gerald Ford is getting off to a very good start, insisting that the recession is over and the country is on the way up again when you can find page after page of statistics saying it's just not so. The man's just not telling the truth."

And truth is what Fran has lived for. So now I put my question to him as brutally as I could. Had he felt any bitterness about how the country had been during the first half of his life when he was in the hospital facing the possibility that there might not be a second half? Fran said he thought about that possibility briefly. "But I have always been kind of a fatalist in that sense. If it is, that's the way it is. It's not good or bad. It's just a fact. And I don't know, maybe it's having come up in the Depression. I always thought that nobody owed me any-thing. And that any good thing that happened to me was just a great stroke of fortune. I don't particularly deserve it because in life there are no rewards and no punishments, really. Nothing that can be matched up with deeds, anyway. Some people are lucky and some aren't." It was only later, listening to the tape, that I realized how angry a statement that was, a life view more hopeless than any I was to hear. And yet more philosophical, more sane, than much I had been think-ing.

At the moment, still feeling that I had somehow failed to elicit from Fran the anger I *knew* must be there, I put one more question to him: "After those ten years in Latin America and the time you have spent since then back here, if you had a choice, where would you live?"

"I'd be here. I think it was Alistair Cooke who said the other day everybody in the world criticizes this country, yet they're all trying to get here. I think people who insist that living somewhere else is better are fooling themselves. I haven't lived all over the world by any means. But I know twenty countries in this hemisphere that I wouldn't give a nickel for."

It was a sparkling day when I played the tape of our talk, came to grips with what Fran had said. Afterward, Glenda and I were walking the dogs in the little park near our house. Late afternoon sun was glowing in a perfect blue sky. I said to Glenda it is almost as if Fran is trying to guide me, to say don't get too shrill, find real perspectives.

66

Evenness, as he spoke of how a news story ought to be written. Calmness. Perspective. The perspective of other countries in the world that always have been and still are far worse than this one, and the perspective of all the people in the world now and throughout history for whom life has held no hope, who never expected it to, who made out the best they could, seizing on good fortune when it came, with appreciation of how rare a thing it is, living, like in the country song, one day at a time.

We walked with our arms around each other. Glenda grinned at me. "After all," she said, "aren't you happy right now?" Given such a moment, how could a man be happier?

How I had needed Fran's guidance, if that is what it was. I was to hear many awful things from middle-aged men, infuriating and frightening, and I needed the perspectives he had given me to deal with them. I also needed them to deal with my own inner turmoil. I couldn't just fume and Goddamn this and Goddamn that through the rest of my quest. I needed my energy for hearing, for understanding what I was being told.

5

So much of what I was to hear had to do with belief. Belief and the lack of it, disappointed belief, belief held to despite public contempt, belief that is burdensome, and belief that sustains. I had my own problem with belief, still worried about how much of it I seemed to have lost in people. All my disdain of workmen had bubbled up unexpectedly, talking with Fran.

And if ever I needed Fran's perspectives, it was when I talked with John Somerville, whose dramatic decision to give up his American citizenship seemed the final disillusionment. So much of what he said turned out to be about loss of belief in people.

We talked in the modernistic apartment he and Laverne had been renting in the Sandy Springs section. All about were the boxes and crates they were packing to move to Ontario the following week. Glenda and I had driven out there in the afternoon through all the garish shopping centers that line old Roswell Road for miles; Sandy Springs is the city's super-suburban retreat. We had to wait at a big old gate at the entry to the apartment complex while a guard called John to find out that we were not a pair of those villainous muggers everybody out there dreads. Glenda and Laverne cooked ribs while John and I sat, like gentlemen in a drawing room, talking in his office. John is a big guy, tall, broadly built, big hands, big feet, big features to his open, earnest face, horn-rimmed glasses adding to the look of earnestness. He wears a moustache, and his sandy hair is cut short and sort of skews in different directions. For all the anger in what he was to tell me, he was hale as ever and his underlying excitement and happiness about moving to Canada kept bubbling out of him.

On the wall of his office was a collection of framed, autographed originals of comic strips, including a Doonesbury. John had been a damned good political cartoonist and had tried his hand for a time at a comic strip. None of his own work was on the wall.

He was born in 1921 in Lymon, Colorado. He grew up and finished high school in McCook, Nebraska, and went to junior college there. He finished college at the University of Missouri School of Journalism, at that time probably the best journalism school in the country. It was 1941 when he finished, "just in time to go into World War II." He served and saw action in the Navy. His first job was on *The Denver Post*, which suggests how good he was. After four years there, he and his first wife, Barbara, took off for a couple of carefree years in Mexico. I asked him if that time of being an expatriate was anything like this time now of leaving the country in disgust. He said not at all. Then they just wanted to learn about another country, how other people live.

When they returned to this country, they went to Mobile and bought a schooner and lived on it for a while, and then went out to San Francisco where John worked on one of the papers a couple of years. Then they moved to Jackson, Mississippi, of all places, and John worked on the *State-Times*, an ill-fated newspaper. I said I didn't know he had worked there. He said, "Yeah, started the paper out. I'll never forget. The governor pressed the Goddamned button on the presses, you know? And nothing happened. That was an omen, believe me."

It was back out to the West Coast and then to Atlanta, where I knew him on the paper in the 1950s and early 1960s. He and Barbara had two sons about the age of my children. Carey-Tim and Robin used to play with Patrick and Ellen. Neither of us could remember the year he left to go out to the West Coast once more, and thence to Philadelphia, where Barbara became women's editor on the *Bulletin* and John tried the comic strip. "The comic strip didn't make it and that's when I went into syndicate selling."

I asked John about all that moving around. How come? He said he just never felt the need to put roots down, liked to live in different places, liked the feeling of being able to go after better job opportunities. He and Laverne had bought an old house in Ontario; they showed us proud pictures of it. It was, he said, only the second home he had ever owned, the first having been a retreat in Florida where his first wife now lives. "I've resisted home buying because I felt it was another trap." But now he was enthusiastic about fixing up the old place in Ontario. Again, how come? "Maybe it's psychological. Maybe it's an emotional commitment. You feel like here is where I am going to stay when you buy a home."

"Anyhow," I said, "here you are spending your last week as an American citizen." It's not quite that simple, John told me. You have to live in Canada for five years before you can become a citizen. He and Laverne had qualified to become permanent residents, and would take out citizenship papers at the end of five years. John spoke of how lucky he was to be able to keep his job. He would still be traveling in the South as well as in Canada, and we agreed it would be good to keep seeing one another.

I had Fran's perspectives but I was, nevertheless, eager to hear someone really angry about matters other than joblessness. So tell, John, tell why you are going to leave this country to live in another country. Tell all the things you find wrong with this country. He said he was leaving because of his despair over where this country seemed headed, and because of the love he had come to feel for Canada.

This country, John. Tell. There are two levels, personal and philosophical, he said. "Philosophically, I think the country's headed in a bad direction, maybe even into a dictatorship. Vietnam was not an isolated incident, not a one-act play on which the curtain rose and closed." It was but a step in the direction in which we had been (still are) heading. And even though we're out now, the causes of Vietnam remain. We're still acting like a world cop. And selling armaments, millions of arms, all over the world. And playing power politics all over the world. "I tell you, Pat, it's wearing on you to always have to be number one. If you're number one, that means everybody else is less than one. We all ought to just be equal." He said he knew we couldn't just lie down and let other countries take us over. But we have gone to the opposite extreme.

I asked him when he became aware of all this. "I was first aware of it when Johnson was lying to us on television. That's when I first became aware of the powerlessness of the American citizen. I watched him lie and I knew he was lying." People now concede that he was lying, John said, but back then you would be called a traitor if you said our President is standing up there lying to us. He said the presidency has become a sort of public-relations operation in which statements are prepared in advance and the President makes them for political effect. The country isn't responsive to its citizens' needs any more. (The same things I had realized listening to Ford. And how often I was to hear about the need for a government to serve all the people.)

John said taxes are higher in Canada than here, but he didn't mind because that country is responsive to its citizens' needs. "You've got a medical system that works up there. They don't have rampant ripoffs by dentists and doctors." The medical profession here has ripped off even the puny efforts we have made at modified social medicine, he said. "That's part of the ethic of this country. The ethic is make your buck."

John said he had a good health insurance program with his company, so he didn't really need Canada's health program. It was the principle of the thing. I thought of my terror at the prospect of losing my health insurance. *That's a mighty important principle, John.* He said he knew, he knew. An editor up there had told him about treatments his child received for some serious disease, many treatments, and the whole thing cost him only about forty dollars.

Canadian medicine is definitely better, John said. And I said medicine is such a basic part of existence. "Yes, and another basic of existence, Pat, is that you should be able to go downtown and feel safe. There's no reason you should have tension and be looking over your shoulder all the time. You go downtown in Toronto and suddenly you're relieved. You don't realize the tension here until you experience the lack of it there." That was one of his personal reasons for leaving.

I could understand. Glenda and I had laughed about that guard at the gate, and I have contempt for suburbia's paranoia about the inner city, the inordinate fear of muggings on downtown streets I have walked safely every day for thirty years. But I knew that feeling John had described: the sudden lack of a fear that has become so habitual you aren't aware of it until you get to a place where you don't have to feel it. We had experienced that spending the previous Christmas with Glenda's folks in the tiny little town of Timpson, Texas. It was the second night and we were walking the dogs in the quiet of near midnight, enjoying being able to see the stars in the big old sky out there, and all of a sudden it came over me. I wasn't apprehensive, wasn't on my guard against the possibility of real danger.

John said the fear of violence was not caused just by the black problem in the country. "But the black problem is certainly one of the biggest problems in the country. And I think it's insolvable. It's a tragedy. Americans like to think there's a solution to everything. You just have to get the right program and the right amount of money and that'll solve anything. Some human problems you just can't solve. It's like the Arab-Jewish problem. It's been going on for two thousand years. President Ford isn't going to solve it."

John went on about the blessed lack of crime in Canada. They don't have the huge black population that we have, he pointed out. And they don't have the huge population we have of near-illiterate whites that nobody wants to talk about. (I had seen them doing the story on crime.) When you get to thinking about why you're leaving a country, John said, you get down to fundamentals. "I just think that the pluralistic society doesn't work." America is not a country where people have the same general outlook and philosophy and morals. There are all these differences in people, cultural, regional, ethnic, and religious. In some ways, the differences are stimulating, but in others, they spell competing interests. So Washington, D.C., becomes a brokerage house trying to handle all these competing interests. "The leaders in Washington become power brokers. They trade off this for that to maybe get something done. But that means politicians instead of statesmen." For example, he said, there is the tremendous pressure of American Jews on the government to send more millions to Israel. He was all for Israel—"I believe in democracy"—but he didn't think the special interests of a single ethnic group should determine our foreign policy.

The government is not run like that in Canada, he said. "In Canada it must be like it was in this country fifty years ago. There's a mutual feeling everybody has of hard work, a fair day's work for a fair day's pay. There's not so much of a handout feeling up there. People have a feeling of self-reliance, like the old pioneer days here, and less of a feeling that the government has to take care of us, that there has to be some kind of a program for everything." Deterioration again.

I asked him about the separatist movement in Quebec. He said even so, even if it should succeed, the two cultures have more in common than many of the cultures in conflict in America. Then John laughed and said he could just hear what people would say when they read what he had said about the Jewish lobby and black crime. "They'll say —why, that guy—he hates Jews and he hates blacks."

"Yeah," I agreed. "A damn bigot."

"Well," he said, "I'll give 'em something else to be shocked at. I'm a Wasp—white Anglo-Saxon Protestant. When I'm in Canada, I feel like I'm among my own kind. Doesn't it seem fair that I should have the right to enjoy being among my own kind—Scottish, English, Irish —without being accused of prejudice?" After all, he said, Jews, Italians, all different ethnic groups congregate together and love their own kind. There's nothing wrong with that. "America is a melting pot that didn't melt. And it just doesn't work as a nation. There's no national consensus. The feeling in this country is that this is a great place to make your own pile and to hell with everybody else. And to hell with the country, too."

By that he meant the lack of environmental control. Just a handful of people were really interested in it, he said. There's no real commitment. Yeah, I agreed, an ineffective few, and they were really cut down during the oil crisis. John said there were simple solutions, really, to all such problems. Why couldn't there be a tax rebate to industries that took care of their pollution? "Except that they say we can't afford tax rebates to industry. But we can afford all kinds of billions of dollars' worth of armaments. Our national priorities are haywire.

"We have absolutely no pretense, even, of any kind of moral attitude in world affairs today. Anything the CIA wants to do to other countries is fine. We're no different from the Russians. And we as citizens have no say in what the foreign policy is to be."

Hell, I thought, we haven't even known what the bastards were up to. Then I asked him if he *ever* felt he had any say in foreign policy. "Well, at least back when we had Roosevelt," John said, "the Congress did *declare* World War II. Roosevelt didn't conduct a foreign war without congressional approval." How many were killed in Korea and Vietnam, wars that Congress never declared? It's been since those two wars that John felt he lived in a "manipulated society," still a democracy, but one where our freedoms are eroding, "eroding very fast." A case might be made, he went on, though it would be abhorrent to him personally, for more controls in the interests of better serving the people. "But to date that kind of control hasn't been for any good reason. It's been for these—these wars." He spat the words out like bitter medicine. "These concepts that Washington has about our world role."

He said he had been anti-Vietnam from the very beginning. "Vietnam made me very bitter" because it was based on such grotesquely false premises. Escalating the conflict and thinking the enemy wouldn't escalate it, too. Everything the government did over there was a complete failure, even in terms of what they wanted to do, "let alone from my humanitarian standpoint." And it was intelligent men in Washington who had done all that. Absurd.

He said he felt just about as powerless in regard to domestic policy. He felt he was in a no-man's-land between the liberals and the conservatives (that sounded like a very familiar place to me). He agreed with the conservatives that violence should be more strictly controlled, that the judges and laws are too lenient. "There's no justification in my mind for some guy with a rape record a mile long going free." That thinking, he supposed, put him in the Wallace camp. But on the other hand, he was with the liberals who want something done about unemployment as an antidote to crime. He mentioned young people and said he suspected "some of them don't even have a concept of what it's like to have a job." That is exactly what I found to be true of nearly all of the many young people I had interviewed in jail for that magazine story. "Most of 'em never have had a job," I told John.

John thought about that. "You know, everybody that goes around with pants on and speaks English is not necessarily a civilized human being. And we've got a lot of animals. They're violence-prone. They have no civilized frames of reference in their heads. They've lived brutish lives ever since they were little. So what do you expect? I can see why they are that way. But I don't want to get knifed by one of them. I'll never get so liberal that I'll want to go out tonight and get stabbed by one of them, or have my wife raped by one of them. I think they ought to be stomped on."

I hadn't been with him much in all that he had said about the melting pot not working, wasn't sure what I felt about that. But this I could respond to. So many liberal efforts to improve the lot of people, and people were no better off and crime was getting worse and worse. Was it the fault of the programs or the people? Later I was to talk with Charles Weltner, who had been in Congress, where he was a strong supporter of all the antipoverty efforts. He said he had come to feel that people couldn't be helped by such programs. Something else, he didn't know what, was needed. He, and John, seemed close to giving up on the idea that people can be changed, that environment does make a difference. Was I at that bleak point of lack of belief in people? Close to it, I had to concede.

John said, "I tell you, we just feel so helpless in this country, so impotent, completely victimized by everything. There's nowhere you can turn and see reason prevailing, or justice prevailing, Jesus." Justice, he said. "If you rob a bank, you get fifty years. But if the bank president embezzles from one, he might get three months. More likely probation. If a corporation pulls a swindle, nothing happens. A fine—which is about like you or me getting a parking ticket."

Helpless? Why you're supposed to be the most powerful kind of American, John, white, middle-class, middle-aged, and male. What of this, John? "I think the white, middle-class, middle-aged man with a good income is just a sitting duck. Whatever he can take home, and whatever he can avoid having happen to him, he's all right. But, Pat, his son is on call for Kissinger at any time. At any time, they can put that machinery back into action, overnight." He said he expected America to engage in more and more brush-fire wars because that was the only way the government could make a show of force now. "A world war, obviously, and the game is up for everybody. You just forget it. We've blown ourselves up."

That final bang is always in the consciousness of those of us who knew the world before it was threatened with insane annihilation. I had been startled by the shift John's thoughts took when I asked him about middle-aged men. I had expected plaints about his own situation, and was moved by his expression of concern for his sons, who could be summoned to die in one of America's damnable wars.

John said he had been prepared to help his oldest boy, Carey-Tim, now nineteen, to get conscientious-objector status. Both his boys could be called up any time in the next decade. "This is another reason for going to Canada." He wanted his boys to become Canadians, too. "Why should they have to go through some horrible thing like Vietnam—for what? During Vietnam, I was concerned for their very lives. I was really for a time there very, very concerned about my oldest son."

Surprisingly, John was the only man I talked to who mentioned that peculiarly horrible ordeal. Patrick barely missed it; the draft ended just after he had signed up for it. He had said he would go to Canada if he had to. Remembering how our children used to play together, I told John about another kind of worry I had discovered during all my inward looking, one about Patrick and Ellen. How I remembered myself, Christmas Eve after Christmas Eve, crouched, muscles cramped, bone-tired, in the early morning hours putting together the flimsy tin or plastic toys that would bring them no real pleasure, would only satisfy the need in them (and in me) to be like all the others, caught in joyless giving, greedy taking. I was part of it, and the schools were part of it, and the hapless kids they played with were part of it, and television was probably the biggest part of it. In their childhood, without my doing anything about it, they absorbed a value system, a way of life that at heart I despised. But then I didn't even have the impulse to say to hell with it, I won't acquiesce any more in this cold and cruel exploitation by business at Christmastime of what was once an expression of so simple a thing as love, real love, for children. And so when they revolted conventionally with the rest of their generation against the value system and way of life I despised, they thought they were revolting against me, too.

During my talk with Charles Weltner, he was to say that his four children had turned out all right, but "why they've developed that way, I don't know because I certainly didn't have much to tell them." I was shocked to hear him say that, considering how much a sophisticated and wise person like him did have to tell his children. Then I realized I had as much to tell my kids, and hadn't either. Some of the things they have revolted against, I value. I might have told them about them, too. I asked John whether he had worried about the way America had shaped his boys' values and life view, and whether he had tried to tell them what he knew.

He said he sure had. "You know, by the time you're middle-aged and you've worked this long, you know how it works. You know how people are motivated and you know how in many ways it's a grubby, sordid, unidealistic existence. Just about everybody's materialistic and self-centered. I worried about it because I knew I was raising my children with ideas that weren't necessarily going to help them get along in this kind of country—like being idealistic or socially motivated. I knew what it took to survive in this society, and the attitudes I had given them were not the right ones for that." Lord. What a devastating admission: a man gives to his sons the ideals he most deeply believes in, and then fears he has handicapped them, I mentioned this to John.

"Well, I think it's important to bring up that back in those days I was an editorial cartoonist. And I still believed I really could make a contribution to the world. A little light, you know. Point up some of the errors of our ways and the validity of some of the truths that we all pretend we believe in. I believed I could do a little good. I wasn't crazy. I didn't think I could change the world. But I thought I could make a little contribution. Expose a little evil, here. Do a little preaching against the wrong, there. My attitudes as an editorial cartoonist, I knew, I was giving my children. And then later on I got disillusioned with editorial cartooning."

Tell me about that, I urged. It happened on the *Atlanta Journal*, he said. It wasn't the paper. It was a great place to work. And he had as much freedom as any cartoonist could want. I told him I had not had as much as a columnist could want. Well, he said, cartooning is different.

"But I was drawing cartoons exposing corruption in Georgia politics. Of course, if there was ever a place to light a candle, it was there." We laughed. "And nothing happened. The same with the editorial writers, exposing all this corruption. Nothing happened. Nothing changed. Nobody went to jail. Nobody ever mended his ways. It was like beating your head against a stone wall. I guess I got tired of doing that. Enough of that. I just couldn't see anything happening."

But John, but John, some small things have happened. Georgia politics is not quite that bad any more. You can take some of the credit for that. So can I.

Yes, he said, and the racial situation has improved. He was here when the sit-ins were going on, remembered when the Fox Theater had separate sections for white and black. Social progress was being made then. "But I felt it was because those blacks were sitting in. Not because I was drawing those cartoons."

I said that seemed to me one more example of our powerlessness. It was a paradox that all these other groups who were supposed to be less powerful than we were somehow made the government and society respond to their needs. "Pat, there again, that whole thing showed me that this society doesn't respond to anything except force. As long as you can get enough people together to walk, to march and sit in, and raise hell, people throw up their hands and say how bad it is, but then something gets done. But you can write editorials and preach in pulpits and draw editorial cartoons from now to Kingdom Come, and nothing gets done. We don't respond to anything except power—counterforce. Maybe this is the way life is. Maybe it's asking too much to expect people to have a rational, compassionate way of handling things. 'Let's do this because this is right.' "

When social change occurs, somebody has to give up something, give up power, John said. So it's power against power. "And I was somebody who was just following the path that was laid out for us in our school days, you know. You get out there and you work hard and you'll get your just rewards. Well, if you're just busy, working, working, working like that, you're out of it. You're not taking part in anything that means anything, as far as changing anything goes." All you've got is your vote every four years, John said, and that means less and less all the time. Damn. He was shucking down the corn. And what he had said about the profession we had shared shook me. I realized that, like Fran, I had never reached that point of disillusionment with newspapers, guessed I still thought they could do some good if only they would do things right.

John said he enjoyed what he is doing now, got real satisfaction out of calling on editors, selling them syndicate material. He liked the challenge of the buyer-seller relationship. Editors were a nice class of people to deal with. And he enjoyed seeing cartoonists in the newspaper offices, men he had known from his days as a member of their national association. They're not doing the world any more good than he was, John said. But they don't know it.

When he changed jobs so drastically, John went on, "I completely short-circuited my whole previous life's attitude toward social activism, toward trying to make a better society, contributing my efforts toward trying to make a better world. I completely turned my back on all of that. Which is the only way I keep my sanity. Because this is a jungle, Pat. It's a jungle. There's no justice. There's just the weak and the strong. As many nice and good people as there are in the whole world and in the States, still—it's just a damn jungle."

His voice was near the breaking point. He had had such a great amount of belief to lose. And obviously, it still meant much to him. I reminded him of how we had all believed that things would work under Kennedy, and he said, "Oh yes. I'm a disillusioned liberal. When Kennedy was in office, I had the feeling that I was being called on—that Kennedy was bringing out the best in America. He was appealing to all our good feelings, all our good values. Whether he was just doing this to meet his own ends, I don't know. But he was doing it. And it's a funny thing. Johnson did too. He did have those Great Society programs. But Johnson came off as a used car salesman, no matter how hard he tried to implement the things Kennedy started. Johnson was a hustler, basically. Johnson is one of these guys who lays his hand on your knee when he's talking to you. Anybody who puts his hand on me when he's talking to me, I want to feel for my billfold."

Did he still think it might have worked if Kennedy hadn't been killed? "Yeah, I do." He didn't feel Kennedy was conning us? "No, I don't. In the first place, I think Kennedy had some kind of bigger view of life and history than anybody after him has had. He looked at things from a more humanistic point of view."

In effect, the killer of Kennedy had killed humanism in the government. Or was it that the death of our humanism had killed Kennedy? I asked John to elaborate on what he had said about not having time to participate in any of the movements for the social change he had so much wanted. "You're so busy hustling for your dollars. All you are doing is watching on the sidelines." And supporting it, I said, by being the one who does the work to make the money so all these other folks can seek their just rights. We can't do that for ours.

"You haven't got the time," John said. "You know you feel trapped, because of all the negative influences—that's the way they get rich, by subverting the interests of the country. The lobbyists of all the vested interests, they've got the time. They're at work all the time."

John told me again how glad he was to have the chance to get away from it. "How did you come to the decision?" I asked him. "Did you just wake up one morning and say I'm going to do it?" He said he had been traveling in Canada a little more than a year. At first, it was just fun and different. But then, on the third trip, he thought, he said to himself, Well, hey now. This is pretty good. I think maybe I'd like to live here. Why in the hell not? Part of it was small things, he said, like going into a pub where they would be having a sing-along. "Everybody just having a jolly, good time. You couldn't have a thing like that here in Atlanta. Everybody sits kind of frozen up in little isolated units. Up there people are open and friendly and community conscious."

He said he believed this was because Canada is a homogeneous society, not fragmented into all these groups we have in America. He talked some more about the different ethnic groups in America, how many, like the Cubans, come here with Fascist backgrounds, how he no longer thought it was possible for such diverse ethnic types as blacks, Latins, Eastern Europeans, and Western Europeans to get along together in the same society, and how they all sought out their own kind to associate with, live among, He said again that, in effect, he felt this was what he and Laverne were doing going to Canada. I still wasn't sure I agreed that these groups couldn't possibly get together. But the picture he painted of an orderly, civilized society was compelling. I felt my own yearning for that.

He spoke of things like the beauty of public buildings in Canada. "While here in the States, any public building is contracted out to some contractor who is going to maximize his profits, and put up an ugly cube." He spoke of the marvelous public transit system in Toronto. "America doesn't have that anywhere," he said, "and think how much less complicated that would be than going to the moon." He said he was so glad to be getting away from dependence on cars. "I think they're a social evil. It's not just the pollution from the exhaust, but the life-style that a car creates." He and Laverne hoped to get along entirely without one. They could, with the public transit. No long waits. Transfers all over town. You could go anywhere for thirty-five cents. It would be a big part of a whole new, better life-style, John said. "Can you imagine getting on a nice, clean subway at twelve o'clock at night and just sitting there with a bunch of nice, polite, middle-class people of all ages quietly riding to where they're going? And there're no hoods, no guys in leather jackets. No filth on the floor. No worries." Again, I was surprised at how strongly I felt the need for something like that, for a life that is civilized, dignified.

John said he knew he wasn't going to find some Goddamn utopia up there. But at least he wouldn't be in a country with a number-one complex. No Pentagon. No military-industrial complex. "They've got to get into less mischief internationally because they're so small and so weak. Small is good. And big is bad." I was to hear that concept expressed again and again, in many contexts. I thought about the Alabama kid in draft exile in Canada who submitted to *Southern Voices* his cogent argument that the South should secede again—for the right reasons this time, manageable size and homogeneity among them.

John said most Americans think that because we're the biggest, everything here is the best. "Well, actually our school systems are falling apart. I think the whole thing is coming unraveled. Really, in the next ten years I foresee very bad race riots, continued deterioration of public services. I think the place is going down the drain. I really do." It's going to get worse and worse, John said. "Why, look at this apartment. We're sitting here behind gates that you have to dial a number to get through. We're living behind a stockade. Jesus. That ought to say something about this country. I don't need to defend my departure from a place where you have to live in a stockade."

All that crap, he said again, about being number one in the world. "We're falling behind the Russians in this. So spend some more billions to do that. When all we have to do to win the world is to turn our attention to our problems and create a beautiful society. Then everybody'll want to copy us. Even the Communists." *It was the essence of his old belief. How sad that the country had killed in him the will to work to make it come true.*

Finally, I asked John what he would do if he didn't have the chance to live in Canada. "Suppose you were sentenced to live in America the rest of your life? Do you see anything that people like you and me could do?"

"Yeah," John said. "Go to a small town."

"No, I mean about changing things," I said.

"I don't see any hope for that," John said. "No. No, I don't."

He had surprised me when he said that about moving to a small town. Glenda and I had seriously discussed such a move during our Christmas visit to Timpson, more seriously when we realized that with the new work each of us had, we could live just about anywhere. We had talked about moving to Timpson, with its peace and safety. But neither of us was sure. And this meant, I realized, that I had not yet surrendered all of my hope, all of my belief—as John had.

When I first listened to the tape of our conversation a couple of weeks later, I wrote to John in Canada asking if, for business or any other reasons, he wanted me not to use his name. He wrote back, "I suppose a good organization man of upward mobility (whatever that is) would say to keep my name out of it. But nothing real bad will happen to me. So it's a chance to be brave at little or no risk. So identify me! Actually the trouble is that no one speaks up any more. More people should."

All during the quest, especially when talking with jobless men, I found myself fooling with the notion that we middle-aged men ought to form a movement of our own, pressure the government in *our* interests. It is a reflex, I would say to myself, of your civil-rights experience. Forget it. But thinking about the movement got me to thinking about Jim Wood again. I had started to go to him when I was having all that trouble finding jobless men. But I didn't want to talk about the magazine then, wanted to get that as far behind me as I could. And I didn't really want to face Jim. He had been treated more harshly than I had by the Council, and he had lost out before that in the business world because of his beliefs. What had been the effect on him? Now, I felt, the time had come to find out, talk with him, compare notes.

So: "Jim, let me ask you where you're at now. Do you have any bitterness about your experience either in the business world or in the do-good business?"

"Naw, I don't. I've been unemployed since the middle of April, and it's August now. I have sent off a great number of applications to federal agencies. Fortunately, we managed to tuck a little money away. I can struggle along for another few months before it becomes really critical that I get out and work. It does concern me to see money being chipped away that could work out nicely for retirement. But I want to work someplace where I can make some contribution to making this country a better place to live. It doesn't have to be dramatic. I can be comfortable with very little progress. That's one thing I've learned.

"I regard, certainly, my experience at the Southern Regional Council as a rare experience. I don't think that many people have the opportunity to do work they really enjoy doing and get a sense of personal satisfaction out of it. And I got that out of a lot of my experience at the Council. The business end, I enjoyed that, too. But I don't want to go back to it. I may end up having to. But—I don't have a lot of killer instinct. And I have even less now than I used to have.

"I'm clearly not bitter about either experience. I'm just not. I *am* worried—don't misunderstand. But I'm not losing any sleep over it."

We talked in the book-lined den of his fine, spacious old two-story home in the ever-fashionable Druid Hills section of Atlanta. All over the house Jim has built beautiful, precise shelves for the books that his wife, Kathy, keeps accumulating. They have been married twenty-seven years and are among the very few couples of that duration I know who genuinely love each other. Jim, his hair and bushy beard still jet black, in one faltering moment, standing up, his trim belly sort of poked out, looks seventy years old. The rest of the time we talk he looks far younger than his years.

He was born on April 26, 1924, in Richmond, Virginia. His father, a Prohibition chief enforcement officer, was killed raiding a still when Jim was five years old. His mother, strong-willed and intelligent, supported him and his younger brother, working as a store clerk, census taker, and the like. She was a strong influence on Jim's life. And, troubles coming in bunches, she died in May after he was laid off in April.

When he was fourteen, they moved to Fluvanna in rural Virginia near Charlottesville. His grandparents on both sides had farms in

Fluvanna, and were the local gentry. Jim enlisted in the Air Force after graduating from high school in 1942. As a fighter pilot in Europe, he flew eighty-nine missions, was credited with four and a half enemy planes shot down, received the Distinguished Flying Cross. After Germany surrendered, he volunteered to go to Japan and was in training for that when the war ended. He entered the University of Virginia in 1946, and finished with a degree in psychology in 1950. In 1947, he met Kathy on a train trip to Memphis, playing bridge in the club car, and they were married the following year. Their daughter, Susan, is finishing college and son Chip is in high school.

Through a college friend, Jim became interested in the commodities business, and on graduation went to work for F. M. Crump and Company, a cotton brokerage in Memphis. Kathy, with the social consciousness of a Bennington graduate, somehow ended up working for E. H. (Boss) Crump's insurance firm in Memphis. The cotton business back then was, as Jim put it, among the last holdouts for cheap apprenticeships. He started at a hundred and twenty dollars a month. Banks were doing this, too, then, he said. I hadn't known that, had fancied, with envy, that friends in those endeavors were getting far more than the sixty-dollars-a-week pittance I got as a beginning newspaperman.

Jim's friend in the cotton brokerage acquired a grain elevator in Mobile in 1952, and Jim went there to be number-three man in the office. The elevator was instrumental, Jim said, in introducing soybeans to farmers in Alabama, north Florida, and parts of Mississippi, helping to free planters from the toils of cotton. His friend was a speculator and in 1954 had the largest holdings in the country across the commodities board. There was a break in the market and, in a bad cash bind, his friend "sold a lot of soybeans that he didn't have." A federal court case ensued and his friend eventually went to jail. The episode caused an artificial drop in the commodities market and "little people all over the country lost a lot of money." Jim said he still feels bad about that. He had no part in the thing. "Technically, I was in the clear. But I knew all was not kosher. Which raises a moral question: should I have run and told somebody? At the time, I knew he didn't mean to hurt anybody." As it was, Jim spent a week testifying in the court case.

He stayed on in the grain business with other firms until the last one he was working for closed its Mobile office in 1966. That's when he took the job with the Council, starting work on January 1, 1967.

I had always assumed that his and Kathy's desegregation activities in Mobile had cost him his job. He said it wasn't that clear-cut. They had led in setting up an organization that supported the desegregation of schools in Mobile in 1965 mainly because there were so many organizations on the other side. Governor George Wallace publicly denounced the Woods and others in the organization, and that had not helped Jim at the state docks. And Kathy had written letters to the editors of the Mobile papers that couldn't have been pleasing to the people Jim had to do business with. In 1966, she was Mobile County campaign manager for Richmond Flowers, a close friend, who ran against Wallace as a racial moderate. And she accepted appointment to the Alabama Advisory Committee to the U.S. Commission on Civil Rights. Jim was active in all these involvements.

"It's certainly possible," he said, "that some of Kathy's and my involvement in racial things may have had something to do with the closing of the office. But it's very difficult to say for sure. It was clearly a business decision as well. They could have just sent me out and kept the office open."

The firm did offer him a job in St. Louis. The main thing then, Jim said, was that they did not want to leave the South. "This was clearly where the action was. It was an exciting time." The Alabama Council on Human Relations had been instrumental in setting up the school desegregation organization, and it was an affiliate of the Southern Regional Council. Jim had gotten to know then-director Paul Anthony and he called Paul to ask if he knew of any jobs in the South. He didn't mean necessarily in the civil-rights field, but just something so he and Kathy could continue their civil-rights activities. Paul told him there was a position open as executive assistant on the Council staff and Jim took it.

"I certainly never have regretted it," he said. "Initially for me, there was a feeling of being totally unfettered in what I could do or say. I swung further to the left, I think, maybe than I really belonged. I think I've come back some toward the middle or maybe right of that. I don't know. Left and right don't make a lot of sense any more. In Mobile, it had been such a dual kind of role. I made my living working with little grain merchants around the South. And these guys are close to being the man on the hill in little Southern towns—super-paternalists. And you had to get along with them. They're the kind of people that maybe on a one-to-one basis, you could influence. But even one to one, you couldn't push 'em too far. You depended on their good will to do business." I could picture him, making his judgments about how far to push, filled with his belief, but needing to make a living, too.

"But once working for the Council," he went on, "you were free to express whatever your thoughts were. When I first came, there was a complete willingness to put your ideas out on the table. Somebody might jump up and down on them. But it wasn't in any sort of personal way. It was a totally abstract thing to do with ideas." Damn, I thought, I never really felt any of that. I avoided whenever I could the tedium of the meetings and discussions. I had, somewhere in those early years of newspapering, shuddering to ride by a slum, put together the small and bleak political beliefs I was to have. I had felt no need to talk about them or build other beliefs. Maybe if I had, I would not have had dammed up in me that tide of despair and anger that surged out all at once when Jim and I were laid off.

Jim said it had been a strong, concentrated learning period for him. "It was to see things a little differently, and certainly to be less sure. The more you try to deal with social change and reform, the more difficult you understand it is, the more complicated you recognize it is. So you're less sure about what might be a solution. You're even less sure about whether you're right or somebody else is right. It's incredible to me now to think that all of us were convinced that something like the '64 Civil Rights Act was going to solve all those problems. I mean, people who were really involved in civil rights, we deluded ourselves. We continue to learn that while legislation certainly has its place, it isn't necessarily going to bring about all the kinds of changes that need to be made."

That was a far cry from my near despair, but as close as Jim was to come to expressing disillusionment or disbelief. He talked at length about how he came to his strong beliefs about racial justice. He never was a white supremacist, he said. Growing up and beginning work in the South, he just never thought about the racial situation. It seemed so fixed and permanent. He had known black people from birth, and as a youth in rural Virginia had the standard Southern paternalistic attitudes toward them. He did as a young man buy the states' rights line against Truman's Fair Employment Practices Code. But he was delighted by the 1954 school desegregation decision, and appalled at the strength of the reaction against it, including that of some of his kinfolks. One aunt was deeply concerned because she could see it would mean strife and killing. He hadn't believed it would—but, of course, she had been right. She could foresee and grieve over the killing—and for her that was of more consequence than how long discrimination might go on.

He talked about the black people he had grown up with. His father took him frequently as a little boy to visit an old black man living on one of his grandparents' farms, and after his father's death, Jim continued to visit with him. There was another older Negro man with whom he was friends, too. "Now I remember both of those old men talking. They certainly contributed to my view of black people as people. And also, they consciously sort of worked at me a little bit about the nonhate. I regarded as totally incidental that the man who killed my father was a black man." (It was the first he had mentioned that startling fact.) "But these two men were concerned about that—that somehow or another I might grow up embittered in a racial way about it. Well, it had never occurred to me in my whole life that I would do that. But these two old men—I remember one day thrashing wheat, I was helping bag wheat coming off the thrasher, and just out of the blue they brought it up. I shouldn't do it. Shouldn't be embittered in a racial way about that. I was just a little boy. But for them to do that was, I think, sort of important."

Sort of, Jim. Sort of. Then he spoke of another matter about which he felt he had deluded himself during his early civil-rights activity. When Kathy would write those letters to the editors, interspersed among the hate calls would be calls from whites who were afraid even to tell their names, but who said they agreed and were glad she had written such a letter. "Those kinds of things delude one. We're always talking about the great number of reachable white people in the South. I think it's been clearly demonstrated we overestimated the number of them. But it was those kinds of things that made you think there were more there. And what happens when you get people one to one. Some person you know fairly well, you get him in a situation where there's no third party involved. It seems to me that then he's willing to be more reasonable than he would be with somebody else around. There's the whole business of what your neighbor's going to say about how you react on a racial thing. But that's not restricted to whites. Blacks have the same problem in another way."

That was as close as Jim came to touching on black racism, whose ugliness both of us, as whites hanging on in civil-rights work, had seen our share of. I asked him to tell me his feelings about the demise of the magazine and our dreams of it as a really effective means of reaching Southerners, of both races, who are reachable.

"I'm very sad about that—and for that reason as strongly as any other. I still think there's a hungry audience. And there aren't many institutions that are really serving that audience. We don't get any good analyses of the alternative ways a society might be. People are introduced to conventional ideas, and unless they really scratch, they don't get beyond them. What the magazine tried to do was to help people discover the need to scratch a little bit. It's too bad it's not there any more."

The magazine, he went on, was able to present a wide range of views in its few issues, and it's hard for people to find that in newspapers or even general-interest magazines. Special-interest ones are esoteric. "Where is the alternate view? There's not much around." The underground papers get more like the Establishment ones.

"And you still can't believe anything you read in them," I said. "I mean, some of it's true and some of it isn't, and there's no way to tell the difference." "Yes," Jim said. "This whole new journalism thing— it's difficult to figure out what's true, what isn't. Much of it in the underground papers is by young people with simplistic views. They might sincerely believe something is true when it isn't true at all."

He had dealt with the foundation people on behalf of the Council far more than I had, and I told him my indictment of them for imposing ineffective programs on situations they had no real understanding of. He struggled with that, and the sum of what he said was that the Council had been lucky for a while because the foundations didn't have any people who even *thought* they knew about the South and race. The foundations had got into the struggle late, and only in the past few years had hired themselves "experts" on the subject. But in the beginning we could go to them and say, here is a problem and here is how we think we can solve it if you will give us the money. Then more and more it became a matter of us figuring out what problem *they* wanted solved and trying to come up with a suitable program. What they are interested in is being able to say we spent thus and so, and thus and so was accomplished.

"And never mind," I said, "whether thus and so really was accomplished, or whether it made any difference anyhow."

"Well," Jim said, "look at the media. It's the same. They don't tell you the issues, the human issues at stake in political battles—only who won, who lost." He cited the struggles between Congress and Ford, like the second veto of the strip-mining act. The news was the battle between the President and Congress, not the terrible consequences of Ford's veto on the Western states. "If the people wanted to know more, maybe they could find out. But it seems to me if we can't deal with something as elementary as strip-mining on a national basis, how are we going to deal with the subtler kinds of things like race and poverty? So I don't mean to excuse or apologize for the foundations in any sense. I think it's the whole damn society."

I put the question to Jim whether he thought we had any power, whether government could be forced to answer his needs, our needs—those of middle-aged men as a class. He said it certainly wasn't doing that now, though he was not as cynical as I seemed to be. Political outcomes, he believed, did make a difference. He cited how much better constituted the Supreme Court would be had Humphrey beat Nixon, regardless of what one might otherwise think of Humphrey. "And decisions of the Court do have an effect," Jim said. He mentioned the spectacle of Justice Douglas, at that time struggling to stay on the Court until after the next election, and we sat in silence a while thinking about that.

We talked some more about Jim's personal situation. He said that it was a time in his life when the burdens were easing. Susan was almost out of college. He would get Chip through college if Chip really wanted to to—but he would really have to want to. Jim confessed that he had enjoyed having a little leisure, and that he looked forward to retirement. "Kathy had said she was concerned about how it would be, us there together all the time, hanging around the house."

"How do you find it?" I asked him.

"I've enjoyed it. I enjoy it thoroughly."

"Me, too," I exclaimed. "I love it. There's something fundamental about it. I never had been in the house during the day in my whole damn life."

He laughed. "And Kathy said she's enjoyed it. She says she's really going to miss it when I go back to work." It was possible that Kathy would get a job before he did, and that wouldn't bother either one of them, never would have. And if she got a job, he would be willing to go to work for something less than he had been making. They would move, if necessary, to get the right kind of job. They were not tied to

Atlanta. "We have a nice house here. We both sort of recognize that we'd never have as nice a house again. And I think we'd miss the house."

I told him of our realization that the unthinkable of selling the house was entirely thinkable now, and he said it was the same with them. "The only thing that bothers me," I said, "is what to do about hospitalization." He had switched to Blue Cross but it wouldn't be nearly adequate for something serious. He was certain the next big reform within the society would be some kind of medical program, if nothing more than to protect everybody from the catastrophes.

Then Jim, his voice starting out uncertain but growing enthusiastic, said, "Now I'm looking around—with the thought of—well, going into some sort of service business. Be on our own. Go to work for ourselves. I'm going to go by the Small Business Administration today. There's a bankrupt marina down in Panacea, Florida. I'd like to know more about it. Why it went bankrupt and all that. I don't mind working—if I'm doing something I enjoy—fifteen or eighteen hours a day. I've done that before. That doesn't bother me. You can be a slave to what you're doing and stay constantly uptight about it, and that's a very bad thing. But it seems to me you can work just as hard and just as long at something you want to do and not be uptight."

I thought of Horace, his capacity for work. My own. We had by chance heard about that bankrupt marina a couple of summers ago, something to do with the channel being blocked, and I told Jim what little I knew. But damn, I hoped he would do something like that. His voice had sounded like a song when he said, "There's a bankrupt marina down in Panacea, Florida."

After that happy vision of the marina, Jim confided, "Another few months, if I don't find something to do, I may get bitter. Who knows? I can certainly see that I'm lucky we've got a few dollars."

I expressed indignation over the general situation of so many middle-aged men out of work and Jim said he certainly felt that. "It looks like they're ready to put us all out to pasture. We've been going through a period of worship of youth. But we may be beginning to get over that. Young people who two or three years ago seemed so absolutely sure of everything seem not quite as sure now. But maybe I'm just not as much in contact with them any more."

That—not being in contact with them—I said, was to me one of the greatest joys of being away from the Council. I went on: "I think the educators just completely abandoned all responsibility during the campus riots and turned loose on the country a whole generation of irresponsible kids bent on tearing up everything, the good along with the bad. It's going to take years to get over them. From what I gather reading about the campuses, educators are getting back their balance now."

Jim said he believed people were coming around to the idea that experience has some value, too. I said I hoped so. Still, he thought legislation against discrimination on account of age wasn't doing any good. "Clearly, people do discriminate. The new efforts being made under Title IX for women aren't doing any good. We'll have to have a Title X, I suppose. A strong piece of legislation for age."

I raised the issue of our political powerlessness again, and asked if he could foresee a movement for us. Jim said he didn't feel the need for it. He saw the John Birch Society in its heyday in the 1960s as an expression of middle-aged frustration. Its converts were, many of them, the sons and daughters of the man in the big house on the hill. They went to college and expected to live in big houses on the hill, too, with all the respect and power that position implies. But they found, once there, that they didn't have any power or influence with the ideas their daddies taught them. I didn't exactly relish the comparison Jim was making, but had to admit it was apt.

Jim said again he had not given up on the political process. He didn't view it as simplistically as he once had. But during his life, there had been some change, even though it hadn't been fast enough or exactly what he might have wanted. He still believed. The whole thing could collapse for lack of enough money to keep it going, though. "But somehow or other I think things are going to work themselves out."

But society is different now, he conceded. "It's a more mobile kind of a thing. But it's far more than just that. We grew up with the idea that a man got one job or two and that was sort of his life. When I changed from my own job in business to work for the Council, that was more of a major change than most people of my generation make. But there are people now who actually make a career out of working at a thing for one or two years and going on to something else. I can see all sorts of advantages to it. But to do that, you have to abandon other sorts of traditions such as permanent homes and that sort of thing. I'm not sure I'm ready to abandon all of those.

"Here we are at fifty, thrown out at the height of our powers, and certainly we are frustrated about that. But what, I wonder, is going to happen to these people who at thirty-two or thirty-three get to be in real positions of influence in business? There are some bank presidents around who are that age now. What's going to happen to them at fifty? Can you be the president of a bank for thirty-five years? What are you going to aspire to? A bigger bank? Or will you have to change fields to get some kind of satisfaction? We're creating a situation where if you don't change jobs, you're a failure. That seems to me a phony kind of pressure. Is it all going to be solved by earlier and earlier retirements? If so, how are you going to condition people to retire early? It takes an amount of maturity to retire."

I had not thought about young people in big jobs and all the job changing that goes on. It was fascinating how we all looked at essentially the same situation and came out with so many different insights. "Maybe," I said to Jim, "we'll have a generation of middle-aged dropouts."

"Where're they going to drop to?" Jim countered.

"Well, either way," I pushed on, "dropped out or retired or just knocked out, what is going to be the effect on society of losing the experience and whatever wisdom we gained out of thirty years of working?"

"I don't know. It's really sort of scary. Where do all the people our age go? Susan's working at a bank and she's in a department where the oldest person is in her early thirties." (We had gotten a letter from our young friend, Amanda Bennett, just starting her first job after college: "These people are all young—about thirty-five is management age—and they all have power over me by virtue of their positions. But, to borrow Glenda's phrase, they are *duu-umb*. And I resent being confused and tripped up by them. Goddamn, I really sound pretentious. What I meant to say is I miss you, Pat, and you, Glenda, who know more than I do, around me while I am working.")

Jim went on: "You keep finding yourself more of a traditionalist than you thought you were. How do you define success? For me, it never was complicated. I didn't have to be the president of anything. It was just satisfaction at what I was doing. And reaching a point where I didn't have to really worry about financial things. I'm still traditionalist enough to be concerned about security."

He mentioned again that maybe if things didn't work out in a few months, he might become bitter. God forbid, I thought. I had asked Jim about his religion. He went into detail, telling me he had left the Southern Baptist Church because to remain would have made him a hypocrite on account of his racial beliefs. Then he had resigned from one Episcopal church in Mobile because the congregation voted 352 to 2 (his and Kathy's votes) to condemn the National Council of Churches for its integrationist stands. After that, he had attended an all-black church that was little more liberal than the all-white one. Finally, he had gotten away from organized religion altogether.

"I don't think the organized church is terribly essential to me. I certainly believe in some sort of God—I don't know just what or why. Beyond that, I'm not really sure. Certainly the Christian philosophy had some effect on me. I'd be foolish to deny that. And whether or not it was a motivation or a justification for my civil-rights stands, I really don't know. It's a chicken-and-egg situation. But one can get quite a bit of satisfaction out of religious experience. Sometimes I'm profoundly moved. . . ."

Jim alone among the jobless men I talked with was someone I had been friends with before. But I realized how little I had really known him during all those years we had worked together, how much of his character I had missed. I came away with far more respect for him than I had had before, and a far stronger feeling of friendship.

Because of that little bit of money he had saved up, Jim was the best off of all the jobless men I talked with. But he was aware that a few more months of joblessness might make him bitter, might damage his belief. Jim Buchan and Horace, even, had not yet had to retrench drastically, sell off things, retreat on their life-style and standard of living. What would be the effect of that on a man, on the degree of his anxiety and anger, on his beliefs? I found out from Ed Lowell, another Americus mobile home man, an executive laid off a year before. And learned from him, too, new understandings of belief, strange and disturbing.

I found Ed in his encampment off a main highway, down a sand road, an isolated little area of cleared earth. He had there an old beat-up mobile home he used to store his tools and possessions, three old automobiles randomly parked, a nearly new mobile home that he had bought cheap before his plant folded and in which he now lives, and his big concrete block machine shop that he built himself during the year out of work. He had gone as far with it as he could: walls up, windows and doors in, but no roof. It would cost at least seven hundred dollars for materials for the roof.

We stood there in the twilight looking at that fine building with no roof and no immediate hope of one. Ed said he had received this day his monthly GI Bill check for his schooling at Southwest Georgia Tech, and after paying the most pressing bills he owed, his bank account stood at $2.78, exactly as it had before the check came.

Ed wears dungarees and a sports shirt. He is a short, compactly built, neat-appearing man with longish brown hair, a brown moustache. His eyes are sunken, almost hollow. He is younger than the others I have talked with, at the lower limit of my own flexible range for middle age, thirty-five. My friend Royce Bemis, the book salesman, said when I told him about talking with unemployed men that he could identify with them, nearing forty himself. A lot of guys, thirty-five to forty, he felt, worried about what would happen if they lost their job. Certainly in Ed's case, a relatively young age had not made getting a new job any easier.

We went into his neatly ordered mobile home, and he started to tell me how he had got to where he was, and what he thought would be the outcome. He was born in Portland, Maine, June 3, 1940, finished high school there, and went into the Air Force when he was eighteen. He spent four years in the Air Force as a jet engine mechanic, and did radio technician work on the side as a hobby. He just missed having to go to Vietnam, the buildup there starting just as he was getting out. "Of course, if I had it to do over, I'd a-stayed in. I think it would have been the greatest thing that could have happened. Should have stayed in. I'd have in eighteen years now, nearly retired."

He got married six months before he got out of service in 1962, and he and his bride went back home to Maine where he went to work for RCA. He worked for them until he got the mobile home job. They moved to Americus on Easter Sunday 1965. He stayed in the business until he was laid off in June 1974.

Ed started out on the assembly line, wanting to work up to engineering. Sure enough, they soon put him to drawing blueprints. Then he went into production control and worked at that for five years. Then a friend started a plant in nearby Montezuma, and Ed went there to run the whole engineering department. It seemed the thing to do— more money, a little more. "I really hated to leave the old job. I don't like to switch jobs. But I did."

They built mobile homes and modular homes. "We built real nice homes. But we had trouble getting paid for them. The contractors that we sold to were a little reluctant to pay, and pretty soon our accounts receivable got out of sight, and payables got just as bad. So we got on

94

COD with everybody and couldn't get any material. We were in real bad shape." They had to sell out to a larger firm, which had headquarters in Atlanta. Ed said they probably got it for the amount of debts the plant owed, about a quarter of a million dollars. "That can mount up in just a few days in this business. You really have to watch it. So much money flows. There's not much money made. But there's a lot of money flowing."

Ed stayed on. It was another great company, he said. Besides being chief engineer, he was also cost accountant. Then the last year, they made him, in addition to the other two jobs, the comptroller. But things kept going from bad to worse in the industry. The plant shut down the last of May 1974. Ed stayed on another month, closing things out. His last day of work was one day after his divorce became final, he said ruefully.

"All at one fell swoop, I was out of work, divorced with seventy-five-dollar-a-week child support looking me in the eye. Which was not bad at all. It was really in line with what it should be with my three children." They are all boys, nine, eleven, and fourteen. His wife didn't ask for alimony. She continued to live in their house in nearby Plains, Georgia, and he continued to pay for it. "I made last month's payment. I don't know what's going to happen after this month."

He knew, of course, that he would be divorced, but he didn't know he would be jobless. He figured he could make the child-support payments out of his $225 a week salary, and he had bought the mobile home we were in to get by cheaply. As it was, he had sent as much as he could for child support, probably half of what was due, and his former wife had been understanding, had not pressured him, tried to make do on the earnings of her beauty shop. Those child-support payments were top priority among his many obligations.

I asked Ed if business pressure had had anything to do with the breakup of his marriage. "Well, I don't know," he answered. A personal friend had handled the legal work and he told Ed, "The only thing I can say is that you spent too many hours on the job. You haven't been home enough." Ed said he would get up at six in the morning to get to work by eight. The comptroller job would keep him busy usually until five. Then he'd stay on until ten-thirty or eleven doing the other two jobs. It was a thirty-five-mile drive home, so he'd get in every night about eleven or eleven-thirty. "She never said she didn't like it that way." But then one day she just said she didn't want to live with him any more. "I guess it was rough on both of us."

He explained about having the personal friend do the legal work. It was his friend, but the lawyer agreed to represent the wife, since there was no contest. This, Ed said, "was to save her from going to these high-priced lawyers. Gyp artists. I don't like to talk bad about anybody. If I can't say good, I don't like to say it. But when somebody charges you three hundred dollars for fifteen or twenty minutes' paper work, that's stealing your money, just like they'd reached in your pocket and stole it." His friend had charged a hundred dollars and said, even so, that was a steal. They ended up settling for Ed's putting points and plugs in the lawyer's Model-A Ford and hauling it to Atlanta for a car show.

I asked Ed what went wrong to cause his plant to close. He said mostly it was increasing costs and decreasing sales. All kinds of material kept going up and up. Lumber, for example, went from $115 a thousand feet to $145 to $185, then to $200, then to $225. Double. They had always lost money delivering the homes. "We owned our own trucks. Naturally, they stay broke down. They blow an engine out on the road, and that's a thousand dollars, fifteen hundred, whatever they want to rook you for." Electrical wire went from $60-some-odd a thousand feet to $200-and-something because copper got real scarce. "We wouldn't bow down to using aluminum wire. I wouldn't allow aluminum wire—although it was admissible. I wouldn't use it. There were certain standards about the home I tried to keep as high as I could."

Is aluminum wire dangerous? I asked. "Naw," Ed said. "It's just Mickey Mouse, cop-out wire. You got to use a bigger size to get the same results. On the assembly line, if they got to work with bigger wire, it slows 'em down. If you fool with aluminum, you've got to have different types of wire nuts. And you've got to use certain types of material in the fuse box to keep the aluminum from corroding. It's just poor material. It doesn't stand any strain. It breaks. It's—*cheap*."

Ed did not want to leave the area for another job because he wanted to be near his boys. But there were no jobs to be had locally. Someone told him about an encyclopedia-selling job, but he couldn't bring himself to do that. As a youth, he had been high-pressured by a salesman into buying a set, and it had been a bitter, sickening experience for him. A job as dog catcher came open in Americus, but so many people applied, Ed figured it was hopeless. He had gone through one term of unemployment compensation, and had put in for an extension. Someone at the unemployment office thought he was entitled to a new claim and filled out the form for it. Then, by mistake, two applications were sent in and the computer kicked them both back. Ed had an appointment the following week with visiting officials to try to straighten the thing out. Meantime, he'd been getting no compensation for five weeks.

He had a year of GI Bill training due him, and so had enrolled at Southwest Georgia Tech in a machine-shop course. "I'd a-took basket weaving if I had to," just to get the money. He was getting $388 a month. Then, of all things, they overpaid him the first two months, $80 in all. Ed felt he ought to report it and when he did, they took all the overpayment out of the check he had gotten this day. It was barely over $300. He added that to his $2.78 in the bank. Then he paid his note on the Plains house, his light bill, and half of the $140 he owes on his insurance. That left him with the $2.78 again.

Throughout our conversation, Ed would repeatedly go over his obligations, each time thinking of one that he hadn't mentioned before. Basically, though, he was trying to juggle payments on his wife's home and its bills, old credit card accounts from when he was working, his insurance, child support, doctor bills incurred when his youngest boy had had an ear operation, notes on his mobile home, and utilities at his encampment. He owns the land there outright, having sold a brand-new five-thousand-dollar Econoline van for three thousand to get the money. He worries constantly about the bills, would rather go without eating than not pay his debts—in fact, had gotten down to one meal a day several times.

"Right now I'm in as bad shape as I've ever been." He had no money to eat on for the coming month. He would do, he said, what he had done before—sell off some of his beloved antique automobiles. The ones he had sold so far had been at a loss, not even counting the time he had put in restoring them. It had been a case of got to, and git what you can. He sold a Model-T that he had put twenty-five hundred into for fifteen hundred, for example. He didn't list the others and I didn't press him. "It was sickening," he said.

All he had left was a 1936 Ford pickup truck that he had put three thousand dollars into and expected to get no more than a thousand for, a 1941 Ford Tudor sedan in original condition, which might bring two thousand, a 1941 Chevrolet coupe, and a 1947 Studebaker Champion. He said he might even have to sell off his old raggedy bulldog because he couldn't afford to feed her.

Each time Ed ticked off his financial obligations or spoke of how down and out he was, he would add things like: "On the whole, though, I'm lucky," or "I don't lose sleep over it." He said the unemployment compensation was a great thing, the people there as nice as they could be, and the veteran's school money was a godsend, a great program.

The only thing he was angry about was food stamps. He went to apply for them early on, taking all his bills with him, figuring he had an open-and-shut food-stamp case. "I talked to the interviewer. She was a real nice, understanding person. I knew that I had three strikes against me already, being white. That's really not true. But I went in there, saying to myself with the bills I've got and no income whatsoever, they're going to be begging me to take those food stamps. I was afraid the woman was going to try to loan me some money right then." We laughed. But when he got the answer to his application, it was a form with a big old X where it said, "Rejected." The reason: He owned the land at the encampment and the house he was still paying on in Plains. You can't get food stamps if you own property. Never mind that rent would be higher than house notes.

"If that's fair play, I think I'll just take vanilla. Maybe they need that billion dollars to shoot off to outer space." He had seen people who live better than he does getting the stamps. "But I don't like to grumble. I'm glad to be where I am. I'm glad to have what I've got. And I'm proud of what I've got, although it's getting less and less every day. But you know, I think what's right is right. It's like these people screaming and hollering about discrimination. It's just a crutch, something to lean on." He said somebody needed to tell them it works both ways. Black people have the edge, he said—but then, they deserve it because they were deprived so long. "But, you know, when I go up there, they say, 'Hey you got three acres of land and it's worth three thousand dollars—man, what're you doing here?' "

The main thing keeping him going, keeping him from losing sleep, Ed said, was the promise of a very good new job, maybe as soon as two weeks from now. A man he knew was going to set up a plant in Americus to manufacture agricultural storage tanks, and Ed would be the manager. The man needed something over half a million dollars to get started, and with investors brought in, had got all but thirty thousand of it. "So I think that right around the corner I will be working. Of course, I can't wait even two more weeks. Something else will have to give between now and then." He paused, then said, "Really, it's kind of been that way all along, now I stop and think about it. It's always been right around the corner. Maybe it never will come. I don't know."

But then he brightened up, said he felt their needing only thirty thousand dollars was very encouraging. And he was ready and eager to go to work. "Basically, the last ten years, I've had not a super-executive job, but quite a responsible job. So I've got to keep my standard of living as high as I can. I've just got to keep everything up—the image, you know, the whole thing. You can't be a bum and then expect to get back in an executive job. You just can't do it. My hair's a little bit long now. I haven't had time or really the money to get a haircut. I try to keep it combed nicely. It's not really long by today's standards. Longer than I want, though." He said the person who wanted to hire him had faith in him. "He knows I can do it. And I know I can do it. There's no doubt in my mind. Except—when is it going to come?"

I asked Ed my by-now-standard question: Did he have any feelings about what the federal government might do to help in his kind of situation, beyond what it's doing now? "I don't know," he said. "I think if anything could of been done, they should have done it. The overall federal picture is sort of sour grapes to me in a way. I'm not a complainer, really. I'm a patriotic sort of person. I love it here. I wouldn't live anywhere else. But here we are out of work and can't find anything, and millions go to this and that, shot off one time and it's gone. The space program basically is a real great thing. I think we need to stay ahead of all the other countries in everything. I just hope they don't come out with some new invention that we got to stay ahead of 'em on. Because if they do, we're going to have to do it. But if nobody had come up with it in the first place, we'd have been how many billions of dollars better off? We're going to have to stay ahead of 'em. I want it that way. I don't want us to be second in anything." I thought of John: *It's wearing on you to always have to be number one.*

Ed said he thought the Vietnam War was a total loss. But we have so many commitments. As long as we do, we'll never have anything. But he wouldn't say that was wrong either. "There are so many things like this. They're right but they're wrong. What're you going to do? We're a strong nation and it's imperative that we stay that way. If I have to go without work and skimp and save, I guess I'd rather do that than have us fall down."

I found myself liking him more and more in all his tangled bundles of conflicting beliefs and ideals, all his insight into the insanities of this country's current course, though still unwilling to condemn it. He spoke of how ridiculous it was for his oldest boy to be bused all the way from Plains, eleven miles, to junior high in Americus, of the waste there of fifty-cents-a-gallon gasoline. "The schools have been integrated. I don't see anything wrong with that. If I had my druthers, I'd rather they weren't. But I'm not a racist. Probably, you might say that's the best way to bring 'em up. Because you know everybody can live together better when they get to be adults. But why can't they go to school together, integrate together, in Plains? Why bring 'em over here? That's right close behind food stamps."

I asked him about politics, and he gave his assessments of the Presidents he had seen serve. He said he didn't understand much about the workings of government, had forgotten everything he learned about it in school. "I'm pretty good at machine work, welding, mechanical work. If somebody wants to get in a conversation with me about that, I can tell 'em the answers. I don't tell 'em what I think. I *know*. But in politics, if I say something, it might be wrong."

Instead of Nixon in 1968, he had voted for George Wallace. It was the only time he had ever been really interested in politics. He is still a strong Wallace supporter. "He's not a racist—which a lot of people try to say. Everybody's got a little dirty remark they can say to cut him down." Wallace had done more for black people in Alabama than anybody before him. "He's an honest Christian person." Could Wallace do something about the job situation? "I think so. He's a true American with no strings attached." He wouldn't be obligated. He would be free to do what needs to be done. "He would not lift a finger to separate the schools again. But he would make an effort to stop all this busing." He would bring all people, black and white, closer together, Ed said.

But, he went on, the news media can make it or break it, the newspapers and television, especially tv. "All they got to do is take little choice portions of a newscast. Like, if they were at a Wallace rally and he was pouring out his heart to people for hours and hours and telling the good he could do. And if somebody were to jump up and throw a rock at him and he would shake his fist, then that is what would be on tv. That's what would be on tv. You wouldn't hear the good."

I have no use for Wallace, God knows, had just written a diatribe against him for *Dissent* magazine, comparing him to Nixon in unprincipled demagoguery, using the race issue, not believing one way or the other about it, to further his ambition, betraying his people in the process, even on their own unfortunate notions about race. But I know the truth of what Ed said about the media from my experience on another side of the race issue. I devoted a good part of the book I did on the civil-rights movement to demonstrating exactly what Ed was saying—that the media had missed the beauty and grandeur and main meanings of the movement because of their obsession with violence.

Ed said he had met Wallace. Wallace wouldn't know him if he walked into the room. But they had met. Jimmy Carter, the former Georgia governor from Plains, who was seeking the Democratic nominaton, was a good friend. But Ed wasn't sure about him for the presidency. Then he said his vote for Wallace was based as much on his fear of Hubert Humphrey as on his love for Wallace. I feared Humphrey, too, and so asked Ed why he did. It was the things that he said, "all sorts of straight Communist quotes. 'We will overcome.' " In fairness, Ed said, Humphrey seemed to have straightened out some since then. But when he was running, he was horrifying. "I used to be quite a sympathizer with an organization here that kept up pretty well with what was going on in the country as far as Communist infiltration was concerned. And there's no doubt it happened. And Humphrey was right at the head of it.

"And Martin Luther King. He was probably the one person who did the most to hurt his own people as anybody's ever done. He liked to have ruined his own people. If the black people wanted a leader—I used to despise Cassius Clay. I couldn't stand the thought of him. But then I heard him on the type of show where he wasn't being real boisterous. I said, what in the world, look at this, this is a great person. Now there would be a real leader. Instead of somebody saying, 'Get yourself a whole basket of Coke bottles and rocks and destroy this man's store because he won't let you buy.' Just hate. That's all Martin Luther King knew was hate."

All that came reeling into my mind so fast I could hardly assimilate it. I had known Dr. King and the genuine strength and integrity of his nonviolent movement, had written my book about that. Now here was Ed, going on some more, this time about the school-book controversy in West Virginia, parents upset about what their children were being taught. What bothered Ed most was a man who said on a tv show that there ought not to be any patriotism taught in the schools.

"That would make me want to flare right up in the middle of the night and take up arms. This is not the American way. I'm real patriotic. You can see. I've got a flag hanging there, and a flag hanging over there. Maybe you might recognize that picture behind you. I don't know whether you do."

I had noted the flags and his old Edison record machine and his guitar and his two antique rifles and his two Confederate bonds and his Seth Thomas clock and his old cabinet radio. But I had missed that picture behind me, somehow. It was a painting of a white knight of the Ku Klux Klan on horseback. "That's where I used to go," Ed said. Great God. "This is a Christian organization, too. It's not what it's played up to be in he news."

He mentioned recent news, an unfortunate incident at Stone Mountain near Atlanta where a black reporter had been roughed up at a Klan rally. Ed said that if the black reporter had let them know he was coming on legitimate business, it wouldn't have happened. But in he walked, unannounced, and feelings were up. "I know good and well that the people there, and I'm speaking as a Klansman myself—I might as well tell you that—if they had known ahead of time, they wouldn't have abused him."

There again, Ed said, the media played up the bad. "If there was any good that came from the meeting, you'd never know it." I covered only as many Klan rallies as I had to and had never been accosted at the few I did attend. But I knew reporters, white ones whose legitimate business had been announced ahead of time, who were roughed up at those gatherings. But Ed was right about one thing: we didn't go to them to find anything good.

Ed said there had never been much around Americus that required Klan action, which, he claimed, was always confined to protests, talking to people. It never involved violence. One time in nearby Cordele, some people burned a United States flag. "Now you just don't do that. It's just not the thing to do. I wouldn't put up for it. And I know you wouldn't put up for it. And we just went over there. We wanted to have a meeting on the courthouse lawn. But we couldn't. We weren't allowed to use it. We had to get in the dern streets, like a bunch of idiotic protesters, which we were not. So we had a little simple parade and gosh, I imagine fifty percent of the population must have joined in, women carrying little babies even. We were naturally wrong by going over there and being patriotic and being against those people that burnt the flag. We were wrong. They were right. It's always that way. This is the kind of thing that makes a few of us go on and on. It's hard, though, for a few people to change a lot of people's minds." How well I knew that.

"But there are a lot of sympathizers," Ed said. "They don't have a robe or a card, but they're just as good Americans as if they did. Most people don't want to be involved. That way you don't get hurt." He didn't get involved in much himself. "But if some movement came into Americus and started preaching all sorts of hate, like Martin Luther King used to preach—hate, bloodshed, all sorts of violence, exactly the opposite of what he said that he was—then that's the time somebody would have to make some moves."

It was an upside-down world Ed was describing to me. I had heard what Dr. King did preach, had heard my share of Klan hate speeches, and had seen firsthand the murderous violence of the Klan. But I wouldn't argue with the people I was interviewing, a holdover from my newspaper, objective-reporting days. Maybe I should have, to elicit provocative quotes. But I don't think so. I wondered what Ed would feel if he found out later the kind of things I have written about Dr. King, about Wallace, about the Klan. Should I tell him? Out here off the main road, night descended now, those rifles on the wall? Ed kept saying that the Klan was not racist or violent, and that he himself was neither of those things, and I believe that he honestly believed that. But he had been through hell during the past year, and the anger had spread all through him, speaking in his voice and his gestures. Maybe I should have argued with him, told him my views. But I didn't. Not all of my reason was prudence. He had, I felt, built up to telling me about the Klan by testing my reaction to other things he said. I suspected he had been through his share of put-downs for that affiliation of his, and I didn't want to add to them. We talked a long while more about the matter and at the end I asked him if he was sure he wanted me to write about his being in the Klan. Would that hurt his reputation around here? He said no, people knew about it, he was proud of it.

But the main thing was the upside-down rapport I felt with him. He spoke bitterly of how the FBI had harassed the Klan, and we had known harassment from that source on the other side. When he tried to explain the good feeling it gave him to be involved in such a purposeful organization, and to go through its rituals, words literally failed him. But I could understand. I realized that much of my strong attraction to the movement had been rooted in the same kind of good feeling about its mission and my enjoyment in immersing myself in the great emotional outpouring of song and prayer and preaching at the mass meetings. Ritual and spiritual release are fundamental human needs; in America, we are starved for them. Ed found them at one extreme of the struggle over race, I at the other. Most people don't go to such extremes. Football, especially in the South, is about the only available outlet. So it is no wonder that we are so often hostile to each other in this country, or worse, closed to each other. We have been robbed of the releases of public ceremony and real religious experience. It was a strong new insight into lovelessness.

Ed was the first Klansman I had ever talked at length with; it had always seemed to me that the fascination some people in the civil-rights business have for communicating with their enemy is a good way to get killed. But I learned much from Ed about that enemy that I should have known all along, and about myself. It was one more instance of the benefits of returning to the real world.

I had been fascinated with his great capacity for work, and now our talk turned to the machine shop he had built. It would be a place where he could keep all his tools and machines, and work on his cars and other things. He had even considered starting a garage business. Then he told me about other work he had done on the encampment. He had no money when he got through paying for the land, and he had to have water and sewage. So he rebuilt an old Volkswagen he had from top to bottom and swapped it with a friend for help and the use of his equipment in digging a well. They drilled it by hand, ninety feet, Ed doing as much work or more than his friend.

Then he needed a septic tank. "And you know they were talking five or six hundred dollars. So I got out here and in five days I dug a hole. A hole five foot by ten foot, seven foot deep. Five days. Five days now from morning till night, through all these rocks. I completely wore out a pair of boots. I wore holes plumb through my boots from jumping on that shovel. And well—you see my shoes. And these are my wing-tips." Yeah, his cordovans. They were battered and frayed. He held up his foot to show holes in the sole. "You can see my sock, right there."

The talk turned once more to that just-around-the-corner new job. As manager, Ed said, he would be doing a little of everything, would be the hell-catcher, supervising the twenty-four employees. They would work two shifts and he intended to have a hand in both, more long hours. "One way or the other, I'm going to see to it that what we make is going to be done right. And we're going to make a profit at it. We're going to be in good shape. We'll have some real good people to choose from. We're going to have some cream-of-crop labor," what with all the local unemployment. He said he looked forward to the opportunity to work people the way they ought to be worked—not driving them, but encouraging them, drawing out the best in them. I told him that was what I had tried to do when I was a city editor, and that it had worked wondrously well.

"I've been waiting for it to come in for so long," Ed said. "We've got all the local banks, the Chamber of Commerce, the powers-that-be a hundred percent in favor of it." Americus is a depressed area, he said, a good place to locate a plant. "Twenty-four people isn't much, but it'll put a lot of money in the community. And maybe put some smiles on some people's faces. I know everybody is down in the dumps around here."

Ed had said at one point he didn't drink or smoke, and now I asked him about his religion. He said it was important to him. He had left the Congregational Church, where he had been a "pore member," not attending, to become a Methodist with his former wife when they moved down here. He loved it, went for many years. But not too long ago, it seemed to him that the congregation was more interested in gossiping about one another than in listening to the preacher. Maybe it was a cop-out, but he just didn't want to go any more. "I believe that I am a Christian. I don't live a Christian life by any means. I don't do the way I should. This I know. The Lord knows it. But still I believe in it."

He said he was willing to listen to other beliefs. He had a friend back home who was a Buddhist-type person, and smart as a whip. He could make you wonder. "But there's no way he could convince me there's any other meaning to life. I know what I feel in my heart. I hope that when the day comes, I'll be acceptable. Maybe when that day comes, I won't. But this is my hope. I shudder to think that it'd be any other way—my children, not ever seeing 'em, and my parents."

We had gotten down to death, its ultimate meaning. But two other things Ed had said, images that his words created, bespoke life, his reality, what is to be no more, but what might be. When he told about selling the Econoline van, he began, "I had a brand new Econoline van—nice, real nice. Chrome, and carpet in it. Well, see, I had the family—three kids and my wife. I—I liked the van." At another point, he said that when he was first laid off, he felt footloose and fancy-free, and built himself a dune-buggy. "I had a girl friend who thought pink would be a good color. So I painted the dune-buggy pink, and we ripped up and down town and had a great time."

It sounded so happy, so different from most of the careworn words Ed spoke that night, with their burdened weight of worry over bills, and anger, and disappointed hope. Both images built a vision of the fuller man Ed had been and still might be.

We said good night outside under the big, star-gleaming south Georgia sky, the machine shop looming big and fine, but roofless, the beams outlined against the sky. I thought about Ed as I drove back to the motel, and then over a bottle of Scotch lonely into the night. So many things that he believed in had let him down—church, business, leaders, government, his country, which he loves with patriotic fervor, even his work, which he loves most of all. I liked him, hoped so much that the things he wants, the new job, the machine shop, would come to fruition. I admired his capacity for work, his belief in high standards, his wanting to draw the best out of his workers. He is a man with tremendous capacity for good. But he is also, in my judgment anyhow, capable of being led into a lot of evil. And there are a lot of Eds in this country.

The most heartening discovery in the quest was that the men I was talking with had so much strength of character, there was so much about them to like. I felt I had strengthened my friendship with John and Jim Wood and made good new friends of the others. To have found in Ed so much to like and admire was surprising and encouraging. The mobile home business might be shoddy, but his attitude and feeling toward the work were the opposite. I was discovering, at least, how wrong my attitude toward people in everyday pursuits, toward men in business, had been. It was not the men themselves, but the businesses that were at fault. The details of each story I heard confirmed again and again that sad awareness of deterioration. But at the same time, each man I talked with restored in me, little by little, feelings of belief in people.

Soon after I got back from Americus, the call I had so long awaited came from Mrs. Cofer at the DeKalb unemployment office. She had her list of men who had agreed to talk with me, and the one she was most excited about was Forrest Stone. When she had asked him about talking with me, he had said, "Why, for heaven's sake, I went to high school with Pat Watters. Sure, I'll talk with him." When we did talk, I felt that he was bringing together everything I had heard up until then about belief, and building further my understanding of the deterioration of business.

But when Mrs. Cofer first told me his name, I couldn't place him. I had been to my twenty-fifth high-school class reunion five years before, and was startled at how easily I recognized nearly all the faces, and how hard put I was to remember the names. (The thirtieth reunion was to be held the following week, and I was looking forward to it.)

And as it had been that time, when Forrest Stone greeted me at the front door of his ranch-type house out near Stone Mountain, I knew his face (fuller now, round, and remarkably unlined) immediately. He had put on a good amount of weight. But it was Buddy Stone standing there shaking hands with me, Buddy Stone, quiet good guy. I hadn't known him well. But sure, I remembered him.

We went into the den where among the decorations on the brick wall were two "extra effort" award plaques testifying that Buddy had not just made his quota selling heating and air-conditioning equipment, but a second quota as well. He served me a Coke, and we reminisced a little, he much better at remembering the names than I was. When we started in to talk about his situation, he handed me a copy of his résumé, which he said he had been sending out by the dozens since being laid off nine months before. It read:

Education: Graduated from Boys High School, Atlanta, Georgia. Attended 3 years Atlanta Division–University of Georgia, majoring in Business Administration and Marketing.

Experience: Began in 1967 with the Georgia Distributor for Carrier Air Conditioning as a Territory Manager calling on full-line dealers in the Greater Atlanta, North East, and North Central Georgia areas. I've also been Specialty Products Manager with responsibilities for Room Air Conditioners, Mobile Home Units, and Gas Unit Heaters. My accomplishments were maintaining present dealers, selling new dealers, creating sales and advertising promotions and programs, and conducting sales meetings.

Previous Experience: From 1957 to 1967, with Dearborn Stove Company as a District Manager selling heating and air conditioning in the Georgia, Tennessee, and South Carolina areas, calling on Air-Conditioning contractors, Hardware stores, Furniture stores and headquarters, and also Liquified Petroleum Dealers, most responsibilities similar to duties listed above.

Achieving several awards for outstanding sales effort with both companies.

Personal: Age 47 years, height 5'10", weight 175 pounds. Married to Martha Jo Stone, with a son, Allen, age 16, and daughter, Kerry, age 15. Hobbies are golf and reading, and I enjoy spectator sports.

It was a poem, really. To flesh out the familiar-sounding life story it outlined, I confirmed that he was born in Atlanta, and asked about his military service. "I was in the Navy when they dropped the bomb, Pat. So I was fortunate to be in only fourteen months." He had served in the Philippines.

And now again, the familiar depressing story: Buddy had been laid off in February 1975, did a lot of applying, and was fortunate enough to get another job in July. "It was an excellent opportunity. It was good money, good fringe benefits, good insurance program, furnished a car. This company was a national company." The job carried thirty-six thousand dollars in life insurance and hospitalization coverage, all for only a little over seven dollars a month, and fifty thousand dollars accidental death insurance on both him and his wife for five dollars a month. It sounded like a dream. And then: "But it was strange and shocking. I thought the new job was one of the best opportunities I ever had, and they laid me off in two months. This was really the biggest disappointment. I expected the first because the job I had was not producing. I was in the building field, and that's down so bad." He explained he had taken new sales responsibility with his old company back in 1973 and it hadn't worked out well. So he had asked for a territory back. The one they gave him was a poor territory that didn't produce.

"But this second one, I went in knowing that the company had to set up a new branch. They knew they were going to have to lose money. But then they said they had received instructions to cut the overhead ten percent after just starting the branch."

Jesus Holy Christ. To have it happen twice in six months' time. A one-two kick in the stomach. He had spoken in a tone of awed incredulity, as though now, a month later, he still couldn't believe it. They send down a number—cut 10 percent—and it's Buddy's life they're destroying.

The dream shattered. They reduced the sales force from three men to two, and Buddy had been the last hired. The job was the same as the one he had previously had, selling heating and air-conditioning equipment. The company had to open the new branch because its distributor had gone bankrupt. "So I'm back sending out résumés." The problem was the shortage of jobs in his field. Heating and air conditioning had been hard hit by the recession and its effect on the building trades. Buddy could see no hope for an upturn before the coming spring. And this was only early fall. No new apartments or condominiums were being built, and they had accounted for much of his previous business. One company had advertised for a heating and air-conditioning salesman and thirty-five applicants showed up, all but four or five of them fully qualified. Buddy had been the number-two choice among the thirty-five.

Jobs were offered in the classifieds, but they were not in his line. "The sales jobs that you can get are mostly commission jobs, they have no draw, and are real tough to make a living at." He said the only industry that seemed to be hiring a lot was insurance. "But I really am not ready to sell insurance." He thought it would be hard to sell.

"I know I've easily sent out twenty-five résumés before, and I've just mailed out four today. The thing that was disappointing to me is that it takes so long for an answer after the interview. With two companies, I was strung out for more than two months before they decided not to hire anyone." He paused. Then: "Sure—at our age, you just wonder what the future's for."

Buddy said selling was the only thing he had ever done or ever wanted to do. "It still affords a good future." But you have to specialize. That's the main advice he would give anyone starting out. "Have your field and know it and stay in it. You can't just say I'm a salesman now and get a job." (But, I thought, that is the very thing that trapped you.) Food companies were advertising for salesmen, Buddy said, but you had to have a following, customers to take to them. Buddy didn't say anything about the cruelty of a system that demands specialization, and, when your specialization runs into hard times, says that's just too damn bad. I said it, but he didn't seem to want to face up to it.

He did talk about how he felt when his double disaster happened. "Of course, your pride is hurt. You know that, Pat. Fortunately, my wife has a good job and it has helped us financially. The unemployment just buys groceries. That's all that does."

"Were you scared, Buddy?"

"Naw. There were times—you know, you would be brought emotionally to think that you had a real good chance for a job, and then they'd say they're not even going to hire anybody. Of course, this leaves you at a real low ebb."

The main thing, though, was that it made him angry, really angry. Not the first time, so much. He had kind of expected it because of the bad territory. But even so, of the fifteen salesmen there, only two were over forty. "The trend in the last four or five years in hiring was thirty-year-olds or even twenty-eight-, twenty-seven-year-olds. You could see the age bracket changing. The man that was president was the same age I was." Jim Wood's thing of the young taking over and what would they do with it? "It made me mad," Buddy said, "because my pride was hurt, and because there were others there who should have been released before I was." And it galled him that they haven't laid off anybody since, though the company is still sustaining losses.

"But this second job was what made me mad as hell. They told me they expected to lose money to start. I gave up two other excellent opportunities to be interviewed and possibly get a job. And then in two months—this took me completely by surprise. This has just made me completely disgusted and mad."

No apologies from the firm? "No. 'I'm sorry. I'm sorry we have to do it,' and that was it. He said, 'I tried as much as I could.' Well, I don't know. This really made me mad. And I'm still mad. It was one of the lowest points in my life to have to come home and tell the family. Because, as you can see from the résumé, I've had only two jobs in eighteen years." *Like Jim Buchan. Loyalty rewarded.*

I asked Buddy if he suffered my delusion that some of the fault must be your own. "You do doubt yourself. And certainly you have a reason to doubt yourself and wonder if it's your failure. This second job, I know there was no failure. I had done a good job establishing new accounts. In the other, I was foolish to have taken the territory. I should have left while times were good and gotten another job. But the company was an excellent company and the people were good." *Over and over. You are loyal to them. They are not to you.*

Buddy said he had made one other mistake. "This is the thing, Pat. The politics. Politics is a very necessary part of business. When I had that job as specialty products manager—it's there in the résumé—I didn't play enough politics with the higher-ups. I was reading an article when we were taking a trip to San Francisco and it said that politics is one of the musts for succeeding in business. That is, to always go to the boss and ask for suggestions and everything all the time. I just felt that I was independent and good enough to do my own job. But you can't. This is very vicious. This is the thing probably— the reason I'm not there now. I just like to do my job and not run in and see the boss, playing politics. But I'm afraid politics is a necessary thing. It's sickening. It's just sickening."

I had made that fatal mistake, too. At the Council, and on the paper, I really did believe that if you were good enough, you didn't have to kiss asses and could be, at times, arrogant. But Buddy was right. You can't. I spoke to him of my great feeling of disillusionment. "All of these things that I was brought up to believe in and really did believe in, all of a sudden I could just see 'em all falling apart."

"Yeah," Buddy said. "I know. I told my wife I would have to just play a little more politics with that second job I got. I didn't—though I'm sure it had nothing to do with the reason I was laid off. But it's what you have to do. And to me, it's just so unnecessary."

Thinking of his wife, Buddy said, "But my family's been great. The kids, they've not, you know, shown any shame about it. My daughter mentioned one person who had been out for about five or six months, the father of one of her girl friends. The only thing with the kids, is that they still can't realize how seriously scarce money is, that it is no longer plentiful."

He had one other worry about his children. Another "great" thing that had happened to him was that he had invested the family's savings in North American Thrift Corporation, a firm that had gone bankrupt shortly before he was laid off the first time. (Those troubles coming in bunches.) That money was to have provided college educations for the kids. "That was the only nest egg we had." The house, he said, was their only other big asset. They had bought it when interest rates were low and had a good amount of equity in it. For that reason, Buddy didn't relish the idea of having to move to some other city to get work.

"My wife has been excellent. Of course, she has a good job. The money she makes—with a lot of the jobs I'm ready to take now, she'd make more than I would. This is kind of demeaning to a man that's supposed to be the head of the household." *Supposed to be. They told us all these things we were supposed to be, and we keep on trying to be them.* Did it really bother him, that his wife might make more than he did? "No. No. Because—not with the wife that I have. It's affected her some, but not obviously. I was just, you know, so glad that I did get that second job because she was beginning to worry some. She looks like she's holding up good this time. But I have been concerned about what this second layoff would do to her."

"Do you do like I do and help around the house?" I asked Buddy.

"I sure do, Pat. I've done dishes today and the wash. I folded the wash. I cook supper. It's my part of it. I'm glad to do it."

Buddy said the neighbors had been good, too, had not evidenced any scorn at his being at home during the hours when men are supposed to be at work. They were friends with only one of the neighboring families, and that couple had been very understanding. It was the first time any of the men had referred to the insult of stigma added to the injury of unemployment through no fault of their own. Edward B. Furey, in that anguished column in the *Times*, had written, "It's to see what the neighborhood looks like at 10:30 on a Tuesday morning. It's to feel embarrassed to answer the ring of the telephone at the same hour." Glenda and I had laughed about what some of our neighbors might think about my being home every day—that she was supporting me in my riotous living. But suppose that were really the case?

Buddy talked more about that awful one-two blow. How much had his age had to do with it? He would have to say it was not a factor at the second company. The boss was his age and two of the three salesmen were over forty. That had been another thing that had made him feel so good about the job. But he was sure his age was against him now looking for work. He showed me the classified section of the paper. "I've circled three or four ads in here, and they're in every Sunday. The ad will say college degree and one or two or three years' experience. Now what does that tell you? They want a guy that's twenty-five or twenty-six."

Experience is disregarded or not highly regarded by people hiring salesmen, Buddy said. But surely, I said, they get better performance out of an experienced person? They don't look at it that way, he said. It really makes me mad, I said. A man with twenty-five years' experience is bound to be better at it. Yeah, Buddy agreed. "And he's settled and everything else. Somebody thirty is going to be looking somewhere else. They can't depend on him being there in ten or fifteen years." Buddy said the worst age discrimination was at employment agencies. "I've gone to four and I've not heard the first word from any of them. It's so obvious that age is the real serious factor with them. You have to go fill out the form and it takes an hour and a half to two hours. They look at it and say it sounds good. But you never get any phone call. You never hear from them."

There's a law against discrimination because of age, Buddy said, but how can you prove it? "There's no way that I can prove it with an employment agency or a company." Of course not, no way. Blacks and women have won cases, proving discrimination simply by showing a pattern of all-white or all-male hiring. I mentioned that to Buddy. He shook his head. He didn't have the time or money for something like that. There's no organization to do it for us. The idea itself is preposterous. A National Association for the Benefit of Middle-Aged Men? Laughable. I asked Buddy what he thought the government might do about the situation.

"Well, Pat, I'm as much in favor of the private enterprise system as anyone. But the problem is with companies that don't want to take people over thirty-five—and really, it's thirty-five. This is where they start discriminating. I feel the government should step in and pay the difference in the cost for insurance for people thirty-five and over. This is the crutch they all use, the reason they don't want to hire. Because the insurance benefits cost so much more money. If the government is willing to spend all this money, then surely they should be considering something like this, too. Say look, here's a guy that's forty-eight or he's fifty-five. Well, how much is the difference between insurance for a thirty-year-old and a fifty-five-year-old per month? Let the government pay it."

A great idea, I said. Really great. "Because a person fifty-five," Buddy said, "what's he going to do, Pat? Where's he going? What's he got to look forward to if no one will even consider talking to him? Except these straight-commission people who have nothing to lose and everything to gain."

Buddy mentioned reading in the paper that Arthur Burns had stated that anyone who wanted a job could be working today. "I guess his point was, and this would be a ridiculous example, if a doctor lost his job, then he could go out and dig ditches. I don't buy that in any way. For a man that high up to say this—it's cruel. I've been in the unemployment lines. I did it to register this week. And there were whites and blacks there and I didn't get the impression from any one of those people they were there to register just to get checks. Every one of them that I talked to wanted to work. What's he head of, the

Federal Reserve?" Yeah, I grunted. "And responsible, the son of a bitch, for a lot of the trouble you and I are having."

About politics, Buddy said it bothered him that so few men our age run for public office any more. "They didn't all get killed in World War II. What happened to them?" Nearly all the candidates were younger now, in their early to mid-thirties, Buddy said. As in business, the young were taking over. Still, there were a few older ones at the top, who have been in a long time. But God knows, I said, none of them were doing anything about what's happened to us. I asked him about public works. He said he wasn't saying he was above that, but he didn't really think it would help us. People with less education, maybe. Not us.

Then almost as an afterthought, Buddy brought up one more thing he was angry about. "I've been out of work five months in all now. I got profit sharing on retirement from my old company. I'm going to have to declare that as income. So as far as the government is concerned, that's just like my not losing my job. Now I've got to pay taxes —and steep taxes—on that as income. It's going to take away from what I need as a backup. I don't think that's right. I know that's not right." *I know. I know, Buddy.* We had filed our second quarterly return the month before. The two of them had just about eaten up that precious cushion I had thought the severance pay would be.

I asked Buddy if he thought the tax burden on us middle-income folks was unfair. Once more, I encountered balance, unwillingness to fly off the handle. Certainly it was ridiculous for millionaires to get by without paying any taxes at all. But: "Oh, everybody complains about the tax being taken out, how much it amounts to. But Pat, I've made good money—not a lot of money. I'm just like everybody else. You pay in proportion to what you make. I wish it was lower. But I don't expect any drastic change there. What concerns me is having to declare that retirement pay, and show it as income. It's going to take away from what I need for my family, for my kids." *Ever those concerns. Holding the family together. And anger at the specific injustice, if not the general one.*

When I was ready to leave, Buddy walked out to the car with me. He fell to talking again about all the old Boys High boys, recalling more names I couldn't remember and some I could. He had heard about the death of one of us. I told him I had heard that Danny Zoll had killed himself. Buddy said, "Good gosh, Danny was the king of the jellies." *Jelly* is a Southern term, partly derogatory, partly complimentary, connoting something like "a hell of a fellow," that was applied to those of us (Buddy and me included) who spent our high-school and college days going to dances, courting the girls, dressing foppishly, and raising hell. He recalled even more names, and I had the feeling that he just didn't want to walk back into his empty house, back to idleness and worry and frustration.

He had showed me a letter to the editor of the *Journal*. I had not seen it; I do not take the paper I used to work for. The letter was from "an unemployed father who last year grossed over $28,000." And part of it said: "When I get a letter from a prospective employer, I am elated and I run the 60 some feet from the mailbox to the house. Then I open the letter and I cry inside. You would not know the torment or the agony. I must not allow my feelings to be known to my children. They are a proud lot. I respect them deeply. The longest walk I have ever taken in my life is the 60 some feet from our house to our mailbox. It has become miles."

I thought of that as I watched Buddy walk back to his house, a lonely figure, sadness in his posture. I had told him about the thirtieth reunion that was to be held the next week. He had not received notice of it. That was because, he figured, he had dropped out to join the Navy and had gotten his diploma afterward by taking the GED tests. I told him the time and place and whom to call to get reservations, and he promised to be there.

During our talk, I had asked him about religion. "Oh yes," Buddy said. "I'm a Christian, and this has really held me together. A lot of people at the church, every Sunday they ask me, 'Have you got anything yet?' And you know, a lot of them must wonder, does he just not care? But I have a faith. And I certainly have said quite a few prayers, and pray every day. And that has sustained me."

Jesus Holy Christ. So when you get laid off from the job you've had many years, you get an even better one, and then two months later, get laid off again, you keep your sanity, your balance, your sense of humor, your humanity by resorting to religion. Religion—one more thing cheapened, watered down by this country. Yet Buddy had faith enough to hold to it, and it had the power to sustain him.

6

I went to that Boys High reunion and found it a disquieting experience, far different from the first one, which I had enjoyed thoroughly, only five years before. But one good thing: a guy who had played in the band brought a trumpet and he played the fight song as we sang it, several times during the evening. "On to victory . . . on to victory!" to the tune of "On Wisconsin."

"Boys High Forever!" we also shouted nostalgically that night. The school itself had been dead since shortly after our class graduated. When I went there, it had been one of only four white high schools in Altanta. The others were Girls High, Tech High, and Commercial High. Black high schools were similarly centralized back then. But when they decentralized high schools, set up the present system of neighborhood schools, they lost a strength we had (segregated though we were) of diversity, of knowing people from all kinds of economic and white ethnic backgrounds.

Part of the excitement and pleasure I had felt five years before at the first reunion was seeing so many different kinds of guys, how they had turned out. Most had done well, showed it in the quiet good taste of their suits, the carefree lines of their faces, their easygoing good humor. I looked forward to that again, the youthful feeling of being out on the town in a taxi (taking a cab because the last time I had left the car at the hotel, gone out drinking afterward with the old gang, and was dangerously driven home by one of the old gang, who was as drunk as the rest of us, at 4 a.m.). I overtipped the cab driver and went in full of great expectation, and the first person I saw in the lobby was

Mr. Aaron, our old math teacher, a great favorite on the faculty not just for tolerating our hell raising and hooliganism, but for downright appreciating it, and for his nasal-voiced attacks on the "progressive education" trends of the time: "We'll go out in the park and gather the pretty fall leaves and study the intricate patterns of the veins of the leaves, and that, young gentlemen, is how we will learn the mysteries and magic of geometry."

Good old Mr. Aaron! We greeted each other in the lobby and went down to where the bar was already going full blast, and I fell to greeting guys, surprised again at how familiar the faces looked and how the names eluded me—here a banker, there a doctor, now our federal judge, who insisted on buying me a drink, and I was having a fine old time, just like before. But then I was brought up short. Last time I had been the only one with a beard and there had been much good-natured kidding about it. This time I still seemed to be the only one, but in one encounter with a guy who had been a football star, the kidding was definitely not so good-natured. And something else, slowly, became apparent to me. Although they still wore good suits, the men no longer had carefree faces or seemed comfortable with themselves, full of easygoing good humor. It had, of course, been a crucial five years. That first reunion, we were all just entering our forties. I had found that time to be the best I had ever known. I had felt, then, comfortable with myself, that I finally knew my place in life. Now we were all nearing our fifties. Our time was getting on, and we were showing it.

But there was more to it than that. Jim Thrash got me aside. He had, it seemed, just moved from his television sales job in Atlanta to become manager of a small UHF tv station in Charlotte. "That's wonderful," I said. "Charlotte's a great town." Jim's face was solemn. He said he didn't know. The papers there weren't cooperative, wouldn't print things about their programs. And his kids were unhappy at being uprooted. I tried to tell him that you have to know people in such a town, that personal relationships with the newspapers are much more important in a place like that than in a bigger city. I gave him the names of some good friends I had there, including a couple on the papers. He seemed little hopeful, no more cheerful.

Old happy-go-lucky Jim. Light red, almost orange-colored hair. Red of face since adolescence. He wasn't in character. He started in, still solemn-faced, asking about my health. I said, "Okay, I reckon." He told me I ought to take better care of myself. He mentioned Danny

Zoll and said the reason he had killed himself was that he had something wrong with him that couldn't be cured. Lord. I didn't come for this kind of news. "Do you take exercise?" Jim persisted. No. Swim? No. Jog? Good Lord, no. Nor golf nor tennis. Finally I said, "Jim, I fuck. I do fuck." That did it. His beautiful grin and the thoughtful, appreciative chuckle he had got from his daddy. "You fuck." The chuckle. "That's good. You fuck."

A little later somebody told me of another suicide. Bobby Payne. Damn. At that first reunion, Bobby had gotten me aside and fussed at me about the condition of my front teeth. He was an oral surgeon. "You come let me fix those teeth," he said. "If money's the problem, I won't charge you anything. You just can't go around looking like that. A man in your position." Back then, money wasn't the main problem. It was my morbid fear of the pain of dentistry, of which I had known much in childhood when the brute of the dentist I went to used to put all the force of his heavy arm into pushing those damn slow-grinding drills into the nerves of my baby teeth. But Bobby's concern had made me aware of how really bad my teeth did look, and I worked up the courage to go to a guy who was supposed to be good with dentist-phobic people, and he fitted me out with a set of uppers that really do look great. I realized after I got them that I had quit smiling out of shame of showing the shards of my real teeth. What a pleasure it is, yet, to smile as wide and long as I feel like. Old Bobby. I had thought with gratitude many times of his saying what he did to me: "A man in your position." What position had gotten him to the act of self-destruction? And all these guys tonight—burdened with their positions in life.

When we sat down for dinner, I looked about and realized Buddy had not come after all. I thought about him as we got up to sing the fight song. The guy shrilled it out, off key, on his trumpet, and we shouted out those long-ago, familiar words:

> On to victory,
> On to victory,
> Fight right through that line!
> Boys High spirit,
> True and loyal,
> Touchdown sure this time.
> Keep fighting!
> Fighting ever,

Giving never,
Always be our rule.
Come on and fight team
For we are with you,
Boys High School!

I thought, as I threw myself into the singing, about how we have those words, those simplistic ideals, graven in our unconscious and are probably influenced by them all our lives. Not just us old Boys High boys, but all of my generation who sang such songs, believed the words, and then went out there and fought through all those lines of war and work and responsibility and care.

I looked around again for Buddy. Not out there. I had told him, when I urged him to come, that he might make some good job contacts. He said yeah in his slow voice. Yeah, he guessed most of the guys were officers of their companies by now. And then all the ones who were doctors. All those successful guys. How many others, like Buddy, were not here tonight because of sudden unsuccess? I could see Buddy walking the lonely way back to his house, and thought about what his life had become. Mailing out his résumés and going to those interviews. *Fight right through that line*, Buddy. *Keep fighting!*

The before-dinner booze was working on me, and memories of what each of the men had told me slid through my mind, as we sang the song again and again. Jim Buchan and Horace Smith and Jim Wood and Ed Lowell, hoping for, seeking those jobs just as diligently as Buddy . . . *keep fighting!* . . . and Jim and Ed and Buddy and John, each in his way *true and loyal* to belief . . . all those guys, *fighting ever!* . . . their hopes disappointed, beliefs betrayed, loyalty betrayed . . . but *giving never! Always be our rule! Come on and* . . . seeking the general welfare, holding the family together. *For we are with you* . . . and *fighting ever* against deterioration in work and life . . . *fight right through that line! On to victory* . . . Buddy every day circling those want ads, sending his résumé. On to victory, Buddy! On to victory, all of you middle-aged classmates of mine here tonight! On to victory! On to . . .

What? After the dinner each of us got up and spoke his memories and sentiments about Boys High, and told about himself. And I realized, as it went along, another reason the feeling, the faces of this reunion, were so different from the last one. Except for the doctors and dentists and some of the lawyers, just about every man there had something discouraging to report about his work, the economy. Most tried to toss it off with sardonic humor: "I'm in the care-taking and cover-over business, which used to be called real estate. . . ." "I'm still a stock and bonds salesman. When our firm talks, nobody listens. . . ."

It was depressing. Mr. Aaron got up and recited a lengthy, rambling history of his life, saying after an embarrassingly long time, "And now that brings us up to the Depression. . . ." That didn't help. Neither did the man, in the hard-hit contracting business, who was already word-slurring drunk and kept shouting abusive, bullying remarks at nearly everyone who got up to speak.

Afterward a bunch of us gathered in a bar at the hotel and continued to reminisce, catch up with one another. Someone mentioned a guy who wasn't there because he was a "controlled alcoholic." I wondered, sipping my drink, what that was. Then I was talking with another guy I had known since the fourth grade, an M.D. now, when a big man, football star at Boys High and then in college, loudly interrupted us, grabbing me by the shoulder, drunkenly saying he had something serious to talk about. That menacing grip made me mad and I jerked my shoulder loose, something I would not, in prudence, have done thirty years before. Turned out the fellow intended to run for governor and wanted to know if I'd be interested in writing speeches that would help him get the nigger vote. I said, "Call me up when you're sober." I wasn't angry any more. Just saddened. I didn't want to say to him that you don't go to white folks any more to get speeches to win the black vote. Mainly, though, I didn't want to say to him that you missed your chance, if you ever had one, to run for governor. You're too old to make it on your football reputation.

The evening kept souring. A rock combo had set up and was playing so loud we couldn't hear each other talk. How I hate to try to talk against overloud music—a familiar thing in places like this, in people's homes with the stereo blaring. Six of us agreed to go elsewhere and continue talking. We found a night club across the street, and it was quiet until the stripteaser came on, and even then we were able to talk under the music of her accompaniment. But watching her was a distraction. The M.D. was in our group, and he would gaze at her and repeat, "What a beautiful body," most clinically. I thought of how none of us tonight, even to this minute of watching a beautiful young woman dance naked before us, spoke the sexuality in us, the way we used to openly as teen-agers. *God, I'm horny* was the usual expression of it back then. Or: *Shit man, wouldn't you like to get a little of that?* At that first reunion, the old gang of us went to a bar afterward and one guy picked up a prostitute there, and left with her. A Catholic, he had long been married to his high-school sweetheart, and his act was the only statement (a profound one) that I encountered at either of the reunions about personal life. Suppose we had, each, gotten up and reported on our personal lives, how well or not they were going. Would the dinner have been any happier?

Thinking about it, with a hangover, the next day, I was struck by how little any of the men on my quest had talked of their personal lives. Fran had made his comments on the new morality, and others had mentioned worry about their children. But for the very most part, they did not spontaneously speak of their relationships with their wives, children, parents, the divorces so many of us have been through, their sex lives. That, I realized, was one more singular thing about our generation of men—the wall of privacy we built around ourselves. Without even thinking about it, I did not pry into the privacy, the reserve that was a strong part of the character and personality of each of the men, a characteristic built into our generation. I would not so embarrass them, offend their dignity.

When I was almost done with the interviews, a book came out by my old buddy Karl Fleming and his wife Anne Taylor Fleming. They had gone around asking interesting people to tell about their first time fucking, and this made a good and sensitive book. Maybe, I thought, I should have probed more into the private lives of the men I talked with. But I cringe yet at the thought of pushing such a question at any of them.

I knew from my own experience that part of the anger in them *had* to come from those personal, intimate things. But that is their business. Let this private anger lie smoldering under the public anger. Keep to reports on careers, work. One can assume common causes in the culture for whatever unhappiness and pain they have known in their private lives.

During the new freedom I had found to contemplate my own life, see through to truths about myself I had never had time to realize before, I had come to both painful and pleasant realizations about my relationships with my parents and my children, had come to my new appreciation of the home and to a closer feeling in Glenda's and my marriage, and in so doing understood things I hadn't before about my divorce.

And I had seen through to private truths about my sexuality, the unacknowledged attitudes I had been carrying around with me about sex. Our generation was one, maybe the last (I hope), that still suffered from Victorian conditioning about sex received from our parents, that crippling influence that lingered longer in the folk culture than one would have expected. Many of us have had to fight through guilts and inhibitions to freedom and joy in our sex lives, and even so are still blocked from the kind of natural sexual expression that is claimed as one of the goods of the new morality. I wish that I had known sexual play when I was the age for it, wish I could have as a teen-ager and young man indulged all those fantasies that thrilled my being and at the same time chilled me with guilt. And I look about me today with some wistfulness, and no little wonderment, at lovely women rigged out in youth's most lustful dream of what the well-dressed, high-class whore should wear, and at beautiful women in boots and leather and fur enough to melt the heart of the Count von Sacher-Masoch himself, and at nubile cuties dressed for all the world to see in short skirts and see-through blouses like the slave girls of my wildest dreams. I enjoy the sight of bouncing breasts and nipples showing through blouses and all of today's other healthy display of the beauty of women's bodies, and hold not to the biblical admonition against gazing thereon with lust, nor to the nonsense that this somehow degrades the person whom I admiringly behold. I have within me the makings of a dirty middle-aged man.

But I am glad not to have known sex as something separate from love in my mature years—just another good healthy form of exercise, as I had kidded to Jim Thrash. I told a friend who is unabashedly bisexual that I envied him his freedom to be that, but that inhibition —if no longer the fear of homosexuality—would prevent my being bisexual, let alone, as Fran said, acknowledging it to the world. And again, while I would have enjoyed group sex when I was a teen-ager and wish I could have, I have known so much of the fuller expression of sex as a part of the love of life together with my wife that I wouldn't enjoy it any other way. And, in having time to think through such things, I found at least this belief I had not lost—belief in the marriage vows. For me, if I can't keep them, I ought to end them. Maybe that's Victorianism still clutching me. But I feel it to be part of the good that was instilled in our generation, along with the evil.

There were two exceptions about speaking of personal matters. One of the first men I had talked with was Charles Weltner, the former

Congressman, for I thought his experience in politics and the fact that he now seems blocked from much of a political future would have instilled a lot of anger in him. If it had, he didn't speak much of it. What he said about not believing government programs can improve people's lives was interesting, and I was even more struck by his confession that he had not talked straight to his children. But about personal matters, his anger did come through, though he couched it in the third person and may have been speaking more out of his experience as a lawyer in divorce cases than about his own situation. Anyhow, he summed up common causes of despair among many middle-aged men.

I asked Charlie if he saw heavy financial responsibilities as one of the major pressures causing divorce among people our age. He said he did a lot of divorce work and: "There's no doubt in my mind that at some point in every sensate man's life he says, why am I doing this? He compares his youthful expectations with his middle-aged status and thinks do I want to do this for twenty more years, and he says hell no I don't. And that applies to everything. I think a lot of that is more vocational than domestic. I've used the term *selling widgets*. After you've sold widgets for twenty-five years, and are the best widget seller in the country, then the very thought of selling another widget is abhorrent. This causes a terrible questioning and is a shaking and shattering experience that goes through all your relationships, including family. Particularly if you are under heavy financial burdens. People tend to think of themselves as trapped in the position of producing large sums of money that get gobbled up by other people. They feel sorry for themselves. Of course, everybody has the same problem."

Providers, I thought at the time. Another abstraction. But the jobless men had given an insight here. Though we might feel sorry for ourselves and resent the heavy burden of providing, God, the anguish and terror we feel at the prospect of not being able to do it any more. I remembered those stabbing worries I had about alimony and child-support money, and about having to sell the house no matter what Glenda and I might be able to earn.

I also asked Charlie about my theory that husbands being away from home so much contributed a lot to divorce. He said he didn't know about that—though a lot of women did think all their men do is sit in air-conditioned offices and eat fancy lunches and talk on the phone. "Talking on the phone can be frantic when paying the bills depends on it." He said he had read enough about women's liberation to realize there is something important to it. Then he laughed and said, "This women's liberation has liberated a lot of husbands as well as wives—so far as the bonds of matrimony are concerned."

Then Charlie turned back to what he had been saying earlier. "Somehow our society is such that life for men ends at age twenty-five. By that time you're supposed to be educated and you're supposed to be married and you're supposed to be in your job. And we're all brought up to believe that things as they are at twenty-five are the way they're supposed to be for the rest of our lives. And that's just not right. A change in careers ought to be the expected, rather than the aberrant. So that when a guy has practiced law for twenty-five years and gotten to be pretty good at it, then he would do something else. Two or three careers in a man's lifetime. Because spending forty years doing the same kind of work is stultifying. It's burdensome and it tends to limit horizons to a very great degree."

He paused, then went on: "The American dream is to have a nice house and two nice cars and some nice children. When you get there, when you've got all those things, you find out they just aren't worth a damn. They're fine, but as far as being the significance of your life, they're vastly and woefully inadequate. And yet, when we get to that point, we don't know what to do. Nobody's ever told us, nobody's ever —you know, every man thinks his own experience is unique. Maybe we ought to have a male menopause anonymous society or something. Then when you"—he laughed—"feel like life has passed you by, you can find out everybody else feels that way too."

It was but another way of saying what the jobless men had said about disappointed expectations. They had done what they had been assured would make them successes, and now they were out of work. Charlie was talking about doing what was expected in work and private matters, and succeeding, and still not being happy. One of the unemployed men I talked with spoke of other ways the expectations held out to us in our youth have not been met.

It was after I had shut the tape recorder off and we were just sitting and chatting. I asked him if he would mind my taping what he had started in telling me, and he said, "No, go ahead. I think it's very important." When he was done talking about these things, I told him I didn't see any use using his name, that his parents and children and others might be needlessly hurt by what he had said. The short story of his life that he had given me and the predicament of his unemployment were not so greatly different from the others I had heard that I felt the need to write them. But what he said about his private life, I felt, if not typical of most of our generation, at least touched on most of the sore points.

He began by telling me there were two things that bothered him the most—his parents and his children. The generation before and the generation after. "We're in the middle and have gotten a raw deal from both ends." He said putting it into words was tough because "you don't get to talk out your angers every day—you just sort of let 'em stew inside you."

He had been taught to honor his father and mother, and he had believed in that. He said he accepted that and all the other things his parents had taught him because not only were they telling him these things, but so were the cop on the corner and the barber who cut his hair and the guy at the filling station as well. They all said the same thing and you accepted it. "But today, the kids are getting one thing from their parents, another from their teacher, another from their Sunday School teacher." That had mixed them up, he thought. "But you might say, our generation was well programmed." A lot of good came of that, but some harm too.

Our parents had been through the Depression, were conservative. "They kicked us out of the nest at a very early age. But we, as parents, have carried our children with us in the nest for a long, long time, and it looks like we will the rest of our lives." Which, again, is not all bad. But we were cut short and now we had to provide a standard of living for our children that was as good or better than our own. "It just doesn't seem fair."

The pendulum has swung all the way, he went on. "Our parents dominated us in every area of our lives and now, damn it, our children come along and they're dominating us, too. There hasn't been any period for *us*. We've never really had a time at bat. When's it going to become my turn to be the chief?"

He said he and a lot of his friends even today are still subject to the wishes and whims of their parents, still called on for their time. "Why didn't you come to see me yesterday? And when you came the day before, why did you stay only two hours? You know you were in too big a hurry to go." But he sees his children at their mutual convenience. "They don't live their lives for us. But our parents want us to live ours for them, conform to their standards."

No matter what you do, I said, you're a villain. "Right. You're a bad guy. I visit a little while or a long while, I don't seem to get any credit for it."

I asked him if he shared my feeling of not having been able to get across my real values, my true self to my children. He said oh yes. He encouraged his children to look at all sides of things. "I felt from experience and my parents' and my grandparents' training, that some of the truths that I believed in were solid and right and would be helpful to them. I don't think I got it across. Maybe because of the conflicting views they get." *And we so need to get those good things across.*

Here again, he said, we were caught in the middle. We accepted our parents' views, didn't challenge them. As we got older, we saw that some of those views should be challenged and did so, but only within ourselves—because to do so openly would be to no avail. "But at the same time, we did give our children and the younger generation an opportunity to accept or reject our views. And it seems like the younger generation today a lot of times has taken the opposite view just to hurt and kick at our generation." That was true, I thought. But had we tried hard enough?

He said he thought we were the last generation that has followed in Father's footsteps—and Mother's. It had all been lined out for us. If it was good enough for Father and Grandfather and Great-Grandfather, it was good enough for us. But it's not good enough for our kids. If our children live by what we believe, it will be out of choice, he said. And again, that's not all to the bad.

But we're caught in the middle, he said. "My parents say, why do you let your children do so-and-so. I say, hell I don't have any choice."

He said he was still mainly just confused by it all. I mentioned the new morality and said, "I just can't help but be human and think Goddamn, I would have liked to have been able to sleep around when I was Patrick's age." He said you were wild then even to think about something like that. The most you could hope for was furtive, fearful trips to prostitutes, or the occasional, rare thing of finding a "bad girl," a gang bang. I remember, I said. He said he saw the openness and freedom the young have today as a good thing we were blocked from having by our parents. And those parents still expect us to conform to their standards in our middle age, are quick to criticize what we do on moral or political or any other grounds.

Again, in the middle. "Take profanity. Our kids hear it in the movies, everywhere, think nothing of using it. We never heard it from our parents and they better not have caught us letting them hear it from us, and still better not."

He thought about being in the middle of the old and the young some more and said, "You know all that. If you can just get it said—I haven't done it well. But if you can get that said, it's important. It's true." I told him I didn't see how it could be said any better.

He talked about women. "My grandfather and father put women on a pedestal. Maybe that's a beautiful place for them, but it's unrealistic. My mother was placed on a pedestal and she's still up there. İt makes it difficult to please her, to keep her happy. But it also makes it difficult for us to relate to today's women who want to be treated as equal. Our generation's women, we have to look after them and do everything for 'em, and this is fine. But the middle-aged man, we're getting pulled by our parents and our kids, we're getting pulled by our work, we're getting pulled by these independent women and by our womenfolk at home, to where it's getting to be an almost unrealistic pressure from every angle."

Then he spoke of the effect on women our age of the same parental influences that had shaped and in some ways mishaped us as men. They were taught by their mothers that sex was for having babies, not for enjoyment. We didn't have the closeness and intimacy in marriage at middle age that young folks have in their marriages or livings-together. He had been through a divorce. He spoke of sex during his marriage as something he had had to do something special to earn. But these younger women he was dating now, oh man—they had such healthier, happier feelings, expressions of sex.

He talked about the trauma of divorce. There are times when two people can no longer live together. Yet for our generation and those older than us, it's almost impossible to end it because of the emotional pressure from parents and friends. "And the court. The judges themselves. You go to the lawyers and you've been held in a marriage longer than you should have been because of these emotional pressures, and it is just an extremely difficult thing to go through. You go to a divorce lawyer and he says it's an antagonistic legal situation and therefore you must come as an antagonist. 'You must fight your mate. She will fight you.' Everybody loses, including the children."

Here was one more evil our children and future generations seem to have escaped, he said. Divorces for younger people were easier to get. Settlements were fairer. States were passing more just divorce laws.

He spoke of another blessing our children have. "The generation after us has a more realistic approach to love and marriage. The men treat the women as individuals, and the women treat the men as individuals. This is healthy. Our generation, the wife is to be looked after and protected at all costs. The man is not supposed to cry or get hurt or have any feelings. It's just not realistic for the woman not to share in the husband's work problems and the husband not to share in the woman's problems in the home and with the children. It's wrong."

How right he was. Yet I knew from my first marriage, as he did, how hard it is for either husband or wife to break out of the arrangements society has shaped and become fully functioning partners in a marriage. From the husband's end of it, I got from his words an insight I had missed through all my own experience and my attempts to understand and adjust to the women's movement. Women complain that they are treated in marriage as sex objects. Well, hell. We men are treated as objects, too. Mostly as providing objects. It was the first glimpse, strange and startling, I had caught of the other side of the women's liberation coin.

I shared the insight with the man I was talking with, and he nodded emphatically. "The marriage," he said, "should be a partnership and each should support the other, help the other." The words were wistful. He was describing what Glenda and I were lucky enough to have found our way to. I hoped he would find that too, along with the job he so desperately needed.

That hung-over day after the reunion, I wondered how many of the guys who were there had feelings and wistful hopes like his, how many other middle-aged men he spoke for. When we were giving those reports after the dinner, an accountant whom I remembered as a frail and picked-on kid, ended his little speech by saying that he remembered hitchhiking to school and spending his carfare on sweet cakes in the cafeteria because every day Phil Upchurch would steal his lunch, and we all laughed about that. Then he said simply, "I'd give anything in the world to be back there now, be back doing that all over again."

It was, I felt, a commentary on things beyond economic conditions, and I wondered how much of the malaise of the reunion was, too. Yet in all of it, I felt closer this time to my classmates, felt a bond with them I had not felt before, and again, that sense of admiration for their inner qualities, the decency and dignity nearly all showed, their will to keep going. Fighting ever, giving never. I had enjoyed the first reunion more but felt no real rapport with the men there, no identification with them as I felt so strongly this time. Much of my feeling grew out of the quest I was still caught single-mindedly in. We do have so much in common, we middle-aged men, the good and bad experiences, the background and history we share. And the values we hold.

The feeling of kinship and friendship and admiration had built in me talking with the men with jobs just as strongly as it had with those without them. The men with jobs might question and roil and they certainly did see through to basic inanities and insanities of this country. But they, too, had held, somehow, to the good things that had been instilled in all of us, simple virtues of the fight songs, but more complex ones, too. They do not whine. And they do not shirk their duties. They hold to a balance in even the most bitter things they have to say. And they are not defeated by what has been dealt them so far.

Some of that went through my mind as I sat there that night at the reunion dinner. On to victory. . . . The irony and goodness of the words rang through my mind like that shrilling, off-key trumpet as we sang them once more at the end of the evening. Things livened up when Joe Kelly got up and went through a tour de force of reminiscence, describing what theoretically every single one of us was doing (characteristic acts, then and now) on the day of the annual football game with the arch-rival Tech High School during our senior year.

Old Joe, all decked out in a gleaming white leisure suit, his face under snow-white hair no different from when we had played marbles together in grade school, full of his old pep, his almost spluttering intensity of speech, his humor intact and his love for what we had been back there thirty years ago so unabashedly expressed. I went up to him afterward and tried to tell him how splendid I thought his performance had been and how great his presence.

We talked a little and he asked what was I writing. I told him the title of the book and he said, "Golly. That's it, isn't it? Angry. I may look so happy. I put up that front. I laugh and I smile. But inside I'm boiling. All the time."

7

Seeing the marks of middle age on all those men I went to school with heightened my awareness of my own middle-agedness. I continued the quest, aware more than ever of how much we all have in common. I continued to be fascinated with those echoes I kept hearing in what the different men told me, echoes of one another and of my own feeling and thinking. Those themes had developed, and variations on them of belief and the lack of it, the evil of bigness and the virtue of smallness, the deterioration of business and the quality of life, joblessness, of course, and its attendant horrors (to which Charlie Weltner added the thing about joylessness in jobs), and the different awarenesses the different ones of us had of the different ways we had been made abstractions. When I talked with George Harris, he sounded all the echoes and, in confronting his own poignantly disappointed dream, described an action he might take about it as drastic in its way as John Somerville's retreat to Canada.

George had been with the Southern Regional Council three years. I had liked him from the first minute I met him because when he came down from Princeton for a job interview, he went around to various of us there and interviewed us about what kind of place the Council was to work for. And he brought his wife, Daisy, with him to meet us and see whether she wanted to be associated with the people of such a place. George and I became good friends; there was a bond between us from the beginning. We would on occasion go out for lunch and egg each other on to have more martinis and get grandly drunk and end up at one or the other's house talking, wild and exuberant. For a time, we had evenings together, good and pleasant times of two couples with much in common. But we lived far apart, they in a black middle-class neighborhood, we in our white mixed-class one. And invariably we would drink too much during those evenings and we or they would have to risk the danger of arrest or death driving the long distance home. In one more way, the city thwarts your life, keeps you apart from people you enjoy. In Timpson, Texas, we could have walked home. But, of course, in Timpson, we could not have had social evenings with a black couple.

The bond between us has remained strong. About a year before my spring of disaster, George went through one of those times of trouble coming in bunches, enough to destroy a lesser man. His son, Butch, riding his bike with twelve-year-old abandon down the driveway and into the street, was hit by a car. George rushed him to the emergency clinic of Emory University Hospital, went through a hell of anxiety to learn finally that the damage done was no worse than a broken leg. Relieved, he went home and was cheered by the greeting of his sheepdog, Yaboo, with all the loving joy those creatures have for you after only the shortest of separations. George and Daisy had fallen in love with our Annie the first time they saw her and had gone right out and bought Yaboo as a small puppy. Now he was almost grown, a joy and a beauty, worshipped by Butch and his little sister, Christa. George went on in the house that day and a little while later, his neighbor was at the door lamenting, "George. They've killed your Yaboo." In his distraction, George had left the gate open. The car that hit Yaboo didn't even slow down. And then the dreaded phone call came that night that his mother in Alabama had suffered a heart attack.

When he told me about all this the next week in his little office at the Council, where poetry about the brotherhood of mankind was tacked on the wall, his voice was flat, and when he finished speaking, he just looked at me with dulled despair in his eyes. What do you say? To be thankful Butchy wasn't killed, that your mother is recovering. Not when somebody had known a Yaboo and seen him broken and destroyed, his blood in the street. I reached my hand to George and gripped his and didn't say anything.

When we talked, George was scheduled to be laid off at the end of six months when a grant supporting his research on economic development was to terminate. In his case, black had fared little better than white. But his concern was not about his job except for a strong feeling of wanting to do something more effective. The anger that he spoke ranged over all the themes I had found and over, too, the events of his life.

George was born in Cleveland, Ohio, in 1934. His family moved to Wickwith, Ohio, and then to Wayne, and from there to Huntsville, Alabama. During his three years there as a teen-ager, 1960 to 1963, he became deeply involved in the local civil-rights movement. Then the family moved to Saginaw, Michigan, and there George worked at factory jobs before going into the Army to serve two years, part of it in Germany. He was married and divorced during this period. When he got out, he enrolled at Alabama A & M College near Huntsville, received his B.A. there, and then an M.A. from the Atlanta University School of Social Work. He did settlement-house work in Columbus, Ohio, for two years before entering Princeton under a special Ph.D. program. He was still working on his dissertation while serving on the Council staff. He and Daisy were married in Columbus.

We talked together in the office he has in their fashionable ranch-style house in the East Lake section of the city. Modern art, mementos of the civil-rights movement, including a poster about Dr. King's "I Have a Dream" speech, are on the walls. George sits comfortably across from me, a familiar stocky figure, his very black thrust-to-life face lit with humor and eagerness and intelligence.

He talked about growing up in Cleveland during the Depression. His parents both worked and rode the street car. They would buy one commuter's pass because they didn't have enough money for two. So every morning George's older brother would go with their father to see him aboard the street car. The father would get on in front, show the conductor his pass, then go to the rear of the car and throw the pass out to his son. He would then run like hell all the way home to give it to their mother so she could use it on the next car "to get to work in them kitchens."

Beginning with such a memory, George said, "I've been trying to understand, Pat, for forty Goddamned years, what does it mean to be here. What does it mean in terms of what you did with your mother and father and what they did with each other and what they did with you? What does it mean to be a Christian? What does it mean to be male? What does it mean to be a high-school student? What does a career mean?"

It was important to understand, he said. Why was it his brother was so full of hate for the memories of his childhood, like that about the commuter pass? George didn't feel that. "My consideration has been:

let's try to understand it. It ain't enough to simply hate it. You can burn yourself out so damn fast. I tried that." He laughed. "I've been that route. It simply eats away everything that would resemble what it means to be a man. And I mean a *man*, capital M. What I want to be is Man. What I want to be is a human being. You try to understand so you can protect what your humanity is all about. That doesn't mean that I love. But I don't think it means that I hate."

He wanted to be Man, a human being, and so he said, "I have to understand some of these things that say I can't be that." Like what? I asked. "Like—well, let's take the obvious one. Let's talk about being black. It's complex—to try to be Man if you're black. To express, to articulate, to give, to want to give, and America says back to you, 'But you're black.' I wanted to understand that. I really wanted to. I mean in terms of what my past has been experientially. It's not some abstract kind of thing."

Black, of course, is the ultimate dehumanizing abstraction as it has been applied by whites through history, a terrible one added to all the others for middle-aged men like George. I said as much to him and he said oh yes. Then I told him my theory of how we are all, black and white, abstracted in other ways almost out of our identities. George picked up on that. He spoke of the abstraction of being American, the abstraction of a job. "What purpose do these abstractions serve? They are something else I had to understand for the sake of my humanity. They are essentially devices to regulate the way people behave. That's how I understand it, and I intend to act out of that understanding down the road, where I'm going to be coming from for the balance of this thing."

He said for all the progress in civil rights in the past ten years toward breaking whites and blacks out of behavior patterns regulated by the abstraction of blackness, he thought it would take at least another ten years before most whites and blacks would be able to relate to each other as people. He said that women are saying what any group opposing any abstraction of themselves is saying: that the purpose of the abstractions is constraint.

Our old civil-rights concern for integration was, in a way, based on misunderstanding, George went on. "Black folks were already integrated. They bought all the abstractions of the society." He spoke of the token nigger out front in businesses, of black capitalism. Blacks are told, "Yes, there is room for you in this society to participate but you will participate like we say. You will buy our abstractions of how you make a contribution." This has already made a decided difference in the black community, he said. There were now very clear class distinctions that weren't there ten years ago. He lamented the abstraction of middle-classness.

Blacks are integrated, he said, to the extent that they buy the abstractions. "Who defines what is a good son, a good daughter, a good citizen, a good GI, a good, a good, a good. Where are the sons of bitches who put this shit together, defined all these concepts and then organized the world so that if you do not respond according to what is defined as good, then something is the matter with you?"

Understanding constraints made it possible for him to fight back now, George said. So many people never knew how to fight back. "Or they have beat back against this constraining world in desperate, halting, and sometimes horrifying kinds of ways. For me, during the next forty years, I want to fight back effectively against these abstractions in my own life and everybody's life I know."

George said it had taken him a hell of a long time to come to these understandings. He spoke of the work he had done, the jobs he had held. When he was in high school, he worked at things like cleaning concrete off the floors at housing construction sites, washing dishes at a hotel, minor jobs. When work got serious for him was when he took a factory job in Saginaw, running a double-mat molding machine on the assembly line. He did that for two years. "You know, standing out there on that double-mat molding machine, black sand pouring down on you, breathing dust all the time—just heavy, steamy kind of work." He figured he was bright enough to do something better than that, and when a job testing molten metal became open, he applied for it, sure that he was qualified. "I asked for the job and within ten days I was laid off." It was a job that had been reserved for whites. George told me what he had learned from that experience. He spent a lot of time hanging around union halls, seeking redress, and in the process came to understand unions. None was as strong as he thought it ought to be. He got no real help from them. *One more malfunctioning institution.*

Of his next job, with the U.S. Postal Service, George said, "It was the most stultifying work imaginable. Sorting letter by letter in a case. It had all the benefits of federal employment. But that's a job you can die in."

Then in the Army he came to understand what this whole military business was about. He could have been a very good soldier, he said.

They wanted him to go to Officers' Candidate School, be a career officer. But when he asked himself, what is a soldier? he knew it was something he didn't want to be. "That was an abstraction I wasn't going to buy."

He told of the time his sergeant, a white from Tennessee, was drinking one day and approached him to talk about race. "The way he announced that he wanted to talk about it was, 'What do niggers think? What the hell are niggers all about? Why are you all always raising hell? How come you can't accept things?' " George said he thinks, now, that the man was sincere. "But that's in retrospect. My first reaction was to knock the shit out of him, and that's what I did." That got him three months in the guard house.

But he learned from that, too. There were so many dummies in the Army, he reflected, who had bought so many sickening abstractions about what it is to be a soldier, "what it meant to defend your country." George said maybe his experience of the Army was so sour because it was a peacetime Army. "Maybe that's what was wrong. Soldiers buying an abstraction and no place to practice it." He laughed. "So we're caught up in that kind of shit." It was something to think about. We've got a lot of guys caught up in that kind of shit now.

George didn't buy the abstraction, but he got his honorable discharge, and several commendations. The important thing, though, was that rejecting the Army OCS made him realize he needed to get back into school. He was on fire to do that.

Talking about work, George said, wouldn't be complete without telling about hustling jobs. Twice a month he would drive from Saginaw to Detroit, park his car, go to a movie, drive back, deliver a little package that had been put in his car, and collect three hundred dollars for his trouble. He ran numbers for a while, and that's how he learned about the streets. "As a matter of fact, some of the most significant support I got for going back to school even before I went into the service came from people, quote, in the life. They're out there hustling, hustling hard. They're pros. These were black folks. And they saw some stuff in me and would say, 'This ain't what you need to be doing. Go to school, George. Go to school.' Some of them would say, 'Even if you want to hustle, go to school. Go to school and get the paper.' What they were saying was that even if you want to hustle later, you do it with the protection of an abstraction that is accepted in this country: you're a college graduate. If you're a schoolteacher, something the white community respects, it gets the heat off your back. So there was a kind of cynicism in the advice. But it was a very good, pragmatic cynicism."

The street people helped him understand selfhood in other ways. In this country, you have *got* to make money. The street people felt blocked from making it legitimately, so they did what the country demands in illegitimate ways. And the country sure as hell does demand that you make money. "The name of the game in this society is money," George said. "If you don't have money, you don't eat. You don't—anything." *Echoing John Somerville. Like a Greek chorus, these truisms repeated over and over until their terrible meanings come home.*

So all that was part of the experience of learning: "What went down in forty years." Then George exclaimed, "Women! We ain't said nothing about women. We got to talk about what you learn about women in those first forty years. And children. What do you learn about that you ought to be sensitive to? Sure, you learn to be concerned and supportive and considerate and all that sort of stuff when it comes to kids. But what do you learn about women? You use women. You use them. Your world and all the rest of the world says you use them. Black world, white world, Chicano world, you use the women. That's what they are for. Where anywhere in the world that relationships between people are organized is there respect for a person that is female? The church? There ain't no respect for women in no church. I mean for women as *people*, with all the aspirations they have. And they are half of the people in the world. On top of that, *they* buy it. Or if they don't agree with it, none has organized responses that are coherent enough to make a nickel's worth of difference. I mean in terms of changing the way in which they're treated, the ways respect is shown and not shown." *Right on, brother. You've been there, were part of organizing responses that were coherent enough to make far more than a nickel's worth of difference in the way blacks are treated. Black women were part of that, too. Maybe that is why so few of them buy the women's liberation movement.* We grinned in male chauvinist understanding at each other.

George went on. "People generally treat children as people should be treated. But once the female children pass puberty, it's all over for them. Now that's an abstraction. These are the abstractions, Pat, that I'll be working the next forty years to undermine, to destroy, to uproot, to demythologize. Destroy. So people can be loosed. So I can be loosed to express all that is within me, before it's all over for me."

137

There it was. George had had a direct stake in the civil-rights movement, improvement of his own lot. I had a smaller one, the chance to do my job right. But so many whites who were in it didn't have even that. I came to realize after I was in it for a while another kind of stake I had, which George brought back to me—that I couldn't really be free as long as blacks were not. The whites who didn't know that, who were being altruistic, giving of themselves for other people, did a lot of harm, both to themselves and to the people they wanted to help. That's why blacks finally threw all whites out of the militant part of the movement when it was falling apart, with so much bitterness ensuing. If you're going to try to help people, let it be in your own self-interest, I thought. But how are you going to help anybody if your own self-interest is ignored and denied by the very society and government you seek to push to help somebody else?

George had me going. He went on some more about abstractions. How did he free his family from them? "Values I disapprove of, disagree with, and fundamentally reject, come into my home. It gets to be a matter of how much money do I make compared with so-and-so. It gets to mean, well, you know the kid down the street, for every A on his report card, his parents give him a dollar. They ride in, such values. The 'what's in it for me?' attitude. It's business. And sharing, cooperation, and concern don't take place. So I fight against that, argue against it with my own children. I want to see them become live human beings and not on their way to the same sort of death that I had to deal with. Otherwise we will kill our kids in the most systematic way, using all those abstractions. I don't want any part of that." *The echoes. I should have done what George is doing. How important it was becoming in my mind, this need to tell the young what we know.*

What it all comes down to, George went on, is that the abstractions are not really abstractions. "They become real, live ways of behaving, and in the process, Manness, our humanity, is what we sacrifice. I must be about getting out of that. And I will be—until I'm dead. For my wife, for my kids, for me, I know what I must do, anticipating opposition all the way."

And the basic hook, George said, was the way we make our livings, all of us in America. "The way in which we have organized the wherewithal by which people live—I mean in the fundamentals of food and shelter and clothing—is the ultimate erroneous abstraction. It is fundamentally wrong. I'm opposed to it and its implications." *I was, too, I realized, always had been, since those days of shuddering to pass a slum.* George said he wasn't sure how to combat that, though, what the appropriate opposing political-economic system might be.

"But I know the mixed economy that I have lived in and the two-party political system have not delivered for me," George said. "And they haven't delivered for masses of people who look like me." Or me, I said. "Yes, and masses of people who are shades in between. They don't deliver in support of Manness. They don't do that for anybody." George said the only hope he could see was that people might become more aware of just how much their humanity is robbed by the way the country is run now, and then go to work to change that. "That's the stream of thinking, feeling, being that I have joined. And you have joined. And numbers of other people have joined." I was not quite sure I had joined. But God knows I was aware of the terrible effect of the way things are ordered now on the humanity of our people.

I wanted to believe something could be done. Belief. Disbelief. I asked George when he realized two-party politics wasn't working. That came within the past ten years. "I really began to understand the extent to which the meaning of politics is the art of who gets. It's not a matter of seriously regulating. It's not a matter of protecting the general welfare." *How often these men got down to that basic, terrible fact, the Greek chorus effect of it.* George listed as stepping stones to his disillusionment his awareness of multinational corporations and what our foreign policy had been doing. And, of course, Vietnam. "The Vietnam years were phenomenal exposés of the extent to which our party politics, domestically and particularly in international affairs, are paranoid politics." The paranoia, the fear, he said. Goldwater threatening in '64 to use nuclear weaponry on the Vietnamese. "It's very clear what we are capable of. It is power and wealth and status gone crazy. And we lived all those years with daily reports of the viciousness our national government was capable of. That along with Bull Connors, those same years."

He told of working in sixteen rural communities in six Southern states and of asking the public officials in each, what is the difference between your party and the opposition party? "And the answers were, none. Very little. Or: we are more conservative." Discoveries like that and the one about our foreign policy had led him to the judgment that "we have a political system that is philosophically defunct. It represents nothing. Both parties are equally pragmatic."

And all the while the quality of life was declining. I asked George about the universal plaint of all the men I had talked with, about medical care. I knew Daisy had had whiplash and other problems from an automobile wreck, and expected to hear criticism about the care she got and the cost. But George hit upon an aspect none of the rest of us had. If you can pay the freight, George said, you get too much care. It's overcare. Because of their medical insurance, Daisy had gotten the very best of care. "But, of course, if you don't have the dough, you don't get the care." Overcare or no care, I thought. It ought to be evened out. George said he wasn't really terrified at the prospect of not having medical insurance. Part of that was an awareness that his middle-classness would help him get care some way, hustling relationships, if necessary, with medical people he knew. But he could understand people who would say, "I need medical protection. And if there was no money, and my son or daughter needed medical attention, I would be prepared to bring a physician to my home at gun point."

And he was aware that a real medical disaster could wipe him out. "We're the kind of middle-class folk who live on the brink of destitution. All of these trappings here are ephemeral." This was the first home he had ever owned; he had only recently learned the joys of home ownership. He spoke of the dread that the hot-water heater would conk out. Or the furnace. Or of having to get a new roof. "Home ownership is just another one of those huge abstractions that go along with what it means to be middle class. You want all this stuff —fine. But in exchange for it, you give up a hell of a lot."

Inflation was already tearing at such middle-class people, destroying their investments, their bank accounts that are so important to them. *Taking their things away.* "What will they do when it costs them $1.25 a gallon to get from their comfortable homes to the office? We don't have mass transit." *Only John, happy I hope, up there in Toronto.* George spoke of the middle-class obsession with keeping up with the Joneses. "What else is there for them to do?" he asked. "There's nowhere they can go for support, for encouragement of their humanity. And so they are forced to debase themselves trying to find satisfaction in showing off their literary tastes, clothing tastes, their automobiles, their houses, the status of their jobs, their very children."

And, George said, these things are like drugs for people. "How much crap will middle-class people take before they begin to reject these hooks. The ultimate irony for me is to see George Corley Wallace running for President in 1976 on a platform of what needs to be done for the middle class. How much crap will middle-class people take? Shooting all that materialistic dope into their systems. They are addicted to abstractions that kill. It's almost as though they are bound and determined to overdose. If they buy Wallace (and they do buy the son of a bitch even if he doesn't get elected), they are sure to overdose."

"America is the best-informed society there has ever been," George mused. "So much information available on so many subjects—yet none of it supports our humanity." *It's not in there–the human element.* "Is it the fault of the writers?" George asked. *Is it? What of the fashions we follow? I hadn't thought of that. Not one profession is perfect, not one.*

In an abrupt switch of the conversation, George spoke a strange echo of what I had thought about animals, our realization that we love ours more than we do many people we know. George spoke of people whose human associations were constantly fraught with risk or exposure, disappointment, or disgust. So they developed a relationship with an animal. He said he had seen this particularly with young single women, "brutalized to no end, already," selling themselves, their personalities, every day as a commodity. Up against the threat: if you won't, baby, somebody else will. So such people dump all their frustrations, their feelings of rejection, all their disappointment, on pets—"that cat, that dog, that animal which can't respond, can't talk back. It's always going to be there. It's dependent." He said it was bizarre, the extent to which relationships between people and animals had replaced relationships between people, that our values were skewed when people spent more for pet food than the government spent to feed hungry people. "So have the abstractions separated us from one another. It's frightening."

I asked him what specifically he planned to do next, what work?

"I want to find a rural county that is at least forty percent black, maybe more. And I want to go to work in that county essentially to help the people take control of all the governmental levers of power, and guarantee subsequently that the public resources that flow from the federal government down and through tax sources up get harnessed in that county in behalf of the people who live there. And I want to be teaching people in the process all that I have come to understand—about our humanity and what the abstractions do to it."

His work, George said, would be to make another kind of abstraction real, the one that holds a government responsible for the general welfare of all the people. He said he hoped to attract others who felt as he did and go into a county and organize the people to take over the governments. Using that as an example, he hoped to do similar work in adjacent counties, 'try to spread good government as far as possible, eventually reaching to the state government. "I want to do that in a Southern state."

Would he seek office himself? I asked. No, he said. His plan was to set up a community agency, like a social settlement house, and from it organize local people, "the leadership already there," to take over their governments. And he would have as a base a university where he could work with students, getting them to contribute their time and skills to organizing the local leaders and people. "What I'm talking about doing is making available the kind of assistance that guarantees that local leadership is both effective and continuous in terms of solving the kinds of problems that exist in those rural areas."

I wanted to believe it could be done. If anybody could do it, I thought, it's George Harris. But I had serious doubts about his hope of getting university support for such a project. I asked him if, out of his experience with institutions of the movement, including the Council, he had any real confidence in such an institution as a university.

"No," he said. "It's not a matter of having confidence in them." But he said he was sure he could find a way to be effective through one. "They are amazingly open places. They are far more flexible than people think. A university is really a marvelous kind of place in which to work. The problem that I see with universities is that they have no way of transferring the atmosphere, the attitudes, the potential they have to the outside world. They're very, very frightened people. They're being good. They've bought the abstractions."

But, George said, he believed he could pull it off. Most importantly, "there are enough students who want something very different and you can find a way to work with them." He talked of imparting to such young people the distinction between tactical compromise and compromise of principle: that it's a fact of life that you have to make tactical compromises, but you don't have to compromise on principle. So many echoes in all that George had said. And this one excited me most of all—his determination to impart to others what his half a lifetime had taught him, his awareness that what he had to say was valuable, had to be passed on. The educators, in that fear of theirs George had mentioned, did the young as great a disservice as they did the country when they capitulated before the campus revolts, swallowed the evil along with the good of what the students were proclaiming, gave them the dangerous and damaging delusion that they were absolutely right about everything. And we middle-aged men, people like Charlie and me, who did not tell our own children all that we should have, had done the young and the nation a disservice, too, by not imparting whatever knowledge and wisdom we had from half a lifetime of experience.

In its essence, George said, his work would be an effort to help the people of the counties and the students working with them to express "their Man-ness, capital M." That's what all his seeking of understanding of his life and his inner self had led him to.

It was a grandiose scheme, a drastic attack on hopelessness, comparable with John's retreat. But what interested me most was how it echoed what all the others had said about the loss of human qualities in our national life. As it turned out, George was offered another job at the Council and chose to stay on, but on his own terms of independence. And he did not give up on his scheme. It was something he could turn to, if only in his mind, as an antidote not just against the things that were wrong with the country, but also against the hopelessness within himself and the lure of middle-classness. Meanwhile, he tried to make his Council work effective and to instill humanism into the Council.

"I think I'm whole enough now, complete enough to make a contribution despite the opposition—not because of it," George said. "I'm really ready to go to work." That's beautiful, I said. I was, I realized, trying to find my way toward that same point, toward belief that my effort might matter and that the kind of effort George described to help people improve their lot, improve themselves, could work. "It must be a good feeling," I said to George.

"It is a good feeling. A tremendous feeling." We smiled at each other.

George's analysis of deterioration was perhaps the most poignant of all—the loss of the good of community, the disappointment among blacks that after the struggle up to middle-class existence, middle-classness was not what it was held out to be. But it had been one of the jobless mobile home men in Americus who told, unaware, the story at its starkest. And in so doing, he recapitulated all the other men said of the ordeal of joblessness, made it more real by the undramatic bluntness of his way of speaking, his understatement.

Berle McGunegle. Mac, he is called. He had been purchasing

agent at his plant. A big guy, a little portly, shock of gray hair, prominent nose, chin upthrust, Scotch kind of face to match his name. He was born in Marlette, Michigan, in 1917, went to high school there, then to Albion College and Ferris State Institute. After graduating, he entered his father's grain business. He served in the Army in Japan in 1945 and 1946.

After his father died, he and his brother ran the grain elevator as a partnership. And then: "The economy, the cost of operation got so outlandish. You had to be either big or get out." They got out in the early 1960s and he went to work for the mobile home company in Marlette. He worked his way from the production line to corporate payroll officer to inventory controller at a plant in Lewistown, Pennsylvania. He was there six years and was then promoted to the purchasing agent job in Americus. He and his first wife had one son, now grown. His first wife was killed in an automobile accident in Pennsylvania, and he had married a middle-aged Americus woman.

Mac told me this now familiar-sounding life history in the lovely den of their suburban, ranch-type home, where a glass wall looked out on a spacious, landscaped back yard. "And that's about it," he said. "Then about a year ago, well, September 13, 1974—Friday the thirteenth—I was called into the general manager's office and told they were cutting overhead and were absolutely cutting out the purchasing agent's job." The general manager would assume those duties, which had been reduced because the plant had already cut back on production. Mac had been job hunting ever since.

"I find"—he started right in—"at my age it's just a little tough to convince somebody that you ought to join their group and hospitalization policies, up the rate a little. You don't realize what those fringe benefits are until you don't have 'em. When you step outside of a group and try to pick up major medical hospitalization, you better have a job. I don't have major medical. It's just minimum hospitalization. The retirement pension that I took, it didn't amount to much. I couldn't live a year on it. If my wife hadn't had some long-term investments bringing in income, we'd be down on the food-stamp line."

Her income also made it possible for him to invest his pension. "And we were lucky. We were out of debt when all this happened. I feel sorry for some of the boys who were in up to their ears when they got it." He had been receiving unemployment compensation, seventy dollars a week, with eleven or twelve more weeks to go on the extension. "You can't—no one can live on seventy dollars, I don't care who you are, unless you got a garden and live completely off it. If you're going to fool around with a garden, you don't have time to look for work, or work if you do find a job."

He had obviously considered such a possibility. (You consider all kinds of things.) He sat there serious-faced, and I asked him, as I did the others, what he felt when it happened. "Did you panic, Mac, like I did? Were you angry?"

"I felt some anger, yes. I'd been with the company for twelve years and we'd had some rough times before. We'd had some problems that I'd helped smooth out for the company. Loyalty. It's a damn shame when the employee is the only one that's got to show any loyalty. They expect that, right up to the hilt. But when it goes the other way —oh, they couldn't care less."

They didn't offer Mac a demotion or transfer or reduced pay as they had officers at some of their other plants. "They didn't figure seniority or anything else." On the weekend after he was laid off, Mac talked to the vice-president in charge of the headquarters purchasing office. He was the one who had promoted Mac to the jobs in Pennsylvania and Americus. He had just gotten out of the hospital and had not even heard about the layoff. "He said, 'My God, what kind of security have any of us got?' And he is a vice-president of the corporation." They had previously sent another vice-president down, just before the layoff, added him to the payroll. Mac figured that was part of why they had to cut overhead.

Now, a year later, they had closed the plant, had shipped all the materials to other plants, but not the machinery. The vice-president and the general manager were the only ones left working there. And the division engineer, who was serving as night watchman. He had been offered a transfer, but said he was an old Americus boy and didn't want to move. "He's a good boy," Mac said. "He deserves better than the night-watch job."

Mac said he could see nothing ahead for himself in the mobile home business in Americus. If things should pick up again, the other plants would rehire the people they had laid off, not someone new like him. So he was studying for the state real-estate examination with the thought of putting together real estate and insurance in one of the local brokerages. He had tried insurance by itself several months before. "I tried it," Mac said. "But I'm not—I'm not that pushy. I'm not knocking the insurance game at all. But you've got to be a certain breed of cat to go into somebody's house—when you really can't see how they can afford to buy what you're trying to sell 'em. They need it. Everybody needs insurance. But you can be insurance poor."

It was strictly commission work, and just too expensive starting out. Pouring good money after bad, Mac said. Travel expenses. They had said it would mean maybe one night away from home every week or so. But as it ended up, he was scheduled to be out three or four nights a week.

I had asked Mac why the mobile home business went to hell. He said at first that he thought his company had problems because its products were top quality and high priced, and people couldn't afford them because of hard times. But the makers of cheapies and match boxes started failing, too. Conventional house sales were also down. "So people just aren't buying houses. They're remodeling what they've got, fixing it up, instead of going into a new one." Or buying down, I suggested from my knowledge of Glenda's experience in the business. Mac sighed. "I don't know how this real estate is going to work. But I'm going to give it a whirl anyway. I'll have to work with someone a while, three years I think it is. And they are moving some houses here. One realtor said definitely to come see him when I get my license. When I pass the test."

The test. God. I hadn't even thought about that. When Glenda took it, out of two thousand trying, only two hundred passed. Dear God. Don't let him suffer that kind of defeat. (I had to call Mac later to check some detail on the tape that I couldn't make out and when I asked him how things were going, he said, "Oh fine. But not much doing yet." He had failed the test by .7 percent, he said. Only 12 percent taking it passed. Point-seven, he said, irony mixed with anger in his voice. He had taken it a second time and was waiting to learn how he had done. His voice was as hearty as ever.)

Mac said he would move if he got a good enough job offer somewhere else. But it would have to be worth it. "This is a pretty nice home," he said. And he wouldn't move to Atlanta or any other big city; he was not a city type. Then he offered me some information. He had read about a "forty-plus" employment agency in Atlanta that specialized in getting jobs for people our age. I put it down for future reference should things come to that, and as a possible place to learn more about unemployed middle-aged men. But I was never able to track it down, find any sign of its existence. Mac said he thought it was in Atlanta. It must have been somewhere else.

146

Mac said it was for "older boys, folks like you and me." They were placing people. Some had to take jobs in differerent lines. Some had bettered themselves. It sounded good: jobs being found for engineers, salesmen, architects, and the like, "that have gotten turned out to pasture, you might say, but still got a lot of good years left, and a lot of sense left." The bond of joblessness: Mac spoke with such pleasure about those jobs being found for middle-aged men.

And now he spoke of his blessings. (How we grasp whatever good we can put into the equations of hope and despair. And how much compassion we learn to feel for those less fortunate than we are.) "I'm not disabled in any way. I'm still able to work." But then to the other side of the equation: "I can amuse myself a lot by getting out here in the yard. But that can only go so long. It's beginning to get on my nerves. A year is a long while. I find myself not sleeping. Waking up worrying about little things. Things that don't matter. Wake up, wide awake, and some dern thing, foolish thing, hits you in the head. You don't know the reason for it. Yeah. It's nerve-racking. It's rough." How well I knew those foolish little worries, along with the big ones.

Mac spoke of a big one—the economy. "I don't know when this thing is going to turn around. I didn't think it would last this long. I don't know what the government can do outside of subsidizing or just putting more out the unemployment payment window than they are now, as far as you and I are concerned. But if they're going to give us more, they've got to give everybody more. And eventually you and I are going to have to pay it back. *If* we ever get working again." He chuckled. "It's got to come out of somebody's pocket."

He had heard that the government was trying to work something out to give older people more security than they have now under private pension plans. "A lot of this, I think it's big business, industry trying to get people my age off the pension plan, off the payroll. Of course, if they can't afford the payroll, they're not going to keep a man on. Just because he's a good fellow." *But they should, Mac, they should. Being a good fellow, like you are, has value. It's one more asset they're throwing away. Something's wrong when they can throw away so many assets, the qualities and skills, and yes, the goodness, of a human being.*

I couldn't say that to him. It would just embarrass us both. Instead: "Some kind of federal program, like WPA, to provide jobs makes sense to me, Mac. Man wants to work, he ought to have a chance to."

"Yeah. That's right. But there again—on the WPA or CCC, like

147

they used to have, you and I can't go out there and work with a pick and shovel like we could when we were twenty-five. You could do it, but I don't think you'd last long."

"I sho' don't want to."

"I don't think your health would let you do it. But there's administrative jobs in that, even, that older people could handle, ones who can't go out and do the physical bull work. There's got to be a certain amount of paper work, a certain amount of supervision. And experience is necessary in that supervisory deal."

We let the dream of something like that shimmer for a little while. Then Mac said one of his worries was what his joblessness was doing to his Social Security. He had been paying into it since it started. Suppose he didn't get a job until he was sixty-two. Would his Social Security be based on the last three years he worked, or on years he didn't? That was one I hadn't even thought of. We agreed we needed to find out.

"What bothers me," Mac said, "and makes me worry is that Social Security isn't going to be enough to live on. Then you gotta go to Welfare, you gotta go to an agency of some sort and ask for help, if it gets to that point. I don't want to go and ask for help." *Hell, no. None of us do. We've done for ourselves all our lives, had jobs when we were kids, paper routes, delivery jobs, and done for our families, and all we want is just to keep on doing, keep on working. And suddenly someone says we can't.* I asked Mac if he had had any of that illogical feeling I had that somehow it was my fault. That when you are told you can no longer work at your job, somehow it's your fault.

"Oh yeah. I think you can look back and find mistakes that you made that you could hang on yourself."

"But with me," I said, "it was more irrational. Like—I don't have a job; therefore I don't deserve a job."

"Naw," said Mac. "I think I deserve a job. But you got to find somebody's to *give* you a job. Who thinks you deserve it, too." We laughed. "You got to have a meeting of minds somewhere."

"It's a contract," I said, thinking of Mr. Cole.

"Unless you go in business for yourself," Mac said. "But that's expensive. You got to have an investment. And at our age, how much money do you want to put out there in a private business, in free enterprise? And shuffle the papers and do all the book work and paper work that has to be done in any business. I think small business, the overhead would eat it up today, clerical overhead. Nothing else."

148

I asked him if he had shared any of my feeling of joy at being out of the rat race, free of regimentation. "Well—the regimentation never bothered me. It's not bad. I say it still boils down to loyalty and security." He spoke of the founder of his company, and told me that after he retired, "the loyalty seemed to bounce out the window." *Over and over, that echo.*

We sat there in the McGunegles' lovely home, and chatted some more, talked of lighter things. Mac spoke with pride about his son, a mining engineer in northern Michigan, in the copper industry, who was ambitious and was working on mining safety. He spoke with pride, too, of his only grandchild, his son's two-year-old daughter. Mrs. McGunegle had been with us during most of the conversation, was there now, and talked a little of Americus, her love for the town. She had spoken earlier only once, in response to something Mac had said. "There is no stigma," she said soothingly, "to being unemployed these days."

Mac mentioned again that he wasn't a city type, had grown up in agricultural surroundings. His father didn't farm, but they had a small farm when he was a boy. He loved it. It had long since been sold off and subdivided. As a matter of fact, Mac said, the main plant of the firm that had laid him off was located where the farm used to be.

He seemed unaware of the irony of that. Goddamn, I thought. The grain business done in by bigness. The plant, the very business that had been so disloyal to Mac, was now located on his father's farm. That's the whole story right there. Quality of life done in. Bigness triumphant. And Mac the victim of it all.

Here in this fine home with the sun sparkling through the pine trees in the back yard, Mac should have been able to enjoy the comfort, the serenity. He should have been able to reap the good things of his time and status in life that he had earned. He shouldn't be waking up stark in the night, worrying about things that don't really matter, and spending his days studying for the real-estate exam, hoping he could get into a business he wasn't even sure of, that wasn't really what he wanted, nor what he had done before and done so well. Mac deserves better than that, I thought; and I see him yet as the personification of the jobless men, and his story a symbol of all that has gone wrong with our country in our lifetime, his and mine.

Deterioration. Each man had expressed it in different ways—Horace, so sad missing the quality of life on the farm, Jim Wood and

John Somerville dismayed about the deterioration of their professions, Jim Buchan and Buddy Stone disgusted about current business practices, Ed disillusioned about all the institutions he believes in, Fran Kent about manners and morals, George about the loss of community. And now Mac's symbolic story. As things got bigger, they got worse. These men wanted to return to some kind of human dimension.

I knew that Joe Kelly had, in his way, tried to do that. He had quit the automobile business a while back, and bought an old grist mill and sold corn meal and flour. He had told me that night at the reunion that underneath, he was angry all the time, boiling. What about? Surely he had found tranquility running his own small operation. I pictured talking with him beside the mill pond, idyllic and serene. It wasn't that way. The other men had spoken of all the different ways of deterioration. Joe was to tell me how those terrible things happened.

The mill, it turned out, was not on a pond, but square in the middle of the small town of Austell. Austell is not thirty miles from Atlanta, but looks like a hundred years ago. The mill was powered by electricity; it had been moved from the pond years ago because the pond kept flooding. But the wooden building, more than a hundred years old, was rustically beautiful. Joe showed me all through it, obviously proud of it, loving it, pointing out the huge millstones that he used to grind the corn.

Then he told me that he had to sell the business. This was the last day the mill's office would function. They had quit grinding corn some time before. Damn. The two middle-aged women in the office looked sad. They were very busy and Joe was, too; he had to stop periodically to sign papers they were working on, go over details of forms they had filled out. He and I had been close friends in grade school and junior high. I could picture him back then—his short pants always seemed to droop, his pug-nosed face was ever earnest. When he was in grade school, he had a prodigious *Liberty* magazine clientele, sold hundreds of copies a week.

Joe was born in Greenwood, South Carolina, in 1927. His family moved to Atlanta when he was in the third grade. He finished high school in Atlanta, and went into the peacetime Army in 1946 after a year at Georgia Tech. He went to OCS and commanded one thousand black troops and eleven white ones on Guam. "It was an interesting part of life," he recalled, "but not one I particularly enjoyed." His engineer unit built roads and buildings and water systems all over the island. Joe returned to Tech when he got out and finished there in 1950. He had played first-string football at Boys High and his first year at Tech. But he didn't play those last three years of college because he had been married in 1945 and had to work to support his wife and baby while going to school.

Joe played halfback, and he is not much larger than my own five-foot-six or so. He used to leave his bike at my house while attending Boys High football practice, and I can remember him many an evening, after having worked out until after dark, staggering up to the porch groggy and dazed from the rough training Coach Shorty Doyal used to put his players through. Seeing him like that had confirmed me in my decision not to go out for sports. But I was to know later in the Army the same kind of physical exhaustion, and I thought, as Joe and I talked, of one of those good stories we never did get to publish in *Southern Voices*, about how learning as a young man that you have the strength to keep on when everything in your body says you don't is a valuable thing to carry through life. Ours, I realized, is the last American generation of men to have been put to that test. And that is an important thing about us, I thought, as Joe went on telling me about his life up to now.

He and his wife were divorced in 1970. They have two sons and a daughter, all grown now. When Joe got out of Tech, he joined the Chrysler-Plymouth dealership established by his father, S. Walter Kelly, in Marietta, an old county seat town that is now a suburb of Atlanta. His brother, Walter, was also in the firm and still runs it. Joe's father died recently. Joe showed me photographs of the ceremonies when they dedicated a football stadium at Marietta Tech to his father. "And he didn't give any money to it, the way it usually is," Joe said. "That's how much people around there thought of him."

The dealership was a real good business when he started in 1950, Joe said. But then in a few years the car business became "volume minded—wilder and wilder." Joe said that even though he loved his father and loved working with him, he felt he ought to get into something else. I had bought the car I started my first marriage and my career in from Joe; it had been one of his first sales. The car was a used 1949 Ford, a good one, and the service I got from Kelly Motor Company had been first-rate. I asked Joe to elaborate on what went sour.

He said that when he started out, the car business was a real solid business. "You sold cars and you provided service. But then, as the factories became, as I say, volume-minded, their interest seemed to be only in turning out millions and millions of cars. They had little interest in whether the customer was really taken care of or not. They wanted you to stay open nights and Sundays. I, of course, didn't mind the pressure, but I did feel that since we owned the dealership, we should have a voice in what was done. Competition was severe and the volume concept was to sell a car at any cost, regardless of ethics." None of the three of them agreed with this and resisted it, as the firm has continued to.

Joe had heard that Perkerson's Mill was for sale and contracted to buy it on October 1, 1962, after twelve years with the dealership. As we sat there in the modern office Joe had put in the old mill building, he told me what had happened to him in the mill business.

He said he figured after surviving in the dealership those twelve years, he could take care of any kind of business. "I didn't know a thing about a corn mill, had never been in one when I bought it." He learned the business from the bottom up, working for three months for the sons of the founder of the mill, who were then in their eighties. They signed it over to him on January 1, 1963. That was the same year I quit the paper for reasons similar to Joe's. We had not kept up with each other; I was struck by the parallel.

Joe showed me a picture of himself standing, happy and proud, by the mill machinery on the day he became owner. He had learned all about the business by then, and about the history of the mill. It was founded in 1851 by Jack Perkerson on Sweetwater Creek in Austell. It was burned by Sherman in 1865 and rebuilt right away by its customers, so essential was it to their lives. Perkerson and then his sons continued to make corn meal and grind flour and wheat for farmers of the area through the years. They began packaging corn meal and selling it to grocery stores around Atlanta in the 1930s and became the strongest supplier in the area.

Until agriculture began to decline in the 1930s, the mill would run all day and all night at harvest time. People would bring corn and wheat in horse-drawn wagons and wait in line for their grain to be ground. "The mill was the center of the community, so to speak," Joe said. "While people waited their turn, they would fish and talk politics. Every once in a while, on a Saturday, somebody would strike up a banjo and they'd have a little music." It was a pleasant scene he evoked, and as long gone as those memories Horace had of the farm.

When Joe took over from the elderly Perkersons, the business had sort of been coasting along. Joe started building it back. "I loved the business, the distribution and manufacturing. It was all so new to me. I really got a lot out of it." He expanded distribution in the Atlanta area and introduced more efficient packaging. But he was selling something the demand for which over the years had been going down. "Our grandmothers would buy twenty-five-pound bags of corn meal. Corn meal was a big staple into the 1930s, corn bread an important part of our diet. Our mothers would buy ten-pound bags. When I took over the mill, we were selling more five-pound bags than anything else. Today, the two-pound bag is the biggest seller." People in Atlanta just don't eat as much corn bread as they used to. "Weight-conscious America" was part of the problem. So was the influx of people from other parts of the country who were not corn bread eaters. The cost of delivery had gone up even during the relatively short time Joe had been in the business. The company he sold out to was a large one. They could deliver other products along with the meal.

The obvious solution in such a business situation would have been to enlarge the market. Joe had expanded it in Georgia. But: "My plant's a hundred and twenty years old. It looks it. And the government does not allow anything to cross state lines that's not manufactured in a place with concrete or ceramic tile floors. Everything has to be spotless. Now the corn meal that we produced is a hundred percent pure. But in an old building like this, you can certainly find some germs down in the cracks." But there's no health problem with your product? I asked. "None whatsoever," said Joe.

"The law is ridiculous. Either what you sell is pure or it isn't. If it's not pure, they ought not let you sell it anywhere. But since it is pure, I don't see why I couldn't sell it in Alabama. We could have expanded into Tennessee and Florida and Alabama. Alabama's big corn-bread–eating country still. There're not many stone-grinding corn mills such as ours left in the South. If I could have expanded into those states, people would have been tickled to get my product. I get letters every week from all over the country wanting me to send 'em our stone-ground meal. We did use the millstones. It was ground like it was a hundred years ago, and that does impart a certain texture and taste that you cannot get with the commercial corn meals that they grind on steel grinders today."

The company Joe sold out to uses the Perkerson Mill name on the bags, but puts steel-ground meal into them. So that's how it happens

—down, down, down, the quality of existence, the very taste of corn bread taken out of our mouths. "You can get corn meal," Joe said. "But you cannot get whole-kernel, stone-ground corn meal any more. It has the nutrition in it. It tastes better. It's better for you. Now, it is perishable. It won't last indefinitely. A lot of the commercially ground ones are so highly processed they'll never deteriorate. But think what that does to your insides." He laughed. "The corn oil is ground up into our product naturally. It gives a unique flavor that you just don't get in the so-called city-ground corn meal. The country style, on the millstones, tastes better. There is a difference."

Those millstones weigh two tons and they had to be cleaned of their coating of meal every two weeks because otherwise they would require greater pressure, which would mean greater heat, and that would scorch the meal and destroy its delicate, natural flavor. I thought of the article Redding S. Sugg Jr. had done for *Southern Voices*, "A Treatise upon Corn Bread," in which he extolled the virtues of Southern cooking as comparable with Chinese and French cuisine, and used the range of our corn breads, from the lowly pone to the subtly exquisite spoon bread, to make his point. And he had said that you had to have stone-ground corn meal for the corn bread to taste right. I told Joe about this, promised to send him a copy, and he was excited about it. I asked him if he had tried selling his meal to health food stores. "What about all the talk among the kids about getting back to natural foods?"

"That's all it is—talk," said Joe from his experience with such markets. And then he told me more about other barriers he had encountered in his futile effort to keep a small business and a tradition of quality alive. "The government forms and the amount of paper work are just about the death of most little businesses. The little businesses just cannot support enough administrative help to keep up with all the forms." Exactly what Mac had surmised, contemplating setting up a small business! "My forms have to be just as correct as General Motors' or Chrysler's or General Mills'. And yet I'm just a little fellow delivering corn meal, and if we sell a bag for twenty or thirty cents, we have to deliver it all the way across Atlanta. It takes a lot of bags to pay for a secretary's time. The forms, to a large measure, do no one any good that I can see. It really is a vexation. I'm really bitter about 'em. They don't do any good and there are more and more and more of 'em." Most carry a penalty if you don't comply. Joe showed me a state form he had just signed. It certified that the mill had collected zero sales taxes during the previous month. He had quit selling corn meal months before, but was still required to fill out the sales tax form every month. "It's ridiculous."

Joe said he was busy enough just running a little business. He was the one who worked overtime if the machinery broke down. He didn't have time for all those forms. And he didn't make enough profit to hire people to keep up with them. "The little businessman puts himself into the business and wants to make a reasonable living. We provide the jobs. We're collecting the taxes and we're paying the taxes. We're providing a service. And while I don't think any one group ought to be favored over another, I just don't think they ought to expect me to operate like General Foods or Chrysler or IBM or what have you. I just can't do it. There's just one of me."

Joe's talk about small and big business struck a chord deep within me that I didn't know was there. It made me, later, understand why I respond so strongly to Johnny Cash's song about Cisco Phillips' filling station. Cisco'd give anybody anything they needed, lend them anything he had, "his tools or tires, bumper jacks or wires." And there was always a friendly checker game. Cisco Phillips' filling station was done in by the same processes Joe was talking about; the expressway passed it by, the big cars on high-test gas sped past it, the big chains got all the business.

I thought of the nightmare grocery shopping had become, and of all the unhappiness the other men I talked with had expressed about their experiences buying things. I thought of all the independent shops there used to be when I was a boy, and how much better the service and the quality and the dealings with the people in them had been than these things are now in all the chain stores that have replaced them. And I thought how many of the unemployed men traced the deterioration of their business to when the company had been sold to a bigger one, or merged into a bigger one. That was when loyalty to the employee went out the window and standards downhill.

"It just isn't right," Joe said, "for the big businesses to get bigger and the little businesses to be closed out. The big business is not as interested in the customer and the employees as the little guy. They're not as close to 'em." Then he said, "There's more. You want to hear about that?"

"Aw yeah," I said. I was hearing something I had never heard before in all the years I've looked slightly down my nose at businessmen. Joe proceeded to tell me the final thing that had forced him to sell the mill. The OSHA did it, he said, the Occupational Safety and Health Act, passed only two or three years ago, not one of the risks to consider when he had bought the mill. "Now, our mill's been here since 1851 and the only person that's ever been endangered in it was General Sherman when he burned it, and none of the mill hands could catch him. We've never had any serious accidents, never had a death, not a broken arm, not any kind of injury at all. And yet my plant under no stretch of the imagination could pass the OSHA test. It's very severe. And it requires a lot of paper work, too. They can fine you. They can close you down. They have almost unlimited power over you. I never was inspected, but I lived in fear of it. Had they come in, I would have had no choice but to close."

It would have meant building a new plant at a cost of two or three hundred thousand dollars, and Joe just couldn't do that. So the threat of being closed down that way was what had finally tipped the scales to the decision to sell this business that he loved. And he had employees who had been with the mill thirty-five years, who could tell the government agents that nobody had ever been hurt. If he'd had enough money to build a new plant, he wouldn't have had to work in the first place, Joe said, could have gone to Florida and played golf the rest of his life. We laughed.

"So we're really caught in a bind. It's terrible to think you've worked hard all your life and some guy can walk in and say the handrails on your stairway aren't the correct number of inches up off the floor, and close you up. And the rules are arbitrary; they really don't help the employee."

In this instance, I said, they cost your hands their livelihood. "They sure did," Joe said ruefully. "I feel the government should work with us instead of making us their enemy." And small business was the most harassed, he said. "Take IRS. You try your best to obey all the rules. But the tax laws are complex. If they audit you, they're bound to find something. Again, if they just wanted to be sure all taxes were paid, they could work with you, not against you. They don't offer you any guidance. But they sure do fine you if they find something that you've unintentionally done wrong."

Why can't they simplify it for small businesses so you don't make mistakes? Joe demanded. You don't want to make mistakes. It can get your business in a hole. He told about hiring people for day labor, to cut grass around the plant, unload a boxcar of corn, schoolboys mostly. He paid them with checks, kept records of it. He thought he wasn't required to withhold Social Security. He had tried to keep up with the rules but didn't know about this one. Nor did his auditor. But, of course, he was required to withhold it. They estimated how much such money he had dispersed that way over three years and made him pay his share and the employees' share of the Social Security, plus interest and a penalty. Joe thought it was fair enough for them to correct the error he had made, but terribly unjust of them to penalize him for it. "If I were a General Motors and had a legal department of tax experts, they could say I should have known about it," Joe said.

Of course, he could have avoided the whole thing by paying those folks in cash. Here again, integrity was a handicap. I asked Joe if this was generally true in small business. He said he had a strong belief that dishonest small businessmen were forced out by their customers, their competition, and their own peers. And I thought how untrue that is of big business, how exempt from any kind of human control it is. ITT tearing up Chile, imposing on it totalitarianism replete with torture chambers. Pollution. Dehumanized workers.

I asked Joe my question about whether he saw any hope for political remedy of the kinds of problems he had described. He said, "I had thought at one time—you know that idealism we had as boys—that the good guys win out. I'm not sure of that now." He said he shared the feeling nearly all of us had expressed that we who are supposed to be powerful are entirely without power. "No voice, whatsoever. We are paying more taxes and we seem to get the worst end of the bargain. It is ironic. We do contribute a lot to all parts of society—the family, community, the nation. And yet we're just left out. The rich don't seem to pay a proportionate share of the taxes. The poor—a fellow here in the plant, he's got all these children, so he doesn't pay any taxes. I support him. I support the unemployment rolls. I provide jobs. And yet my business is like a guillotine. It hangs over me and it can cut my head off any day."

Damn, I thought. We're caught in the middle, Joe said. It's not right. It's gotta be corrected. But, I said, is there any way of forcing politicians to correct it? "I have hoped," Joe said, "throughout the last ten or fifteen years that there would be a revival of statesmanship in government. I have lost this hope now. I will not say it's impossible. But it doesn't seem about to happen.

"The solution, as I see it personally, is for our senators, along with our President, to stand up and be counted, to do what's right for the whole country, and not just favor this certain group or that one. No group should have so much control of our leaders as some of them appear to now. The politicians appear to be interested only in getting elected or reelected, and once they get in there, they lose sight of the everyday guy.

"Things should be changed. They can be changed. But I must say I don't see any immediate hope of that. And long-range hope doesn't seem to be much better."

That was that. "I'm tired," Joe said after a pause. "I work night and day. I don't see any letup. I only see it as getting worse. I've always worked for myself. I love it. The long hours I know are part of it. And I don't want anyone feeling sorry for me, the fact that I have to work late at night and have all these problems. But I also would like to be able to take a vacation and go off in the evenings without feeling guilty that I'm neglecting the work or am going to overlook some government form." Then: "But I love it. It's my life. The business that I run is really a reflection of my personality, of my youth and my training from my parents and from my school—it reflects my entire life. I want the customer to be treated fairly. I want to work with my people fairly and help them to a better life if I can. Sometimes I get tired. Sometimes I get discouraged. But I want to stay in it. I just hope I can. If it gets any tougher, I may have to go to work for somebody else somewhere."

I hoped to God that would never happen. Joe said his immediate situation was that he had three businesses going—a hardware store, a dry animal-feed plant and a liquid animal-feed plant. No one of the three would provide a living, but there was a chance all of them together would.

Then Joe said maybe he was too much involved in their operation, that in a way it was a form of escape for him to immerse himself in his work. Both his sons were working with him. That was a pleasure for him, but also a challenge. "They feel like they're pretty much in charge, not so much because they're my sons, but because they feel their generation is so much sharper than our generation." He wasn't competing—but he still felt ultimately responsible for them and his other employees. He started his day about six and worked until ten or eleven at night—with occasional breaks at the driving range or on the tennis court. He worked those hours six days a week, and usually worked Sunday afternoon and into the night. Good Lord, I said. He explained that on nights and weekends, he was free from the distractions of phone calls and employees' interruptions.

Most people in business for themselves have to put in such extra hours, Joe continued. It's a way to get all the things done you don't have the money to hire people to do. He said again the government should do something to help people in little businesses. "We are meeting a need that big business will not meet. We're interested in our employees. We're interested in their families. This takes time—to talk with them, visit them, counsel them or whatever. You make a profit, but you make jobs, too, and you make life better for the people who work with you."

He had introduced me to one of his workers at the mill, a lean, lanky mountaineer with humorous beady eyes. When Joe first took over, he found that this man was indispensable because he was the only hand who could make the antique sacking machinery work. When Joe installed newer machinery, he told the fellow he could no longer expect him to get him out of jail on Mondays after a weekend drunk, because now there were others who could handle the sacking. So straightaway, the man gained such mastery over the new machinery that he was again indispensable.

Joe worried a lot about his business, the jobs of his employees, his own welfare. "Do you wake up in the night worrying?" I asked, thinking of the unemployed men.

"Sometimes I don't go to sleep." He mentioned an associate, his own age, whom he had talked into leaving his teaching and coaching career to come into the business. Now that man was faced with the possibility that the business would fail and he would have to start all over again. I commented that that would be hard to do at his age. "Yes," Joe said. "About all there is left for him to turn to is those bigger businesses that have gobbled the little ones." And they won't hire him. "No, they won't," Joe said. "They're definitely after the younger people." *The echoes. The echoes.*

"It's a waste of human resources," I said. "A waste of the best resource they might have."

Despite all of it, the gobbling and the injustice and the way the government treated him, Joe said he still believed in the free enterprise system. From all that he had told me, I wasn't sure whether believing in it or not made any difference. Old Horace had described so eloquently the human damage done by bigness driving farmers from the land. But that process had begun almost as soon as the country did, though it didn't reach the South until the years just before and after World War II. But the thing Joe had stressed, that bigness was taking over and that mindless government regulations were making this process inevitable, with a lot of human damage (taking the taste out of my corn bread, the chance of a livelihood from his associate, and possibly from Joe, too), all that had happened to the country in the years since Joe and I had been working. I thought of how proud he had been selling me that secondhand Ford and how proud I had been driving off in it to cover the first stories of my newspaper career. The car business had gone crazy so soon after, "wilder and wilder," and the newspaper business had been going downhill before I got into it. (The paper I worked for had been combined with its opposition by a Northern-based chain while I was still in college.) Neither one of us had been able to carry out our dreams and ambitions in the dozen years each of us had put in on our first jobs, and we were both struggling against the odds to do it now. And what those dreams and ambitions amounted to was simply to do our work the way it should be done for the satisfaction of it and for what it could mean to other people, could mean for the healthy functioning of a society that had shaped those sane dreams and ambitions in us in the first place. Both of us had to retreat from the main directions of the society to do what we wanted to do. At least now, from talking with Joe, I understood a little better where and how those main directions had gone wrong.

Belief. "The free enterprise and capitalistic system works," Joe said, "if it's given an opportunity to. I firmly believe that. But it is not being permitted to do so now."

Belief and the lack of it. Each man struggled with that. It mattered so much to them. I wasn't sure any more, now near the end of my quest, what I believed and what I didn't, and worse, whether it mattered. Joe Kelly, prosperous looking, happy looking at the reunion, was as sorely beset as any of the jobless men, feeling just as helpless, powerless. To be an average middle-aged man in this country at this time is to be baffled and frustrated, no matter what your effort has been, no matter how much of a success or failure you are. And angry. The anger abided, certainly in me, though now in a quieter, more rational way. So much of the anger, whether at corporate disloyalty or at a government not responsive to the general welfare, came out of all those disappointed hopes, things we had spent half a lifetime believing in, only to find they were no longer true, if they ever had been. Total cynicism and despair, was, perhaps, the appropriate reaction. Yet none of the men I talked with, least of all the jobless, and not even John, had come to that. We still wanted our lives to mean something.

8

I had a good while back made an appointment with Manuel Maloof, knowing him to be a man of long enduring, broadly ranging anger. When I set out to talk with him, I thought about how he had put me on to Jim Buchan early in my quest. And when I picked up my notebook to go to his tavern, I saw that I had filled up all the right-hand pages and would be making notes about Manuel on the first left-hand page, the back of the page on which I had long ago scribbled: Harold Chapman. Then three phone numbers, scratched out. Then an address with a question mark by it.

I had come a long way and somehow, I felt deep within me, a full circle. The quest was almost over. I had reached out to the other men and learned much from them, gained much insight into the causes and effects of my own calamity. Now it was time to face my own reality again, including the inner one. I still had those questionings about belief. And Manuel was, in addition to being angry, a man of vehement belief and, unlike any others I had talked with, actively engaged in trying to change things for the better. I would ask him all about belief and acting on it.

Besides, Manuel is a great guy and his tavern is a great institution. It occupies all of a short block on North Highland Avenue, and until DeKalb County finally went wet recently, it had been the nearest place to Emory University to get beer. I used to go there when I was a student, before Manuel owned it. Emory students and professors still frequent the place, as do guys like Jim Buchan, middle-class men, and there is always a sprinkling of working-class men, too. Newspapermen, writers, not just in Atlanta but around the South, know Manuel and drop by the tavern for a beer and good talk. (Like Cisco Houston's filling station, it's always there, a little island of sanity and civilization.) It is one of the few genuine neighborhood bars in the South, and something more than that. With Manuel presiding and encouraging people to talk, it is an ongoing forum among the different kinds of people who come there.

I went in it on the day of our appointment and sat at the bar waiting while Manuel drew beers and chatted with the customers, watching him, short and heavyset, almost square, moving about behind his bar. It is big and ornate and used to be in Manuel's father's saloon. Hung on the wall behind it and pasted on the mirror are many of Manuel's trophies and treasures, including the big portrait of John Kennedy and the faded photograph of Roosevelt. The good noise of people talking filled the barroom with its row of booths and the adjoining, rambling old room with its tables. No raucous blaring of the ugly noise that so much of modern music has become. No electronic beeping and bonging of pinball machines.

Manuel has set these aside, out of earshot, in a special game room. Glenda and I, eating lunch out together occasionally at neighborhood places, had become addicted to pinball. I had said more than once that the machines are a near-perfect metaphor for how life ought to be. Most of what happens to your ball is entirely due to chance. But you do have some control; you can hit the ball with the flippers, keep it from going out of play, send it back to bounce around by chance some more. And your skill with the flippers decides whether or not you win free games. That's the way life should be, the way they told us, training us to go out to work, it would be. But my own experience and the testimony of other men showed that is just not so.

Manuel took me into his office, a big, pie-shaped room, to talk, and we sat at the big pie-shaped table built specially for it. Muted noise from the bar drifted in, and Manuel's longtime business and political associate, Gretta DeWald, answered the phone and went about her work as we talked. A huge map of the road system of DeKalb County covers one wall in there, and decorations on the others include old beer ads, a copy of the Declaration of Independence, a pretty good painting of Manuel with a fish-bowl mug of beer in his hand. Manuel's face, like his body, is big, chunky, almost square, with prominent nose and cheekbones from his Lebanese ancestry. Enthusiast of reform politics, true intellectual, self-taught and abreast of everything, he is the last guy you would ever expect to be any one of those things.

He was born May 10, 1924. "Coincidentally, it was the day that J. Edgar Hoover was appointed director of the FBI." Good start, I said. "I was born in Atlanta, Georgia, on Hunter Street, about a block from the state capitol." He said it with pride. That was tough territory, even back when he was a boy. He attended the Immaculate Conception Parochial School and finished Tech High.

"Then I went in the Army. I had to fight my way into the Army. They wouldn't have me because of birth defects. Four times I was refused. But I just had to go in the service. You know. It was different times then." Different, indeed. Fran's thing about the last war we believed in. The Air Force finally told Manuel that if he would learn a trade, they'd let him in on limited service. So he learned to be a sheet-metal worker, "probably the worst one that ever lived." The Air Force sent him to England, where he served two and a half years "behind the women and the children." He met his wife over there, and they have eight children—seven boys and a girl. Two of his sons, Gregory and Jerry, work in the tavern.

When Manuel got out, he worked for a while for his father, who had run his tavern at the corner of Pryor and Hunter streets since 1919. Then he worked for a beer distributor three or four years. He said he was desperate and broke and borrowed money to open a grocery store. "I did that five and a half years and made a complete flop of it." Then he saw an ad that the tavern was for sale. He had served it as a beer salesman and, back when he was a boy, had sold newspapers in it. The man who sold the tavern to him had been his circulation manager at the old *Atlanta Georgian*. It seemed a good omen.

Manuel bought the tavern in 1956 and began developing it into what he thought it ought to be. "I've always had some ideas about a tavern. My daddy was one who never allowed politics and religion, that sort of thing, to be discussed in his tavern. My idea from the start was to have a big place where people would come and talk about everything." He said he wanted it to be like the beer gardens in Germany and the pubs in Great Britain. He thought America had suffered from the lack of such taverns. His idea, he thought, was particularly suited to Atlanta in the 1950s and 1960s, when the population was growing so much and branch office people were pouring in.

They needed a place to meet others, to learn about the city and how to do in it, to exchange ideas. I remarked on how good it was, too, to have a place with such a mix of all kinds of people.

"All kinds of people," Manuel said. "From all the places of the earth. It's a great education for me, a tavern owner, an Atlanta boy, to get to know these people. I'm not that smart, and I've learned from people. I learned about the world, you might say, in all its complexity, from getting to know these people."

Manuel said there was another part to his idea of a tavern as a place where people can talk. "I believe in the right of an individual to express himself to whatever degree he wants to without infringing on other people's rights. The basic rule here is enjoy yourself as long as it's not at the expense of others. One of the things that has bothered me in the last few years is the kind of pleasure some people seem to seek. It's not pleasure from what they're doing, but from what they're doing to other people. It's kind of a weird idea all of a sudden. It's prevalent enough to give you pause. I think it's great to sing. But in a room with a hundred people, I don't think it's right to let somebody sing if it interferes with the right of somebody else to discuss something. Maybe I should have a singing room and say, 'All you can do in here is sing.' Some of my people say singing is what you're supposed to do in a tavern. Well, it might be. But the people who come in who don't want to hear the singing have that right."

I told Manuel I agreed with his rule about singing. Already, he was talking about belief, and he went on, mentioning other rules he has in the little world of his tavern. He recalled how in his father's day, women didn't go in taverns because they risked being thought prostitutes or on the make. "I felt like a woman had a right to go in a bar and have a drink just like a man, and not be bothered." So he sees to it that nobody bothers a woman in his place "unless she wants to be bothered." And the same for men. He said he thought part of the crime problem was that people are no longer taught the basic rule that you don't interfere with other people. Too many people just never learn respect for the rights of others. I mentioned people who play their stereos too loud. "That's right," Manuel said. "And they don't understand that they don't have a right to interfere with you. They have a right to listen to that music. But their right stops when it begins to disturb your hearing. This is the basic thing about a democracy. You can write all the Goddamn laws in the world. But you can't operate a democracy on laws alone. It's got to be responsibility. The

166

individual has to understand his responsibility as a citizen. There's not enough paper to write a law to cover every situation, or time to teach people. There is my problem. How do you make sure that standards continue? People are better than we think they are. But unfortunately some of the standards that we've had have diminished. People seem to take as much pleasure out of looking sorry as they do looking nice."

Echoing Fran. People who deliberately make themselves look ugly. And how, I realized, Manuel echoed all of us in his concern that the good things we know, standards of decency in large matters and small, be handed on, passed down to the young.

Manuel reflected on another part of his life story that he felt was important. "I was born and raised in the South. And I was the son of an immigrant who happened to be in the alcohol business and who happened to be of a religion that was a very small minority." Because of all three of those things, Manuel knew discrimination growing up. And that molds you as a person, he said. "I feel very fortunate to have had that discrimination against me as a youngster, and as I grew up and as I tried to get jobs different places as a married man. You learn how to deal with it. And I learned that most people want to do what's right. It's just ignorance and fear that causes 'em to do wrong." Not a lot of other Caucasians in this country, Manuel said, have had the chance to learn those things from being in a minority group. When someone asks how can you, a white person, understand what's happened to me, a black person, he replies that he doesn't know what it is to be black, but he has known all the things done to blacks because of their race. He said he hopes we can get the laws enforced to the point where blacks have the same chance to achieve that he did, despite discriminatory attitudes.

"I wish to hell we could remove this racial issue," Manuel went on. "I know we can. It's going to happen eventually. One of the good things I see happening all the time as a bartender, Pat, is more and more mixed groups." Interracial couples. Groups of blacks and whites. "And they're not hung up to the degree our age group was. It's hard for a guy my age to take for granted the intermingling of the races. These youngsters do it. They're going to eventually win out. We got to get away from this racial issue and deal with things based on need, class, and that sort of thing. When we do that we're all going to be better off."

I spoke of how we had both worked for improvements on that score and others and had seen some progress during the years we have known each other. Was he satisfied with the progress? "Satisfied? Oh no," with great feeling. What did he see as the big problems now? "Well, let's talk about a guy like me, raised in America, taught by a daddy to understand some things. I was raised to believe that the FBI was the greatest thing ever was. And now I find out all the sorry things they've done. And the CIA. I remember I took a crowd to Affirmation Vietnam, and we were out to support the government. I've always been the kind of a guy who thought my country ain't going to do no wrong. We're the White Hats. I always said the government knows what's right, and if it has the right information, it will make the right decisions. Fine. And not long after we went out there to Affirmation Vietnam, Mylai came out. I've never been so infuriated in all my life. Those guys made a fool out of me. A sucker. I began to realize that the things an old patriot (I guess you'd call me) believed in ain't so. Those guys ripped me off. It was *people*, not the system. The system was weak and needed shoring up. We all got sick and didn't look after it right. So we got to pay more attention to it."

Anyhow, he said, that made him for the first time in his life question his government. He marched in peace rallies, the like. *Belief betrayed. But action on new belief. And belief ongoing.* Now, he said, "I think we've got to purge ourselves. But not overpurge. I worry about overcompensation. Let's get that balance we used to have. And find out how we can stick with the Bill of Rights, which is a precious document, and the rest of the Constitution."

He said he had been raised to believe income tax was a sacred thing. And then he learned that the CIA used our income tax not to protect us from other countries but to spy on other Americans. "I despise a Goddamned tapped phone. When I pick up a phone, I don't want nobody hearing what I'm saying." He talked about his battle against the political foe tapping his phone. I had read that the grand jury was investigating the thing and that the fellow stood a good chance of being indicted. I told Manuel I was pleased. He said that was one reason he was "up" on this day, not "down" the way he was the last time I saw him. Then: "It's an important damn thing. Nobody should tap a phone for no reason. Don't give me the argument that we got to protect this, and do that. That's crap. That's one thing we gotta stick with. And we got to stop these bureaucracies from divulging information that's private about people they have to get information from. We got to make sure the FBI is not utilized as a political weapon. The government shouldn't work against its citizens. We can't have these practices and these rules and regulations that abuse every-body." *The government against the people.* He mentioned capital pun-ishment, the danger of hanging the wrong guy, citing a local situation where seven men had spent years in jail for a murder it had just been discovered they didn't commit.

I asked Manuel what had been the reaction in the tavern to Water-gate. All kinds, he said. Most people knew something bad was being done and were mad about it, but didn't fully understand how bad it was. "The thing that was felt down deep by most people who thought about it was a sense of betrayal. Betrayal. Maybe not understanding it all, but knowing they were betrayed." They had a tv in the big room the night Nixon made his strange farewell address and some people back there, Manuel said with outrage, cheered and clapped for him. "I felt a crazy thing—I wanted to cry. I was angry and I was sad." He said he went to hear John Dean when he spoke in Atlanta and never felt so unclean in his life. "There's something wrong about this son of a bitch getting this kind of publicity."

On Watergate, as well as on the war, Manuel worried about over-compensation. "I worry about all of these holy-roly type guys. They say, well, we're going to clean up the son of a bitch. And what we'll wind up with is a government that don't operate. They worry me, these God-fearing, church-going, Bible-thumping people who're going to clean the world up. They scare hell out of me. You need that balance." *Oh God, yes, that precious balance.* I thought how aptly Manuel had described my own feelings toward Ralph Nader and those legions of equally joyless, equally sanctimonious young people who see him as the Messiah. He has fought against things the other men and I had talked about, things that diminished business practice and ethics and the quality of life. But I heard him speak one night and heard his dogmatism and merciless malice for the enemy, sensed the impersonal antihumanism of his harangue, and felt the shuddering revulsion I always feel in the authoritarian presence of a sure-enough puritan. Show me one of those, old Mencken said, and I'll show you a son of a bitch. He was right and Manuel was right.

"If I had something to say to this country," Manuel went on, "it would be just don't overcompensate by restricting what I can do. Don't stop me from reading what I want to, saying what I want, or contributing money I want to contribute, or working for a candidate the way I want to." He said this damn campaign law that they wrote scared him. He agreed with its provisions against corporations and

---

169

unions making contributions, and its requirement that donor lists be made public. "But Goddamn it, Pat, one of the rights of my life is to spend my money the way I want to. If I make money and pay taxes, I ought to be able to put it behind a candidate if I want to. And I don't like the idea of their limiting it. That's wrong."

That's wrong. How often they uttered that from the depth of their beings, these men who had made their way through half a lifetime, and learned from it, and now look about them and see so many basic injustices, not just against the weak and powerless but threatening their own very existence. I told Manuel I didn't have that problem because I had no money to give away, but I agreed with him on principle. Manuel said, "If I believe in Jimmy Carter and I want to give him five thousand dollars, why shouldn't I give it to him? It's my money. He's got to report I gave it to him. That's as it should be. But this damn government telling you what to do all the time, it's the most fearful thing I know of."

I allowed as how it was one more example of things being done in the name of equalization that turn out to mean just the opposite. Corporations shouldn't give. Unions shouldn't. The poor man can't afford to. So nobody can. "And the po' son of a bitch can't run," Manuel said. "Here I am, a good guy, and I want to run. And here's this guy worth ten million dollars and he wants to give me half a million dollars to run. It's his money and everybody knows he gave it to me and it's going to be an albatross around my neck. It's my right to take it. I ain't got the money on my own." He paused. "Yet the toughest thing for me to do in politics is to take money from people. It's something I don't know the answer to yet." His campaigns had been financed mostly by small contributions.

I thought it strange that here, as in every other vocation I had encountered, the despised politician, the runner of the government itself, was beset with governmental barriers to good performance. Crazy. Manuel, echoing Joe Kelly, said the government considered us the enemy, and echoing so many of the men, claimed it had lost sight of the common good. When he spoke of efforts to revive capital punishment, he said, "It's abuse by politicians attempting to further their own ends, not caring about the people involved. That's wrong. That's wrong."

But can we right the wrongs, all those wrongs? "Do you believe," I asked Manuel, "that this country is still capable of reform?"

"I really do," he answered. Some parts of national life have diminished, including the family unit, the respect for one another within it. He spoke of the need for mavericks to assert the values of something like the family unit against what seems a majority will to let it wither. *(Hold it together.)* Men like Madison and Jefferson asserted the principle of separation of church and state against probably the majority will back then, and they prevailed. The same with Lincoln and the Emancipation Proclamation, which was even against a Northern majority will. Wilson went to war to preserve democracy. FDR arranged the lend-lease program. Truman fired MacArthur. "We've done these things all through history. We get to thinking that we are diminished in our heritage and all of a sudden somebody asserts it and people begin to feel good again. I think we're not any different today than the country was a hundred years ago. Maybe we're a little bit lazier now. But I'm not afraid of the people. I think the people are better than we want to give them credit for."

I had heard all those ways the country is not as good as it was a hundred years ago, all the ways it has deteriorated. And I still didn't know about people. Certainly, the men I had talked with were better than anybody gives them credit for being. But people in general? Even if they are, I said to Manuel, what about the leadership? That worried him, he said, the mediocrity of the leadership. The system had caused this to a degree. "Able men, for financial and other reasons, and especially exposure reasons, have felt they couldn't afford to run for office. That's a weakness. We've got to rectify that. We've got to protect our people who do run. Compensate 'em enough so they can afford to run. Too often, it's only been rich people, for whatever reason they were rich, who could afford to run. A successful man going up the ladder couldn't afford it."

It was the best explanation I was to find of why the very word *politician* was uttered as an epithet in so many conversations. And here Manuel, who had gotten into politics because he felt so deeply about issues and the general welfare, still believed so deeply. He first ran for the DeKalb commission in 1972, a sacrificial lamb, he said, against a strong Republican. He did it on principle. "And it was an enlightening experience. I never thought a Lebanese bartender, as ugly as I am, as fat as I am, could even stand a chance. But by jiminy, we got forty-two percent of the damn vote." He won with 65 percent of the vote in 1974. He said he used to be afraid to go into DeKalb County when he was a youngster, but now they had elected "a guy like me." It proves the worth of the people, he maintained, the toleration of a populace generally considered to be rock-ribbed reactionary. "Because I really am as minority as you can be in DeKalb County—religion, my racial stands, age, profession, and looks."

So there he was, a politician. How had it been? Was he aware of the contempt so many people feel for politicians? Oh yes, Manuel said. He described a special phase of it, the attitude of young reporters toward him. It was strange, but the principles and ideas he grew up with seemed foreign to a lot of them. "They have almost a cynical view of life. They might have read about a guy like Truman, but they don't really believe people like that ever existed. And that's frightening. I get discouraged about it. Goddamnit, I ain't no different as a politician than I am as a bartender. But they look upon me differently now that I'm a politician. To me, politics is a beautiful game and I know how to play that game on issues of principle. They don't understand that. I hope they'll begin to. I never had to explain to a Jack Nelson or a Reese Cleghorn, reporters like them, what I was talking about. They weren't going to be sucked in, but they knew what the hell I was talking about. Pat Watters knew what I was talking about."

"And still do, Manuel. Still do." Jack and Reese and me, all middle-aged. Fran had worried about those young reporters, not grounded in the basics and ethics of newspapering. The fault was not all with the politicians. "How do things work now," I asked Manuel, "in the operation of a local government like DeKalb's?" He said that as a businessman you learn quickly the inefficiency of the bureaucracy. But it's there and you've got to deal with it. He learned about all phases of the government first hand by watching the bureaucrats as they did their work. "The great thing about being a commissioner," Manuel said, "is the capability you have to do things that you always wanted to do." Appointing the right kind of people to jobs, people with the right kind of thinking, with good mixtures of race and age.

"And you can seek to rectify mistakes that have been made. And you get into the very personal thing that I love—where people have problems and you can deal with them. Then you can come back to them and say your government's working for you. I love that more than anything else. This sombich has got a street problem or a drainage problem or something, and he's been fighting that bureaucracy, and then you go over there, know where to go, and talk to this guy and that guy, and all of a sudden you've solved it. And the guy with the problem believes in government again."

It was what all the other men, in one way or another, had been calling for: government for the general good, human intervention into the cold workings of the machinery of government. I tried to tell Manuel how much disbelief in government I had found, talking with the men. He said he knew. But on the other side of the coin, "I find there are a lot of people in government who are really dedicated to doing a good job. But it's becoming such a tremendous job. The hours are not good. The money is short. In spite of that, they make it work. Not as good as it should. But they make it work."

I thought about all the lawmen I had interviewed doing that story on young criminals. I had in my mind come to accept the dehumanizing word *pig* for all people involved in law enforcement. Yet those lawmen I interviewed were decent men doing their best against terrible odds, just as Manuel said. This was true of prosecutors, judges, probation officers, wardens, even of some cops—though I still fear them as an uncontrolled force, a part of America's meaningless will to dominate, just as much out of control as the FBI and CIA. But most of these men I had called pigs stood, however ineffectively, for the basic tenets of our civilization. So did the institutions in which they worked, however corrupt they might be. The left's attitudes toward law enforcement have been fully as damaging as the right's stern call for law and order. The left's zeal to root out abuses and injustices has given people like me a distorted view of law enforcement, an unconscious willingness to ignore the good of it because of the evil attached to it. Manuel was right about the need for mavericks to speak out against such popular oversimplifications.

"The government is doing the best it can," Manuel said, "and somehow the citizen has got to understand the need for his input into the government." And on matters beyond his personal self-interest, he said, "The citizen ought to realize that the government belongs to him. But you're right. People are estranged. Government is very foreign to 'em. That's wrong. One of the reasons I ran, Pat, was to give people confidence in government again. It's as big an issue as any I know of."

And among the most difficult. How can you restore belief in governments that lie? How can you get the Joe Kellys in touch with the Manuel Maloofs for the benefit of all? And how many Manuels are there in all the governments we've got?

Get involved, he said. I asked him how people could do that, the way things are now. "Get with all these different groups," he advised, tax-payer groups, conservation, all of that. And the two parties. And:

"A primary thing is to write letters. There ain't nothing that impresses them sons of bitches more than to get a few letters on one side or the other of any issue." That was still true? I asked (my own feeling being that such letters are dropped into a void). "You're damn right," Manuel said. "And telephone calls and petitions, what have you."

I still had my doubts, and sensing them, Manuel went on. "You can rationalize your thinking in any situation you want to. But if you really care about this place that we inherited, that a lot of people spilled a lot of blood for, you've got your responsibilities if you care to assume 'em. You've got to spend some time." And it does take time, he went on, away from home and family and recreation. It's up to you. "But if you don't participate, don't blame anybody but yourself."

It was a challenge and a basic call to faith. Manuel spoke of Oregon, how it made him feel good to think about Oregon because they had started the ecology kick up there—and they won important fights. That was one thing I could hearken to: winning. Manuel spoke of his own participation in a local fight against a toll road. It had been the first victory in a series that finally blocked all the mindless expressway planning in Atlanta, stopped that one through Virginia Highland by Mother's old house. "There were only a few of us who began the toll-road fight," Manuel said. "But we beat government. We beat city hall. We did it because we worked at it." Yeah, I said, and turned the whole thing around. "Turned the whole fucking thing around," Manuel shouted. "It proves that you can. If you really care about winning, you can win. If you sit on your ass, you get what you deserve. It's up to you."

I wasn't convinced. But I was sure as hell tired of the no-win attitude. I told Manuel my discovery that though middle-aged men were supposed to have all the power, they didn't seem to have any. And were unhappy, at least the ones I had talked to. Manuel dismissed some such guys as cop-outs. "They were raised like I was, that you get to a certain point, make a certain amount, it's supposed to be all rosy. So we got there and we found out we've got money, a house and a car, and a good job. But we ain't happy." But here Manuel made an abrupt switch. "They ain't happy because they didn't understand how to develop all the other areas, too. They didn't participate. I think those who did are happy. I ain't got enough time to do anything and I love it. It's precious, this life we have. Don't waste it. A guy that sits around deploring his lot in life and not doing anything about it—it's his fault."

Manuel said that, of course, when he gets depressed, he doesn't feel like that. But he always comes back around. "You're just one among four billion people," he said. "When you're dead, it ain't going to take more than thirty minutes before everybody forgets you. So do something while you've got life." Exactly my own thoughts, after contemplating death. I admired Manuel for feeling that way, despite his physical problems. Heart trouble. Problems with his legs all his life, circulation problems. Diabetes. "That's all beside the point," he said. "As long as I can still think and speak out and do things, I'm satisfied." He didn't know what he'd do if he couldn't participate, but "I'd find me something to do. Never give up." *On to victory.* And I was so close to giving up on everything Manuel holds belief in, clear-eyed and maybe effective belief.

I had mentioned his medical problems to get his views on health care. They were vehement. He spoke of his admiration for Hubert Humphrey and his sixteen long years of fighting for Medicare and Medicaid. (Fighting. Winning. And how I had come to despise Humphrey.) Now we needed to expand his program, Manuel said. "Ain't nobody supposed to be sick and can't get well because they ain't got money." He spoke of a friend who had saved his money for his and his wife's old age and for their two children. He got cancer of the brain and it used up all his savings in the six or seven months he lasted. His wife had been faced with the cruel decision of paying for hopeless treatments for him or providing for her own future and that of her children.

I trotted out my other big grievance. What could be done about all the umemployment among middle-aged men? Something had to be done about retirement programs and medical programs that make age such a liability in employment, Manuel said flatly. Buddy's insight, echoed and expanded. Manuel said he had found the older an employee, the more dependable he was. A job ought to depend on the individual's capability. "But unfortunately things don't work like that. We're too involved in generalities and computers and statistics." *The human element gone.* "I think we'll work that one out, though," Manuel said. "A man has to feel like he's worth something on this earth." But, he went on, a person's whole life was more important than the work he does. America was too hung up on the kind of work a person does. If a man had to take something less, he shouldn't feel demeaned. A job ought to be mainly to provide the wherewithal to enjoy life the way you want to, live a full life. I told Manuel that is what I had come to. But I was lucky. What about all those guys who did everything they were supposed to do, got all the things they were supposed to have, and still were not happy?

Such a man, Manuel said, needs to understand himself better. "The old red-neck or what have you who is used to going out and hollering for football and gets bored with it. Maybe there's something better in life. Maybe painting. Maybe walking with his kids in the woods. Maybe sitting in a bar discussing things with other people. Some people look at it as 'My daddy did it that way.' You got to look at it from what you want to do, not what your daddy did." He respects his parents, he said, but he doesn't like all the things they did.

"I just hope more people begin to understand what life is about. I think life can be most pleasant. You can have an exhilarating conversation. You can enjoy a nice day. And if you've really got some feeling, that suffices." *Yes. Yes. Walking in the park with Glenda, the dogs romping up ahead. That's beyond and impervious to all the problems all of us struggle with, big and little, personal and public. That much I did know, did have faith in, believed.*

Manuel had mentioned relationships with parents. Now he spoke about the young. He said the biggest problem he had heard middle-aged men discussing around the bar was their kids. They had a hard time communicating with their teen-aged kids. Only a few had succeeded in "holding their families together," he said. Most couldn't compete with television, peer group influence. Monetary needs had formed much of his own life, pushed him to do what he did. "That same fear is not in the kids. It's not their fault. They weren't born in my time. Their objective in many cases is to contribute something to make this a better world in maybe a different way from what I would. A lot of parents don't understand that to the degree that they should."

I thought of the unabashed and uncompromising humanitarian impulse in my own two children. And I had strong feelings about the need to communicate with the young. But I wasn't willing to concede that everything the young were up to was to the good, and told Manuel so.

He didn't think kids were really much different now, they were just more open. Kids who came into his place during the fifties were all screwing around as much as they could, getting drunk, having wrecks, getting busted, all that. They didn't smoke dope (which Manuel said he deplores), but back then everybody was an atheist or an agnostic, and that had bothered him. Now we had all these young Jesus freaks.

"You can't worry about it. It keeps changing." But people our age had to understand that we couldn't make our kids do everything the way we did it.

"Certainly, though, there's some fault on the part of the children. They haven't learned responsibility largely because of this estrangement. I've had the problem and it worked itself out. I had to learn I had to give a little bit." I guessed that I needed to learn that, too. All of us do. In dealing with our own kids and with all the generation coming up now, we should find the good in them and give them the good in us. Manuel, a smile on his big old leathery face, was going on: "My optimism is today a little bit high. But you know, the things we think are going to inundate us today somehow have a way of disappearing tomorrow if you work hard enough. You can't just hope for it to go away. But it will if we all work at it. We got to talk to folks. My pleasure is talking to kids and trying to teach 'em something. We were taught by our people. I think we don't do enough teaching of these kids. At least, give 'em a chance to find out about it, whether or not they accept it."

All through my quest I had been excited by how much men my age needed to be heard, how much (more than they know) they have to tell their children, this country's young people.

"I'm glad you came," Manuel said. "It makes me feel better. So I could really unload. Because some days I really get down, Pat. I cuss the whole bloody world. I know where I'm at ninety-nine percent of the time. But I do deviate some. I'm hypocritical. No, that's not the right word. What's the word, Gretta?" She wasn't listening, she said. Sorry.

"When I get down and start cussing the world, what is that?"

"Well, I call it the Lebanese funk," she said.

We all laughed. Manuel said he despised being seen feeling that way. But he was too honest to hide his feelings. He wished he could disappear when he felt like that. I said, "Good Lord, it keeps you going to talk about it. You can't bottle it all up inside you." Manuel said he knew I got that way sometimes, too. "But I can write mine out of my system," I said. And I asked myself again how much all of this, the awareness and outpouring of outrage, had been, after all, an exercise in catharsis, an unloading of anger and hurt at an excess of personal calamity so as to get back my own balance. I was glad I had come for this last of the conversations to Manuel Maloof, to Manuel's Tavern, a little island of sanity and civilization.

"I'm glad I hit you in a good mood," I said to Manuel. "Because one of my big problems with this book is to state what I think are legitimate problems and grievances, and then pull it together with some kind of balance, and say what the hell we can do about these things. You've given me directions I hadn't gotten before. And I thank you."

"Well," said Manuel, "it boils down to the old idea that a man gets what he deserves. He makes his life. He's responsible for what he does, no matter what the circumstances against him." I was about to protest, thinking of Horace, all the unemployed men. But Manuel was going on about his experiences in England during the war, when he used to say, "The only way the Nazis'll ever take this place is to kill every bloody Limey over here. That's the only way they'll get it." You don't give up, I thought. And none of the men I had talked with gave up, least of all the unemployed.

Manuel and all his belief. I couldn't respond to much that he said the way I wanted to, I couldn't suddenly rekindle belief. But I did realize from talking to him that I wasn't ready to give up, to quit trying to change things now—because there ain't going to be no next time.

A week or so after we talked, I read in the paper that Manuel had been hospitalized after collapsing during a turbulent session of the DeKalb Commission over the phone-tapping business. I went by the tavern and asked his son Jerry how bad it was. "Aw, you know him," Jerry said. "He's a little down now. But he'll be back up again soon. He'll be okay."

And sure, I felt, relieved, sure he will. But what about the rest of us, all of us who had talked together, and all of us across this land? Are we going to be okay?

Manuel would come back to fight again, he would keep on trying. But when you come right down to it, I said to myself, Manuel—for all his beautiful spirit and tough determination to do something about things—is little better off than the rest of us. He is beset and bedeviled by major and minor problems and worries and frustrations that drive him into his Lebanese funk. He controls the little world of his tavern, but outside of the tavern he is faced with such things as phone taps and the campaign fund limitation law. Like the jobless men, like all of us, he is powerless, not in control of the forces shaping his life. He believes and acts on belief, and ends up tilting at the windmill of county-government bureaucracy. In one way or another, mostly in our work, that is what we all have done—tried to make do with inadequate, malfunctioning institutions, the way we tried to keep a worn-out, broken-down car running, replacing the parts, patching, mending, pouring in solvents, limping along in it.

We accepted powerlessness when we were young as the beginning of the process of working our way up in the world. But the expectation, the hope held out to us, was that by middle age we would have a degree of power, would certainly be secure and in control of our lives. Disappointment of that hope in public life, politics, work, and private life was the substance of what the men had told me. The jobless were at the point of desperation. Joe Kelly was frantic, George Harris was gearing up his grandiose plan to change things, John Somerville was resolved to escape to another country and a different mental landscape.

Manuel spoke of the kind of thing Fran had helped me find, existential happiness at just being alive, joy in the small things of life beyond work and worry. Others of the men I had talked with had that, too. But what of those who don't? Middle-aged men across the country were miserable, the successful along with those in bad straits. Were they to be condemned for not developing inner resources? George said there was nowhere they could turn to build their humanity. I was surprised to find as much religious faith among the men as I did, though precious little of it was supported by their churches. Ed and I were prime examples of the lengths you have to go to in this country to satisfy the all-important need for spiritual release, meaningful ceremony.

The reason work is so important to us is that we seek in it the very meaning of our lives. We were raised, our generation of men (one hopes the last), to center all our existence on work—jobs, careers, getting ahead. When work turns sour or a job ceases to exist, no wonder the bottom falls out and we are terrified and nearly destroyed.

The deterioration of the country that the men had described so chillingly was seen almost entirely in terms of work. Two images came into my mind thinking about that, two parts forming a whole in my understanding of those men. The first was of a meeting of my high-school fraternity, always held on Sunday afternoon, only this was the Sunday of December 7, 1941, Pearl Harbor Day. I was not yet in high school, was a junior-high "pledge" in the fraternity, and with the others of my age I stood listening to the older guys talk about what this day would mean in their lives. They were the "jellies," the good-time boys. Now they were sober and serious, talking about quitting school right away and joining the Air Corps, talking about what a terrible thing that we should have been attacked, talking about going off to war. In their talk, I didn't sense the dashing, hell-for-leather lust for war and killing we are told characterized the Rebels, from whom so many of these boys were third-line descendants. The feeling that long-ago Sunday was entirely sober, a sudden seriousness and getting down to business for seventeen- and eighteen-year-old kids who had lived for four years with the knowledge that such a day would come, but who had lived, too, with fun-loving happiness, graceful dancing to Glenn Miller tunes, who had lived the way kids of any generation ought to be able to live until the time for that is over.

The other image went back to Albany, Georgia, where I started school and began to learn to read. I would spell out the words on the billboards and ask what they meant. *Quillty* was the way one of them looked like it ought to sound. What is quillty? I asked. *Quality*, I was told, and given a definition I could understand. Another of those billboard words was *Inc*. After so many of the names of what was advertised, it would say Inc. What is Inc? Dad laughed. "It is what the Depression has turned most businesses into," he said. He tried to explain to me about corporations.

And for all of us, the ones who had to fight the war and the ones coming up just behind them, quality and corporations have been central themes in the life we have known since the war. The ever-growing, ever more uncontrolled corporations are symbolic of all the bigness and mechanism that has destroyed quality in just about every-thing and removed the human element, leaving us with those broken-down, rattletrap institutions that we struggle to keep going.

This is what the men were telling me during the quest. I had no coherent notion of any of it when I set out. Throughout, I had the excited feeling that I was hearing important thoughts, important expres-sions of feeling from men who are not considered important them-selves and, sadly, do not consider themselves important. Why in the hell should they feel that way? I would say to myself. And why have they not been consulted about the important matters of the day? They **have** that half a lifetime of experience during a period of great changes, bewildering difficulties, to draw upon for knowledge and judgment and counsel. The pollsters canvass us with preselected issues that are not issues at all in our minds, and they ask us to say yes or no, right or wrong, approve or disapprove. Why doesn't somebody ask us what *we* think the real problems are, what *we* feel about things. Had anybody ever actually listened to men like us? And then it hit me. Ernie Pyle had. These were Erie Pyle's men I had been talking with, and I had found in them the same decency and dignity he had, the same heroism without the first sign of heroics. He caught them in their youth, fighting that last of the wars that could be believed in, and told the country about their lives and their character, the quiet courage with which they faced and found, so many of them, death.

I caught them at middle age, facing the natural forebodings, talking about problems unique to their generation, describing what they felt in terms of their work, their vocations. And it was truly in the sense of vocation that each man I talked with regarded his work. To each, it was a calling. The vocation of real-estate man, of assembly-line worker and farmer, of newspaperman, of political cartoonist and syndicate salesman, of grain merchant and do-gooder, of plant manager and mechanic, of heating and air-conditioning salesman, of double-mat molding machine operator and hustler and organizer, of purchasing agent, of automobile agency manager and grist-mill operator, of tavern keeper and politician.

Thinking about the striking devotion they each felt for their vocations, I realized that they were also Bill Mauldin's men. Mauldin had bothered to know them, too, when they were young, and he found them totally unfooled by the nonsense and needless cruelties of the military life, but determined nevertheless to do the best they could in it, adapting the military to their style, brewing coffee in a steel helmet from a jeep radiator's hot water, making military life human, making it work. They won the damned war that way.

Now each, in the same spirit that Mauldin had portrayed in his drawings, was struggling to maintain the integrity and importance of his work, despite all the deterioration, despite all that had been done to take away what Manuel called the right to feel you're worth something on this earth. And each had, in his own way, succeeded amid corrupt systems in holding to standards and ethics. Each had fought the deterioration and adapted the broken-down situations to make them work, make them human. Each was still trying to win that kind of war.

I had gone to them with all the prejudices I had accumulated, that unlovely disdain I had for business and businessmen. But I found myself filled with sympathy and admiration for each man struggling with his vocation, dedicated to its best values—those in such a lowly regarded business as mobile homes, Manuel in the sneered-at vocation of politician, even those men in law enforcement I had interviewed for the crime story. I thought for a time that I ought to talk with a doctor, just to prove that men in a profession so universally damned in America today can be true to the best tenets of their calling. What I came to realize was that I had accepted a prevalent fallacy in this country, which is to blame and condemn people who are caught in the sorry broken-down institutions we have, rather than try to build some new-model institutions.

We all live with prejudices in us, and for most of us they suffice. Worst of all, middle-aged men have come to accept the sneers and disparagement directed not only at their work, but also at the things they believe in. Again and again in the conversations, men would apologize for asserting the highest beliefs of our heritage. I know this is old-fashioned, fuddy-duddy, they would say. So many of them just don't talk any more about what ought to be, not even to their own children. More than once as I was writing, I would pause in some one or another of my preachments and say to myself, who are you to be saying that? And oh God, what an unfashionable thing to say.

But if I learned anything from my quest, it was just how much middle-aged men do have to say and how much they need to be heard. If we don't tell what we know, it is likely we will be the last generation of Americans with a fixed set of standards and values. Conflict between generations is as old as mankind. I wandered from my parents' teachings when I was young, and like the unemployed man who talked anonymously about his personal life, I came back to the ones that seemed life-giving and wise and discarded the ones that seemed harmful. But when our young people come along and tell us everything we believe in is a crock of shit, we falter in our beliefs and start apologizing for being fuddy-duddy. What will they do, these young people, when the time comes for them to know what they believe, who they are? They will have no storehouse of beliefs to pick among for the good and the bad.

So I resolved that I would speak out from now on about what I believe and what I think ought to be done, speak to my own children and, as Manuel said, take pleasure in trying to teach other young people, at least give them the chance to know what they might be missing. And that is my advice to other middle-aged men. Hell, tell 'em. They need to know.

One of the most important things we can tell them is about time.

How it is not limitless, as one feels when young. And yet how it stretches, with so much time and so many events in a ten-year span. So they should feel free in time, know that it is not to be wasted in unhappy situations, as so much of the time of my generation has been, and that there is enough of it to allow continuing change, so that even at middle age one can set off a on a new course, sure of time enough ahead to work it through.

We need to be heard on political matters, too. If the powers that be are not going to come asking us—and they're not—then we ought to go tell them what we think and feel. Always before, middle-aged men were consulted; their opinions counted higher than most. We have the right to have ours weighed evenly with opinions of others in society. Let Presidents know they can't get away with lying to us—or can't pretend, anyhow, that we don't know it. Fling "liar" in their faces.

In so many of those conversations with middle-aged men, I had the feeling we were discussing the real political issues of our times, the most important though altogether unacknowledged. When Manuel talked about his rule against singers in the tavern, I thought surely this is one of the most important hidden issues. How many restaurant lunches, dinners, entire evenings have been ruined by loud and inane music, whether Muzak or rock gone berserk, and the noise of people too crowded together, to begin with, trying to talk over it?

Just as government could and should impose realistic regulations on such a thing as the purity of Joe's corn meal, so should it impose sane and human standards regarding density and acoustics in public places so that it will be possible in this land to enjoy a meal out in peace, with quiet conversation.

Noise as an act of aggression ought to be punishable like any other assault. I've lived in apartments where some fool with a stereo turned up full blast held a building full of people at his mercy for entire evenings. And some other fool mindlessly racing a motorcycle with no muffler, a blockbuster of belligerent noise, over and over some course he has chosen, can close a streetful of front porches to people for hours at a time, robbing everyone else of the peace they have a right to enjoy. Surely our technology is capable of producing a soundless motorcycle. What better thing for government to regulate, along with chain saws and the omnipresent power mowers. Proclaim and enforce the right to Saturday morning sleep across the land, a peaceful Sabbath. Stop the churches, for God's sake, from blaring out bastardized, electric-organ versions of hymns over electronic loudspeakers. The highest mark of our civilization is the traffic light, which regulates what otherwise would be a chaos of technology out of control. So much else of our rampant technology needs similar control, whether by cooperative compliance of citizens with mutually protective laws, or by regulation of manufacturers, or both.

There were many other hidden issues in what the men talked about. The need for a return to personal responsibility, an end to casual violation of the persons of others. An end to the government's considering the citizens that own it as the enemy. Why should people be fined for unintentional mistakes in computing their taxes? Why, for that matter, should we be fined for unintentional traffic violations? It's bad enough that our cars get torn up and we get injured and killed. Let there be criminal sanctions only where criminal negligence or recklessness is involved.

And let there be again that sane and simple enough principle that all the men, in one way or another, called for—government in the interest of the general welfare. And (as they also called for) a return to humanism in all our national life—government as well as business and agriculture, the professions and education, and even the churches and the do-good organizations. Let's get things back to human dimensions, make our institutions reduce forms to an absolute minimum, and tailor them to the human brain. Let's break free of the clutches of the military and quit killing people over the globe and selling them weaponry to kill one another. Let's demand control of all these cops we've got, local, national, and international.

These seemed to me the important things the men were saying. Most of them are middle class, and these are middle-class concerns. But when George Wallace (at the time the men were talking to me) appealed to the growing discontent of the middle class, he talked about opposition to busing, discontent about high taxes and inflation, distrust of the United Nations, distrust of détente with the Soviets, belief in a strong military. It is a mark of our political bankruptcy that Wallace was then the only presidential aspirant who even tried to list the issues, and another that the respectable candidates soon picked up on his list. (The most hopeful thing to have happened since was the success of Jimmy Carter, with his promise not to lie.)

With the exception of taxes (their unfairness rather than their amount) and inflation, Wallace's issues were not at all the ones the men I talked with wanted to hear politicians address. The unhidden issues they wanted to hear discussed were things like the need for national health insurance, for subsidies of private retirement plans to eliminate age discrimination in employment, for better unemployment compensation, for full employment, for a federal works program geared to our times.

So, hidden or unhidden, our real interests are not being met. What to do? So often the human, controllable quality of smallness was evoked as the solution. Corporations, perceived as symbols of bigness gone crazy, were seen as evil. I am not sure it is possible to return to smallness in many areas of national life. But some effort, surely, can be made to control the bigness, to regulate the corporations, to insist on human qualities in business and government and other institutions. If not the form of smallness, perhaps we can reinstate the essence of it. This would, I thought, be the way to begin turning the country back toward sanity and civilization.

Still, at the end of my quest, I had no real hope or belief that the things the men I talked with wanted were going to happen. Health insurance was probably the only thing we would get soon. But the other things are important, too, I would say to myself. I had regained, I realized, the ability to tell the difference between big and little issues and worries. The catharsis of talking with the other men, of writing about their and my anger, had been healing.

At some point soon after being laid off, I had written a strong denunciation of shower drains. "I have never known a shower drain that worked in any of the houses I have owned or lived in," I wrote with seething rhythm back then. "I remember them all back to childhood, that awful feeling of the dirty water swirling around my feet and dirtying the tub. In only a few hotels and motels have I experienced ones that work, the altogether reasonable thing that the water drained out as fast as it poured in." Now I could see that this was not really important. The drain I have now works right if I don't turn the water on too hard. Let Nader and his puritan followers bring us forward into the utopia of purified consumerism, a land of perfect milk and honey. I have more important concerns.

Personal calamities had not ceased for me. I was involved in a minor traffic accident. Then a hit-and-run driver backed into the side of the Mercedes while it was parked and destroyed the door. I discovered that I had inherited Mother's glaucoma and would have the effort of controlling it the rest of my life. But these things did not possess me, drive me to new frenzies of anger. I could be angry at the specific outrage and then let it go. There were enough good things happening to balance the bad. I no longer had the daily terror of joblessness that made life seem intolerable. And Mother's situation continued to improve. Now she was chirpy, had her sense of humor back. Glenda and I had gone out and looked at some old houses that had been restored in the West End section of Atlanta, and when we told her about them, she said, why that is the street I lived on when I was a young girl. It turned out that one of the houses, beautifully restored with complete authenticity, was where she had lived. We drove out there in the sparkling Thanksgiving Day sun, and she walked about the yard and on the porch and peered into a home she had known when she was sixteen, and lived in her memories some of the good and simple pleasure of that time in her life.

I had gained from the quest (from Fran, actually) another perspective: that other countries were worse than this one, and that most people through the ages and around the world have had no hope, and this helped me find my balance again. Then I discovered, or rediscovered, one more perspective. It was entirely by chance. I was beginning to organize my notes and think through the words of the men I had talked with when I was asked to review a book by Paul Good called *The Trouble I've Seen*, about the civil-rights movement. It turned out to be the best single book I've seen on that subject (and I wrote two myself). The reason it was so excellent was that Good was able to convey how great the movement was at its height and why the country killed this greatness.

Good wrote movingly of how the spirit of the brotherhood of man was the best part. I had known that, too, but had pushed it out of my consciousness during the bitter ten years after 1965, when so often it was people formerly of the movement who most blatantly violated that spirit. Like blacks now who are ashamed of the anthem "We Shall Overcome," I had come to disparage my own memories of the spirit that was there for a while, to believe that it really hadn't been. Good's book made it real for me again. I was in full agreement with Good when he wrote that once you've known that, you'll never settle for anything less, and was grateful to believe again that the years I gave the movement were worth it.

The other part of what Good wrote, how and why America killed the sweet spirit of the movement, was in accord with all that the men had told me about joblessness and deterioration. Good's thesis was that, in its essence, the movement exposed and challenged the schizo-

186

phrenia of what we say we believe in America and what we practice, the old conflict between the West's spiritual and philosophical ideals and its economic system. So, he said, the movement had to be destroyed because it was a threat to the status quo, to America's capitalism and its convoluted perversions of capitalism.

Then I realized that the cruel ordering of the economic system in this country is what the men were talking about at their angriest. The terrible desperation the jobless men felt. Joe with his business like a guillotine suspended above his neck. Horace saying he'd steal before he'd starve. George's will to bring a doctor to his house at gun point if he had to for his children. And George's picture of the street people, told they've got to work to eat, but barred from any legitimate work to do. These are realities so terrible that we can't face them, won't think about them. It took a chorusing of specifics, over and over, to make them real for me.

Destitution is indeed one payday away for most Americans. Its threat is peculiarly horrible to us middle-aged men because we were raised to be (and for the most part still are) the providers. This is instilled in us, and it is not all bad. But God knows, the kind of marriage Glenda and I have moved toward, with mutual responsibility and support and importance, is far superior to the kind described by the man who talked about his personal life.

The abstraction of being a provider, as I was so startled to discover, is the other side of the women's liberation coin. Women justifiably have protested and to a degree rid themselves of different dehumanizing aspects of being abstracted by the same set of institutions—marriage, parenthood, work—that abstract men almost out of their identity. From my own experience and from what the other men told me, I think men are quietly shedding such abstractions, too. As the man who talked about his personal life said, we are able to cry now, too. But the main thing is that both sexes have been dehumanized by the same set of broken-down institutions. Yet all too often the women attack not the institutions but their fellow victims, hurling that ugly, dehumanizing word *pig* at us. It is the same as with business or medicine: blaming those who are caught up in the institutions instead of trying to make the institutions sane.

Of all the letters that came lamenting the demise of *Southern Voices*, the one I cherished most was from the writer Barbara Smith. A woman. A black woman. It said: "I was so hurt to learn that it would not be resurrected. It meant a good deal to me. The only American magazine I know of that actually acknowledged there are various and valuable people living here, not just one race, sex or class."

That is where it is at. Out of my experience, the reflexes from having known the movement, I had set out on my quest with at least the half-notion that we middle-aged men could form yet another group, a bloc, a lobby. But I knew as I talked with the other men that it was not going to happen. If for none other, it won't because of the reasons they gave—they were not interested in it, they didn't have enough time for it.

But deeper down, I think it is not going to happen because part of the wisdom that middle-aged men have to give is that all this splintering of people into arbitrarily defined groups, each conflicting with the others and calling outsiders pigs, is not going to get the country, its people, us, anywhere. That is what is wrong with the government now, as the men kept pointing out. Special-interest groups and blocs are treated preferentially and played off against one another, to the detriment of the general welfare. We middle-aged men still have within us a strong will to hold the family (community) together.

So let me be done with this one last artificial grouping of human beings. Let me dare to be old-fashioned, say what I really feel and believe and know from a lot of bitter experience.

After all, joblessness is not a predicament reserved exclusively for middle-aged men. Its terror and trouble are just as real to middle-aged women, older people, and young people. The central thing about joblessness and all the other real grievances of middle-aged men is that if we have them, just about everybody else has them or can expect to have them, too. We were once, and in myth still are, a powerful element. If you let this happen to us, baby, think what is going to happen to you.

All those confident young people—the one thing they're going to be, if they endure, is middle-aged. So we're all in it together. Why in the hell can't we work together instead of working solely in the interest of this benighted group or that one? Why can't we work for the *common good?* As George said, we have to fight for the humanity of women, not just for their sake, but for the sake of us all.

The final thing the middle-aged men I talked with had to say was that they are not the only ones who need to be heard. Somehow we have quit listening to what other people can tell us from the struggle and defeat and occasional victory of their lives. There used to be two strains in American writing: one snobbishly sneering at and condemning everyday people caught in ordinary pursuits (Mencken), the other seeing the glory and the beauty of their lives (Agee). The Mencken strain has come to dominate the country's writing and thinking. The only fit subjects for glorification any more are the downtrodden and the aberrant. It is time we looked to the good again in ordinary people. I found so much of it when I set out on my quest. And I would find it, too, I am sure, in any other small sampling of any other kind of people. We need to believe in one another again, and in ourselves.

The reason I discovered so easily the humanity of the men I talked with, especially the unemployed ones, was that most of them were caught in adversity. And so it was with Ernie Pyle, who discovered that the evil of war brings out the best in people, and with Agee, who wrote his one masterpiece about poor sharecroppers in Alabama, and his other about a death in his own family of ordinary people. If the memory Paul Good and I share, and the dream John has given up on, of the brotherhood of all mankind is ever realized, it will be by universal acknowledgment of common adversity. All mankind faces nuclear annihilation. Awareness of that most central fact of our existence was present in the conversations with all the men. Yet, I thought, what difference does it make to any one of us how death comes—whether in the absurdity of being smashed by a berserk cop's car, or in the indecency of lying in a hospital in the painful clutch of cancer, or in a big blast at the end of the world? Yet something in all of us that knows we are mortal nevertheless cringes from and stands against that last kind of death. It is the intactness of animals that we still have, the blind desire that life continue, the knowledge beyond all other knowledge and wisdom that this is why we are here.

I had conceded to myself that there is not going to be any middle-aged man's movement. But I know that middle-aged men are angry, if the surface of them that I scratched, with all that outpouring of outrage, means anything. This is not the anger, as Mrs. Cofer could see, of young, rebellious people. It is stronger and more enduring; it is built of such things as lost belief and disappointed dreams. And it is going to express itself, one way or another. There is the danger that it will be harnessed by a demagogue and led into evil. But I believe that it will express itself in positive ways, against the idiocies and indecencies bedeviling all our people, that it will force us to acknowledge the beliefs we still have.

I am with them, yet, in anger. But I had to face it that Manuel was right when he said nothing is going to get better if you just sit on your ass and deplore your lot. Whether I believe it will do any good or not, I will, as he urged, participate. Speak out whenever I get a chance. Write letters. Try to influence powerful people. I won't waste my time with organizations, attending meetings. But for those who can tolerate the tedium, that, too, may be worth the effort. Making do, like Mauldin's GIs, with broken-down institutions, inadequate and absurd—that is yet the road ahead for my generation, without much hope, really, that the road will lead anywhere.

I had reached the end of my quest and pondered its meaning, and that was the bleakest point. Not much of a belief that we will be able to find a sane world in our lifetimes. But the hope that perhaps we can help to influence the future, for our children or grandchildren. And that is worth the effort because people are worth it.

We will make this effort, many of us, and the most important equipment we have is what we know from our own living and the good things we have held to in our heritage. If we can pass down what we know and believe, guide the young, then if they are able to change things, it won't be for the worse.

It is evening and I load the dishwasher. I love to get all our machines going at once, the dishwasher, the clothes washer, the drier, humming and thumping. It gives me a sense of well-being, of things getting done. Glenda is out showing a house. Glenn Campbell is singing on the radio about being middle-aged and a success in LA, but wondering if he wouldn't be better off singing for nothing back home in Tennessee. We had a good walk in the park a little while ago with the dogs, enjoying dusk-dark there. The phone rings. I start to answer it. Dad has had a mild heart attack. It might be his good wife, Sue, from down where they live in Valdosta, Georgia, calling with bad news. Or some other voice of disaster, unexpected. Or it might be someone with good news, an assignment for me, a sale for Glenda. I walk across the dining room to answer the phone. I am ready now for whatever it is.

In that way, at least, we'll be okay, we middle-aged men. We will survive, despite it all, will go on answering phone calls of disaster, and coping with them.